Everyday Knowledge and Uncommon Truths

THE EDGE: CRITICAL STUDIES IN EDUCATIONAL THEORY

Series Editors   Joe L. Kincheloe, Peter McLaren, and Shirley Steinberg

---

Everyday Knowledge and Uncommon Truths: Women of the Academy
edited by Linda K. Christian-Smith and Kristine S. Kellor

Intermediality: The Teachers' Handbook of Critical Media Literacy
edited by Ladislaus M. Semali and Ann Watts Pailliotet

Power/Knowledge/Pedagogy: The Meaning of Democratic Education
in Unsettling Times
edited by Dennis Carlson and Michael W. Apple

The Misteaching of Academic Discourses: The Politics of Language in the
Classroom
Lilia I. Bartolomé

Teachers as Cultural Workers: Letters to Those Who Dare Teach
Paulo Freire

Revolutionary Multiculturalism: Pedagogies of Dissent for the New
Millennium
Peter McLaren

Kinderculture: The Corporate Construction of Childhood
edited by Shirley Steinberg and Joe L. Kincheloe

Pedagogy and the Politics of Hope: Theory, Culture, and Schooling (A Critical
Reader)
Henry A. Giroux

Literacies of Power: What Americans Are Not Allowed to Know
Donaldo Macedo

FORTHCOMING

Discourse Wars in Gotham-West: A Latino Immigrant Urban Tale of Resistance
and Agency
Marc Pruyn

Presence of Mind: Education and the Politics of Deception
Pepi Leistyna

Education and the American Future
Stanley Aronowitz

Everyday Knowledge
and
Uncommon Truths

Women of the Academy

EDITED BY
Linda K. Christian-Smith
Kristine S. Kellor

Westview Press
A Member of the Perseus Books Group

The Edge: Critical Studies in Educational Theory

Copyright © 1999 by Westview Press, A Member of the Perseus Books Group

Published in 1999 in the United States of America by Westview Press, 5500 Central Avenue, Boulder, Colorado 80301-2877, and in the United Kingdom by Westview Press, 12 Hid's Copse Road, Cumnor Hill, Oxford OX2 9JJ

Library of Congress Cataloging-in-Publication Data
Everyday knowledge and uncommon truths : women of the academy / edited
  by Linda K. Christian-Smith and Kristine S. Kellor.
    p.   cm.—(The edge : critical studies in educational theory)
  Includes bibliographical references and index.
  ISBN 0-8133-3460-8 (hc). — ISBN 0-8133-3461-6 (pb)
  1. Women college teachers—Biography.   2. Women college
administrators—Biography.   3. Feminism and education.   4. Critical
pedagogy.   5. Discourse analysis.   I. Christian-Smith, Linda K.
II. Kellor, Kristine S.
LB2332.3.E84   1999
378.1'2'082—dc21   98-27912
                                                                                       CIP

The paper used in this publication meets the requirements of the American National Standard for Permanence of Paper for Printed Library Materials Z39.48-1984.

10   9   8   7   6   5   4   3

Contents

Series Editor's Foreword, Shirley R. Steinberg ix

Acknowledgments xi

Introduction xiii

1 Feminism in New Times, *Carmen Luke* 1

2 Unsettling Academic/Feminist Identity, *Jennifer Gore* 17

3 Her-story: Life History as a Strategy of Resistance to Being
Constituted Woman in Academe, *Kristine S. Kellor* 25

4 Strangers in a Strange Land: A Woman Studying Women's
Literacies, *Linda K. Christian-Smith* 45

5 The Backlash Factor: Women, Intellectual Labour and
Student Evaluation of Courses and Teaching, *Magda Lewis* 59

6 Can Feminist Voices Survive and Transform the Academy?
Ava L. McCall 83

7 Deconstructing Feminist Pedagogy: Seeing That Which Is
Ordinarily Obscured by the Familiar, *Janice Jipson and
Petra Munro* 109

8 Asian Women Leaders of Higher Education: Stories of
Strength and Self Discovery, *Lori M. Ideta and Joanne E. Cooper* 129

9 Dancing on the Sharp Edge of the Sword: Women Faculty of
Color in White Academe, *Frances V. Rains* 147

10 Negotiating Daily Life in the Academy and at Home,
Jean I. Erdman 175

11 Feeling Blue, Seeing Red, and Turning Fifty: Moving in
    from the Margins, *Sue Middleton*   191

12 Against the Grain: Reflections on the Construction of
    Everyday Knowledge and Uncommon Truths, *Linda K.
    Christian-Smith and Kristine S. Kellor*   219

About the Editors and Contributors   231
Index   235

Series Editor's Foreword

So much to say, so many voices . . . using everyday knowledge, the authors of this book collectively and individually discover and reveal truths. Decidedly female, their records and life histories dance above the page forming a union of the themes within the collective consciousness of women in the academy. Using the lived world as curriculum, these scholars uncover the layers which have accumulated into the stories we are reading. *A caution to the reader, we must always be aware that the stories (even though they are in print) are not stagnant and final—they are tentative and fluid, subject to change and re-group as life is lived and interpreted.

Each author is aware of her positionality as she choreographs the pages to express her thoughts and actions. She is aware that we have been living, as Carmen Luke mentions, in "new times." These are times in which we are carrying forward and developing the messages of third and fourth wave feminism. The stories come to us with the agonies and ecstasies of girl/woman/academic-hood. Melding theory with life history, this book exemplifies successful rigor in scholarship. The authors clearly are able to fuse intricate feminist and critical theory equally with a pedagogical and affective recognition of nurturance.

When we re-tell and re-form our life stories as women in and outside of the academy, I caution the adoption of the voice of victim. Empowerment and equity do not result from our victimization; they result from our own self-analysis and theoretical frameworks and the actions we take in light of them. Naturally, we acknowledge and name our sufferings—but we must beware the traps of essentialism with its comparative suffering. I believe that as we discover ourselves as women and scholars, we must also study and position everchanging/mutating masculinity. To reduce masculinity to the status of enemy lessens the validity of our ability to view and make sense of the world. Naturally, we eschew the absurd notion of masculine mandated objectivity in our lives/research/careers—we celebrate subjectivity and recognize it for the bias and history it carries.

When I revisit my own growth, first as a girl and then as a woman scholar, I position myself and the academy in a way in which I am able to heal and grow through critical critique and the knowledge of how power works. I recall during the pursuit of a Master's degree, my personal confrontation with many of the issues dealt with in this book. My voice was silenced and ethics ignored by university administrators regarding my major professor's sexual harassment/blackmail of me (subsequently he was promoted to Dean of Education). I am able to reflect with a healthy shade of cynicism that indeed, my naiveté as a student led me down paths that did not guide me to an understanding of the patriarchal hegemonic tentacles that pervade the everyday life of colleges. I am now able to use my experience to help other women and marginalized people identify power dynamics and to protect themselves. I understand dominant culture and do not allow myself the luxury of thinking that "just this once" it won't affect me.

We all have many stories, histories to tell, re-tell and to re-examine. This book introduces us to the dance, it allows us to expand and apply what we read and to know that we are partners in our experiences and feelings. This collective bond allows us the true evolution of collegiality and personhood.

Shirley R. Steinberg

Acknowledgments

This book represents the many visions and efforts of several people. We express our appreciation to the contributors and to our colleagues and friends at the University of Wisconsin at Madison and Oshkosh. Most of all, we appreciate the generous support of our partners, Bill Camperlino and Kenneth Smith, as well as the comforting attention of our faithful felines.

Linda K. Christian-Smith
Kristine S. Kellor

Introduction

Situated Knowledge/Discerning Subjects: Women, Life Writing, Discourse, and Activism in and Outside of the Academy

We proposed the anthology to potential contributors using the working title: "Situated knowledge/discerning subjects: women, life writing, discourse, and activism in and outside of the academy." In the prospectus, we delineated the broad theoretical framing of the anthology we envisioned. We were aware that theories informing chapter contributors's research and practice would necessarily alter the framework we outlined—this was critical to the work we hoped the anthology might perform. The text of the prospectus we sent to the women we invited to join us in our project read:

Lately, there has been considerable interest by women in the academy in a discernment process involving examination of the historically, politically, and culturally situated nature of their knowledge of the world, their work in the academy and other activities in which they engage. This inquiry, which contextualizes and politicizes personal experience, takes the forms of critical examinations of how women's subjectivities and professional lives are shaped within these six sites: the ways home and domestic matters impinge on academic life, (Erdman, 1996), the constraints on women becoming educated (Tokarczyk & Fay, 1993), the contradictions surrounding teaching and teaching practices (Lewis, 1993); (Luke & Gore, 1992), the background factors that shape research and writing (Lather, 1991; Maynard & Purvis, 1994) and women's activism within and beyond the academy (Davis, 1981). Research within and across these six sites calls for critical understandings about the constitutive and potentially regulative nature of dominant academic discourses and practices for women.

Appreciating that experience is socially constructed and negotiated, those engaged in this discernment process explore women's subjectivities as embodied, historicized experiences that may be named, analyzed and transformed, in part, through posing the following questions:

- Who am I as a teacher/student/researcher/writer/activist?

- Where do the perspectives guiding my practices as a teacher/student/researcher/writer/activist come from?
- What do I bring to the activities in which I engage?
- How do I interpret the world and my position(s) in it?
- How do these interpretations affect my future commitments and actions regarding these commitments?
- How does life writing, narrative inquiry and discourse analysis in the academy relate to these questions?

Language, especially in the form of narrative inquiry, life histories and deconstructive language practices such as discourse analysis figure prominently in breaking silences and giving voice to the many tensions that women experience in the academic workplace and other settings. Viewed as embodied and historicized narratives of experience (Connelly & Clandinin, 1988; Kaplan, 1993; Mairs, 1994; Steedman, 1987), these approaches have potentially powerful pedagogical implications for recognizing and working across socially formed differences such as race, ethnicity, class, gender and sexual orientation (hooks, 1994; Middleton, 1993; Williams, 1991). As forms of personal and collective testimony and critique of such testimony, narrative inquiry, life histories, and discourse analysis can serve to surprise, disrupt, and create crises which have the potential to transform previously held assumptions and beliefs about self and others and foster agency and activism as well (Davies, 1993; Felman & Laub, 1992; Felman, 1993; Phelan, 1993). Within this politicization lie possibilities for imagining alternate constructions of experience for women inside and outside the academy.

This book which consists of twelve chapters by women academics from diverse social backgrounds in the United Kingdom, Australia, New Zealand, Canada, and the United States addresses a variety of issues pertaining to women's homelives, education, teaching, research, writing, and activism. To provide diverse perspectives on women's experiences of being and knowing in and outside the academy, the contributors draw on a range of critical approaches derived from feminisms, poststructuralisms, postmodernisms, critical education theory, discourse theory and analysis, narrative inquiry, and life histories. The book is organized around the aforementioned six sites and addresses the discernment questions through a variety of approaches.

Too Common Truths and Dark Victories

Everyday knowledge and uncommon truths: women of the academy contains twelve chapters that explore through life narratives women's shifting academic identities. This anthology also represents a series of performative texts which provide new ways of seeing and different kinds of analysis and understandings. The contributors reject the confessional mode, moving into the realm of testimony/witness. Through this move, life history becomes more than a testimony to a private life, but a tactical text which has agenic potentials for writers and readers. The writers compellingly give witness to a too common chronology regarding women's alienation and silencing in academe from the moment of entering graduate school and throughout their careers even when they are senior faculty. However, these chapters are also "victory narratives," stories of perseverance, strength, and courage in the face of adversity as well as of commitment to changing the very institutions and political climates that inspired their writing in the first place. Within these accounts of women as graduate students, teachers, administrators, and researchers is a rich variety of experiences where academic identities intertwine with being family members, friends, domestic partners, and mothers. Yet, these multiple subject positions are contradictory and often in conflict with one another as is evident in the chapters by Jennifer Gore, Jean Erdman, and Sue Middleton. From this nexus of conflict, the contributors speak loudly, often for the first time about their life and work experiences. Breaking the silence is, however, not without pain and fear. For contributors Kristine Kellor, Jennifer Gore, Carmen Luke, and Jean Erdman, writing their chapter has been a personally and professionally transformative experience which not only gave them a loud voice, but the courage to carry on.

Several broad themes tie together these testimonies of women's lives inside and outside of the academy. All writers emphasize what Carmen Luke and Jennifer Gore call the "embodied situatedness of women" in which personal and work experiences are historicized and politicized. Academics, suggests Kristine Kellor, bring to their professional studies, research and teaching "storied bodies." The contributors give witness to the impossibility of excluding personal and collective experiences from teaching and research practices. Kristine Kellor and Linda Christian-Smith especially demonstrate the possibilities and strengths of historicizing the ethical frameworks informing research and practice. By writing life narratives, the power-knowledge regimes that structure work and private life are made public, especially in the chapters by Magda Lewis, Ava McCall, Linda Christian-Smith, Jean Erdman, and Sue Middleton. Another theme concerns feminisms old and new. Carmen Luke compellingly writes of the conflicts between old and new feminists and how the latter's ideas and actions are often read through the lens of earlier feminisms. In a sense, this collection is about the new feminist politics of survival in a world where patriarchy still reigns, especially for women of color and those who confront the international colonialism of the West. These feminisms are less about lamenting "women's lot" and involvement in resisting widescale social conflict. They are more often about the daily routines of women's work where women, in particular those of color and the working class, resist victim stances and demand that each person take responsibility to learn about and work across socially formed differences of race, class, and gender. Chapters by Lori Ideta and Joanne Cooper, Frances Rains, and Linda Christian-Smith represent very nuanced accounts of those topics. Yet another theme of this volume involves feminist pedagogies and social consciousness development strategies with students of predominantly European background. Chapters by Carmen Luke, Kristine Kellor, Magda Lewis, Ava McCall, and Janice Jipson and Petra Munro show how the use of these "liberatory pedagogies" are highly contradictory and have different consequences for women teachers. These chapters contain rich accounts of compassionate and deeply engaged pedagogies within the classroom atmospheres where women teachers are often the object of backlash.

Everyday knowledge and uncommon truths: women of the academy represents a future chapter for transformations of the politics of gender and academic life. Just as the contributors have become transformed through writing themselves into history, it is our hope that the readers of these narratives themselves change and in turn effect change as a result of becoming participants in shaping the meanings of this book.

Linda K. Christian-Smith
Kristine S. Kellor

References

Connelly, M. & Clandinin, J. (1988). *Teachers as curriculum planners: Narratives of experience.* NY: Teachers College Press.

Davies, B. (1993). *Shards of glass: Children reading and writing beyond gendered identities.* Cresskill, NJ: Hampton.

Davis, A. (1981). *Women, race & class.* London: The Women's Press.

Erdman, J. (1996). Time to Read. *Taboo, 40, No 2. 8–41.*

Felman, S. (1993). *What does a woman want? Reading and sexual difference.* Baltimore: Johns Hopkins University.

Felman, S., & Laub, D. (1992). *Testimony: Crises of witnessing in literature, psychoanalysis, and history.* New York: Routledge.

hooks, b. (1994). *Teaching to transgress: Education as the practice of freedom.* NY: Routledge.

Kaplan, A. (1993). *French lessons: A memoir.* Chicago: University of Chicago Press.

Lather, P. (1991). *Getting smart: Feminist research and pedagogy with/in the postmodern.* NY: Routledge.

Lewis, M. (1993). *Without a word.* NY: Routledge.

Luke, C. & Gore, J. (1992). *Feminisms and critical pedagogy.* NY: Routledge.

Mairs, N. (1994). *Voice lessons: on becoming a (woman) writer.* Boston: Beacon Press.

Maynard, M. & Purvis, J. (1994). *Researching women's lives from a feminist perspective.* London: Taylor and Francis.

Middleton, S. (1993). *Educating feminists: Life histories and pedagogy.* NY: Teachers College Press.

Phelan, P. (1993). *UnMarked: the politics of performance.* NY: Routledge.

Steedman, C. (1987). *Landscape for a good woman: a story of two lives.* New Brunswick, NJ: Rutgers University Press.

Tokarczyk, M. & Fay, E. (1993). *Working-class women in the academy: Laborers in the knowledge factory.* Amherst: The University of Massachusetts Press.

Williams, P. J. (1991). *The alchemy of race and rights: Diary of a law professor.* Cambridge: Harvard University Press.

1

Feminism in New Times

Carmen Luke

Since Jennifer Gore and I wrote "Women in the academy: Strategy, struggle, survival" (Luke & Gore, 1992), in 1991, much has changed in our own lives, in the academy, in public debate, in feminist and social theoretical debate. Here I would like to revisit the issue of struggle in feminist praxis, but this time in terms of what Stuart Hall (1996) has termed "new times." The term implies various inflections of the postmodern turn—in economic realignments, structural workplace change, media cultures and new technologies, public culture and debate, and theoretical priorities. While I don't have the space here to go down the road of each of these turns, I agree with Hall that there is something fundamentally different today in people's social and economic relations, cultural experiences, and in public sentiment in both the west and western client states. Racial tolerance is down, work intensification is up. Cultural, technological and economic globalisation are no longer the stuff of future studies but are empirical facts. Backlash politics are rampant and the intellectual and political agenda of feminism seems not to have been able to stem the systematic dismantling of many equity programs. It seems to me that the current state and public face of feminism are under siege. Part of the current impasse of feminism may well have to do with its perceived relevance to women of a new generation, and its intellectual and political responsiveness to economic, cultural and social conditions in new times.

Feminism in new times takes many culturally distinct forms and here I will focus primarily on my own context in the Australian university sector and draw on some of my recent experiences in and around feminisms. I want to address what I have observed as generational tensions among competing interests between established first-wave feminists and feminist doxa, and this generation of feminist Gen-X women. To elaborate on these tensions and differences, I will refer to my recent experiences of establishing and subsequently heading a women's studies center. I will also try to illustrate the generational "struggle over meaning" among women with reference to the feminist project of 20-something women as I encounter it in my own university context and among the young women in my social and professional network. But first: the more immediate changes in Jennifer's and my own situation.

The year *Feminisms and critical pedagogy* (Luke & Gore, 1992) was published, was the year a group of women, at the university in which I was then teaching, got together to begin deliberations over how we could establish a Women's Studies Center. Some three years later, I was appointed founding director for the first Women's Studies Center at that university, one of the last among Australian universities to have made it into the 1990s without dedicated Women's Studies. In our personal lives, Jennifer married and became a parent. My daughter, an only child, left home for postgraduate studies. For both of us, our experiences of 'family' and 'identity' changed dramatically: Jennifer gained a daughter and I 'lost' the immediacy and intimacy of my daughter's presence. We both launched into different dimensions of the 'mothering' construct. In 1996, my partner and I left the small rural university in northern Australian where we had worked for the past ten years, to take up new positions in a large ivy league university in a southern capital. As with any new job, this move required that I establish new collegial relationships, find ways to fit into a very different university culture, and 'prove' myself yet once again. As well, in the last few years Jennifer and I both received hard-earned promotions to associate professor. In different ways and contexts, then, our professional and personal identities have undergone significant changes.

In the last few years, I have learned a lot about how feminism works institutionally and professionally. In the early 1990s I was still among the junior troops in my department, untenured and on contract. In a conservative department and university, I was cautious of going public on feminism: in my teaching, writing, and on committee forums. Then came tenure and promotions, job security and more senior status, which I assumed, would guarantee the academic freedom to pursue openly my political and theoretical interests. And so I set about to establish a women's studies center which, over the course of about four years, brought me in contact with many women and many feminists, young and old, academic and non-academic. That experience changed many of my understandings of what the enactment of a feminist politics means. In retrospect, I can say now that I got into institutional feminist politics somewhat naively. The feminism I had cherished—the astute theoretical works by feminist scholars whose latest books or articles I couldn't wait to get a hold of—was a feminism I encountered in text, in theory, in the private space of my study. It hadn't prepared me for the politics of struggle among women. I thought then that feminist struggle was about countering white supremacist rule of the father enacted by arrogant men. I now know a bit more about the complexity of feminist struggle and the layers of differences of interests and standpoints among women.

Feminist Politics: Women's Studies in the Academy

The years leading up to the establishment of the Center taught me many lessons about how academic men and women react to "feminism." It taught me how to package and play the feminist card to anti-feminist women and men, to male university administrators paranoid of seeming too left-wing if seen to support 'radical' initiatives such as women's studies, and also paranoid of seeming too right-wing if seen to oppose equity related programs. It taught me how to negotiate among competing and sometimes hostile women's interests in the university and community. Throughout three years of lobbying, proposals for other academic centers and units repeatedly and unproblematically passed the gatekeeping bodies of faculty and senate boards. The women's studies Center proposal, however, took three runs to senate before it was finally passed in 1994. On every turn, the proposal was vehemently debated, queried and dismissed on 'separatist' grounds—special interests such as women's studies, it was argued, would open the floodgates to other "non-disciplinary special interest" areas. I was well aware that the general opposition to the proposal was due to a lack of understanding across the university of what Women's Studies means. In response, I developed a range of scripts—arguments based on 'equity', on statistics for Women's Studies Centers in Australia and worldwide, on student and staff questionnaire data supporting 'strong' demand, etc.—that I delivered to department heads, deans, and so forth. What I had not anticipated, however, was the strong opposition to the Center by other senior academic women. The three-time defeat of the proposal at senate was repeatedly argued down by women, several times with support of letters from deans and other senior academics.

The tensions and divisions this debate generated over a two-year period set the tone for the kinds of support the Center eventually received. The Center was allocated a start-up budget of AU$ 20,000 (U.S. $15,200), and provided with an office temporarily vacated by a staff member on sabbatical. In other words, the Center's institutional presence was in a non-place. In the second year, the social science faculty offered me a spare window-less experimental room literally the size of a closet but further divided by a one-way mirror. The purchase of a filing cabinet, a computer and printer, bare bones stationery, and five-hour a week clerical support chewed up most the annual budget. I ended up raiding my other research accounts to pay for visiting speakers, lunch snacks at seminar series, printing of brochures, etc.

The not so hidden agenda, of course, was this: we'll give the 'girls' the Center but then hamstring the operation through under-funding. It seemed obvious that we had to prove the success of the Center on sheer determination and the goodwill of many other women who were willing to put in voluntary time over and above their own research and teaching commitments. I headed the Center for two years in addition to my teaching, research, and administrative commitments in the education faculty. In the first year of operation, there were no students since no courses or programs were available. That first year was devoted to the development (and getting past faculty boards) of degree and diploma courses, curriculum development, and establishing the Center's operational structure. With no dedicated staff assigned to the Center, no research productivity indicators could emanate from or be assigned to the Center. Once degree programs were formalized by the second year, five students had enrolled which was far from what was required to fund five students. In short, with a review target of five years in which the Center was supposed to demonstrate financial self-sufficiency (through student enrollments, external research grants, conference profits, quota funding on publications), the university's undermining strategy looked like it might work after all despite our best efforts. In fact, the year following my departure, the Center had been collapsed and absorbed as a 'woman's studies program' within the behavioral sciences faculty. In retrospect, those years highlighted for me the politics of "strategy, struggle, and survival" in ways much more concrete and multi-layered than the meanings I attributed to these terms and issues Jennifer and I grappled with back in 1991.

The antifeminism permeating both public discourse and the academy (Clark, Garner, Higonnet & Katrak, 1996) is always situated and localized, and my experience in that particular site was produced by many other local histories and political interests that coalesced at that particular moment in the university's history. I would argue, however, that despite the localized context and history of that particular event, there are some profoundly entrenched ideologies and practices—in the university sector generally and in both pro- and anti-feminist camps—which extend far beyond localized sites. Let me elaborate on this a bit further.

The hierarchical structure of masculinist models of doing business in the academy—whether in research, administration, teaching, funding and grant regimes, or publishing—remain virtually unchanged despite some 25 years of feminist attempts at intervention. For example, the continuing under-representation of women at executive levels of academic management is endemic to universities worldwide. Moreover, the incorporation of women's studies centers and degree programs in the higher education sector has been largely a gesture of formal inclusion with the common price of institutional, financial, and intellectual marginalisation. By intellectual marginalisation I don't mean a lack of scholarly output or lack of theoretical development or 'maturity'. As we know, feminist scholarship has increased exponentially throughout the 1980s and 90s, constituting a knowledge industry that far outstrips adjacent 'newcomer' contenders such as postcolonialism or cultural studies. By intellectual marginalisation I mean the tacit digs often leveled (most often by men but not unknown among women) at feminist research and theorizing in 'mainstream' disciplines and (mostly undergraduate) courses. It is also evident in the widespread refusal—again mostly in 'mainstream' traditional disciplines such as sociology, psychology, philosophy, the natural sciences, and even education—to incorporate feminist scholarship as core subject matter, standpoint, or course readings rather than as an add-on last lecture or 'recommended reading' in a course.

Knowledge and control, as new sociology of education alerted us to way back in the early 1970s (Young, 1971) has pretty much remained in the tenacious grip of a profoundly masculinist ideology, embodied and enacted by men and hegemonized women. That control, as feminist educators have long pointed out, is enacted through the curricular exclusions and inclusions from grade school to graduate school. As a general point then, my claim is that feminist intellectual work is marginalised because it is *not* the mainstream. But to return to the point I wish to make about anti-feminists and the anti-feminist stance: it seems to me that patriarchal power and control, and broad-based resistance to the feminist project has remained relatively constant even in its more benign pro-equity variants, and certainly in the more virulent inflections of backlash and PC politics. In that sense, a generalized 'patriarchal politics' is easy to read, the targets for contestation and reform are relatively transparent and more or less stable.

On the other hand, the pro-feminist camp comes in many more colors. By that I mean that the visible targets of patriarchy against which women develop strategies (and struggles) to subvert and reform anti-feminist and anti-woman regimes, are relatively straightforward, the goalposts visible and tangible in comparison to the far more nebulous goalposts of internal opposition, more complex and often invisible alliances, covert tensions and oppositional discourses that often subtend relations among self-professed 'pro-feminist' women (Hirsch & Keller,

1989). I wish in no way to detract here from the many supportive networks and politically powerful and affirming relations that do exist among women and feminists, despite their various and complex differences. I do, however, wish to raise the issue of generational and political differences within a politics of feminist struggle, particularly as these become institutionalized in the academy.

Since the late eighties, "best-seller feminism" (Denfield, 1995; Fillion, 1996; Garner, 1995; Paglia, 1992; Sommers, 1994; Wolf, 1994) repeatedly has made the point that first generation feminists are still carrying an anti-male torch in an era when the conditions for women allegedly have changed for the better. Disgruntled first wave feminists, so the argument goes, are giving feminism a bad name because of the strong anti-male stance, a separatist ethos, and because the first wave agenda no longer represents the interests or interpretations of a new generation of women's social reality. Whereas today's 40 and 50-something feminists threw off the mantle of dutiful daughters of the masters, this generation of women born in the 1970s is rejecting their dutiful daughter status as daughters of 70s and 80s feminism. This rejection worries many feminists who often misread it as a lack of political commitment among younger women who allegedly are taking for granted all the gains struggled for by their older sisters. Over the last few years, my professional relations with many feminist educators of my own vintage, and my relations with many women postgraduate students who have feminist agendas but would not publicly label themselves 'feminist', has confirmed for me that something indeed is amiss in the generational dialogue among pro-feminist women, and that the 'old-guard' has fossilized into a rigid dogmatism and ideological purity crusade that is turning off younger women by the droves.

Part of the generational diaspora is evident in the university sector where senior women have fought long and hard to get to the positions they now hold. Young women coming up through the ranks of academia do not have to fight the same battles that feminists engaged in 20 years ago. The landscape of gender equity appears more balanced to them: women have moved into middle management and administrative posts in the public and private sector, more women than men now enroll in undergraduate studies, and more women are in visible and middle-status positions to act as "role models," mentors and supervisors. Young women today "see" a very different picture than that encountered by women entering university some 25 years ago.

In contrast to the male model of sponsorship and "club" induction of young male recruits, women's ascendancy during the 1970s and 80s into senior ranks has been a tough road because the glass ceiling was then a lot lower. The marginality of women's presence and their low authority standing, and therefore lack of female sponsorship networks, meant that most first-wave feminists had to pioneer new paths up the ranks alone. I have encountered many women who are bitter about the struggles they underwent in the 60s and 70s, and the open door career opportunities many young women today allegedly take for granted. I would argue that it may not be unreasonable to suggest that first wave feminists' academic struggles may have resulted in the tendency (among some but not all women) to close the door behind them or pull the ladder up with them. Significantly, these strategies don't seem to be isolated incidences; I have heard these same stories again and again in different universities and countries.

In the case I described above, I found that older women who had been in the movement since its early beginnings—women in the academy and activist women working in the community—tended to take what I would characterize as a more "separatist" and anti-male stance to what women's studies should mean and how it should function in an institutional site such as the university. I found none of these separatist tendencies among the younger women who participated in the run up to and establishment of the Center. Moreover, I don't see this stance among the young women in graduate studies today.

Let me provide just one example related to managerial issues in women's studies. Today, under Total Quality Management and Quality Assurance regimes pervading the higher education sector in all western countries, issues of accountability and transparent financial and human resource management are paramount. Hence, an academic unit such as a research and teaching center, particularly one labeled women's studies, would be under particular scrutiny in terms of financial management, strategic planning, and performance measures (Luke, 1997). As Director, it seemed to me that the need for committees, terms of reference, systematic policy and curriculum development, course and financial planning, outcomes and performance reviews, was paramount in a context where economic rationalist arguments had been mounted against the establishment of what was considered an economically non-viable center right from the start. However, among the older women, I found a wall of covert and overt resistance to developing "male models" of management in favor of "women's ways" of doing things. What are these women's ways of doing things? We were to have informal meetings to debate course content, to vote on expenditures, to get all the pro-feminist women involved and keep the hostile science women out. Men weren't supposed to teach or be in the Center. Attempts to include courses or course readings on masculinities were ridiculed. Before I was even fully aware of the winds of change, factions had developed that split different epistemological and political visions along age differences.

Women's ways of doing things are commonly associated with informal networking among women. Within the Center's first year of operation, women were indeed very busy building networks, which very quickly developed oppositional ideological camps. On numerous occasions these factions launched into veiled attacks and subversive strategies in public forums such as faculty meetings where, in full view of senior academic males who could make or break the Center, the tensions among younger, "new wave" feminist women and older established feminist women surfaced. Identifying the targets of patriarchy, as I said, is relatively easy: we've lived with them all our lives and are pretty good at reading the signals and negotiating the map. Identifying the strategies of opposition among feminist women is much more difficult for it is often masked, hidden under pro-feminist rhetoric and, in my view, calculatingly deceptive.

Through the informal networks that bind the relatively small community of Australian feminist academics together, I have learned that the incidents I have described here are not isolated. As participant in several external reviews of Women's Studies Centers in this country, I have heard the same narratives of conflict, tension and division—some focused on 'personalities' but all testimony to forms of struggle among women in addition to the day to day battles they fight against the self-serving male culture of academia, and the consequences of economic constraint and uncertainties of new times.

New Times: New Generation

New times in higher education have meant the closure of many departments, women's studies programs, and Affirmative Action and Equal Opportunity Units. Structural downsizing has led to an increase in contract work on one hand and, on the other, to increased teaching workloads and research productivity expectations among remaining staff. It has meant increased competitiveness for scarcer resources and job opportunities. Young women entering academia today face a lifetime of contract employment, limited tenured positions or scarce tenure-tracks that can easily be revoked through redundancy tactics (Tierney & Bensimon, 1996). But these issues are not exclusive to women. The partners of many of the young women entering graduate school today face similar limited job prospects in and outside academe. And this shift in economic conditions is what I think partially marks the generational difference between what young women demand of feminism and how they define it, and what many first-generation feminists define as a proper feminist politics. It has been my experience that, despite recent theoretical gestures to a politics of difference, too often within the movement and within feminist enclaves in the university, assumptions of one generalized feminism still prevail. There are many feminisms and differences in perspectives within feminist schools of thought. There are many ways to enact a feminist politics and yet old-guard feminism has tended to promote a rather purist view which allows only one way of seeing, critique, and action.

Young women often tell of the pressure they have felt in the feminist classroom to display a moral and political stance of a 'proper' feminist politics that is often rooted in the ideals and struggles of what to them is a former and outdated feminism. Often diversity of perspectives is silenced, and the obligatory assignment essays on, for instance, sexism in curricula, media, or educational policy, turns many women off. Women seemingly are tired of writing essays or theses on girls' disadvantage, on the plight of female teachers or administrators, sexist representations in popular culture or curriculum. Particularly in my own field of media and cultural studies, there has been a tendency among feminist scholars and educators to force students to read media narratives in only one way: looking for near seamless and universal sexist portrayal of women, girls and things feminine. The common mantra is that media violence is unilaterally bad, that all boys are socialized into aggressive behaviors through violent video games, TV and movies, and that girls and women are innocent and hapless victims of a male culture of violence. Such positions construct women and girls as ideologically duped and at the mercy of a conceptually totaled, male dominated culture industry. I don't discount the social consequences of gratuitous sex and violence in the media and public imaginary, but there are many ways to read the media (cf. Luke & Luke, 1997), to read the world, and to construct meaning. In academic circles particularly, anti-media, anti-technology, and anti-popular cultural rhetoric is endemic and much feminist writing is part of this levisite bandwagon dismissing popular culture and new technologies as exclusively male products and fictions detrimental to women.

It is clear to me that many women are resisting the feminist narratives and analytics of a generalized oppression leveled against women by a still undifferentiated category of 'men' and 'masculinity'. Instead, women want to investigate girls' academic achievements in science and math, or how girls use popular culture to construct their identity and social relations in affirming and empowering ways. Their analytic and political interests are more focused on theorizing gender dynamics in positive and affirming terms rather than writing the same old tired narratives of oppression, marginalisation, and disempowered women. For instance, among my students, doctoral work is proceeding on family life headed by single male parents, women's career histories who have pushed aside seemingly impenetrable glass ceilings, women's roles in formal and informal support networks for refugee women, identity politics among the new generation of Gen-X cybergirls, women's professional advancement in relation to home and workplace use of new technologies. Rather than spend three years of doctoral research writing victim narratives, women are choosing to write victory narratives: to document 'best practice' or exemplary models of women's achievements both in local sites and in newly industrializing nations in the south-east Asian and south Pacific regions.

Many of the young women coming up through the academic ranks today have grown up in single parent households, with full-time working mothers, many of them college and or university educated. Equal access to the workplace or higher education is a right inherited from their mothers' struggles. Today's women grew up expecting to go to college or graduate school, to have reproductive rights and choices, to sole parent or not to parent. In many ways, I think that the struggles young women have seen their own mothers go through in attempts to raise families, work full-time, go to nightschool and finish degrees, has made this generation more committed to what we often dismiss as 'family values' and strong family structures. It may also have made them more determined to get an education first, to defer family, and to support social programs and workplace reform for women *and* men that would make it easier to balance family and work.

Whereas 1960s, 70s, and 80s feminism drew sharp lines between women as victims of and oppressed exclusively by male perpetrators within a generalized patriarchy, today's young women see feminism less as a battle between the sexes, and more as a tool box with which to fight for political reforms and social justice agendas that would serve their (female or male) partners, their daughters and sons, as well as themselves. Women fight on behalf of their sons by supporting anti-bullying strategies in schools. In my institution they fill our gender study groups (coordinated on a rotational basis by women and men) to study feminist theory and politics to problematicize ideologies of culturally diverse masculinities. Young women today believe that there is no generalized patriarchy, no global army of potential rapists and abusers, but that what first-wave feminism has totaled as male culture is constitutive of differences among men that are as complex as they are among women. For example, my own 20 year experience in the academy (ten as student and ten as faculty) has provided plenty of evidence of the siege mentality of white and male academic culture which, however, "othered" me as much as did it my partner who is not white and who is not "one of theirs." Such othering tactics are fundamentally about divide and rule and they are widespread, not the exception, in women studies departments and centers. It's about out-groups and in-groups: self-professed feminists against non-feminist academic women; lesbian against the hetero camps; the liberal CR "soft" feminists against the (often younger) deconstructionist "hard" theory (read "male") feminists. Granted the ideological and political splits aren't quite that simple, located in neat binarist pairs. Nonetheless, no matter which vantage point one takes (or is othered into), the divides seem to be underscored by generational differences, which in turn align with distinct positions on the "men in feminism" question. These ideological alignments surface in debates over male/female managerial models, leadership styles, in the unwritten rules of feminist dress codes, the use of male symbolisms, and so forth (cf. Bauer & Rhoades, 1996). But to return to my point about younger women's rejection of an anti-male (and often anti-theory) feminism.

Women are tired of going to feminist classes where they are coerced to go into confessional mode: spilling the beans on how bad men have treated them, how the media misrepresent women, how men harass, rape, and leer. Indigenous and international students find this kind of pedagogy particularly invasive and culturally inappropriate: it makes them feel uncomfortable and often silences them in face-saving strategies of passive resistance. Sexual harassment, as one of my doctoral students argues, has long been unproblematically associated with exclusively male harassment of women. We know this is not the case: women harass and come on to men, men harass men, and women harass women (and here is another story to be told). Sexual harassment is not exclusively a one-way street between the male academic perpetrator and female student victim, although this is the model on which sexual harassment theory and policy has been founded (cf. Matthews, 1994). Moreover, cultural variation in what is perceived as sexual harassment and by whom has not been taken into conceptual or analytic consideration. With the increasing internationalization and globalisation of educational delivery, intra-cultural and cross-cultural dynamics of sexual harassment are a pressing concern.

I take Rene Denfield's point that for many women, and I include myself here, men aren't always and everywhere the enemy. There are men in our lives whom we love and are committed to, and who do not victimize and oppress us despite the heterosexual structure we enact. These men are our sons, brothers, partners, and fathers. They are our best friends, and often our colleagues at work. Denfield (1995, p. 257) puts it this way, and she is worth citing at length:

Young women today have men friends. We attended the same schools, sat in the same classes, played together in the streets as kids. Today we work side by side, discuss our problems with one another, and respect one another as individuals. And just as women of my generation believe in equality, so do the men. There are countless men today who have never raped or sexually harassed a woman, never attempted to deny a woman her rights, respect and love the women in their lives, and yet, like their sisters, wives, lovers, and friends, don't feel welcome in the women's movement. Even more than women, they have been made to feel gun-shy around the feminist label, as if convicted of a crime they didn't commit.

So what does this mean for feminism in new times? Young women today are coming to feminism at a different time in its intellectual and activist history, from experiences and life histories quite different from the life histories and vantage points of women who got into the movement two decades or more ago. And because it is established, older feminists who are now pretty much in charge of writing the feminist canon, it is their voices and politics that are setting the terms of feminist debate and pronouncing the daughters, especially those mounting challenges to orthodox feminist dogma, as "soft" feminists, as failing to carry the feminist political torch into the next generation and century. It is my sense that there is a profound generational difference in interpretation and "ways of seeing" feminism and women's issues which, to take one example, Helen Garner's (1996, p. 216) observations illustrate "The current wave of new books by women in their thirties who wish to dissociate from feminism argue that there are silences between us that need to be broken. . . our students misperceive us and our aims as teachers." In my view, it's not that young feminist women want to "dissociate from feminism" but that they want to break from "old-style" feminism. There's a significant difference in interpretation at stake here. Moreover, I don't think "students misperceive us" but, in fact, probably perceive quite correctly a feminism that does not speak to or for them. Again, I think it's a question of interpretation: accusing the next generation of getting it all wrong turns a blind eye to "crisis" signals and reflects a defensive and chastising posture that won't help break the silences or mitigate the tensions. Consider, for instance, what Betty Friedan's, Germaine Greer's or Gloria Steinem's celebrations of post-menopausal femininity might mean to 20 year olds? How can we appeal to young women with agendas like this: "feminists should promote pregnant hags, menopausal and postmenopausal feminist academics who persist. . . in a prolific, horrific, semiotic, and political performance that continues way beyond the usual limits of a foreseeable 'prime'" (Carpenter, 1996, p. 160). My point here is not to critique these women, deride their positions, or trivialize their pivotal contributions, but to illustrate generational interpretive differences of vision for feminism, of women's experiences, and feminist political action. Potentially the most dangerous difference in terms of divisive consequences is how establishment feminism is interpreting young women's engagement with feminism: as anti-feminist, as misperceiving "the truth" of feminism, as backsliding into soft-core vanilla or lipstick feminism.

I agree that many 18-year-old women who enter undergraduate studies reject the message that gender equity remains a pressing and ongoing social justice issue, but once these women enter the workforce and later return to postgraduate studies, many are indeed strongly committed feminists—albeit to a feminist project enacted by women unapologetically wearing stockings and lipstick. These women want feminism to work for them in their everyday work, family, and personal relationships. In their research, they focus on practical issues facing women today—from childcare to healthcare, reproductive rights, technology, and workplace reform. What they are looking for in feminism is a more conceptually and politically inclusive framework. For many women this requires retheorizing many of the traditional assumptions and theories of 70s, 80s, and 90s feminism. It requires that young women are given the intellectual freedom to pursue areas of inquiry that might exceed the traditional feminist boundaries of what used to be considered politically appropriate topics.

The nineties have seen profound structural economic and workplace changes at national and global levels, and the higher education sector has not been exempt. These are indeed new times. Throughout the decade, middle class women in the west and in developing nations have become more visible in middle management positions, and yet millions of middle-class and working-class women worldwide have been relegated to part-time and contract work with few workplace benefits and virtually no job security or career path prospects. Many of these are the young women who enter postgraduate studies today. Their struggles almost always have a common denominator: balancing studies, which they hope will improve their professional opportunities, with family commitments and part- or full-time work. They don't want to be made to feel guilty for coming to class after work in full business suit regalia— makeup, stockings, and cellphone in hand. Women "with attitude," as many such women consider themselves, don't "look" or act the part of the traditional stereotyped feminist student, and many claim that they are often made to feel as outsiders in the feminist classroom. In highly competitive and restructured workplace environments, their struggles are different from those faced by women entering the workforce some twenty years ago, and their take on and demands of feminism are different. Whereas we struggled to compete with men, fought hard to achieve wage parity, gate crashed into male dominated occupational and professional territories, and reshaped policies in favor of more woman friendly workplaces, young women's struggles today are in the context of competition with other women, climbing up professional ladders that are often headed by senior (older) women, and their activism is focused on "family-friendly," rather than exclusively "woman-friendly," workplace reform.

Whereas we came of age during the so-called sexual revolution, this generation grew up after that revolution but during a time when sexual practices were profoundly mediated by the specter of AIDS. We were the single-medium TV generation. Today's students are the multi-media cybernaut generation who grew up with Game Boy, Walkmans, TVs and VCRs, computers, and the digital datasphere of internet. This generation's experiences and ways of seeing are different, as is the political and economic context they have inherited.

New times shape and are shaped by new and transformed social identities and social issues. I'm unconvinced that feminism has transformed its identity, politics, agendas, and analytics in tandem with and in relation to new times. As one of the "old-guard" in generational terms, I believe that feminists, feminisms, feminist practices and politics, largely have not been responsive to new times: to the diverse cultural, economic, and political shifts that have saturated the public and private sectors throughout the 1990s. The current wave of scholarly and mass-market challenges to feminism, which many young feminist authors argue is an outmoded and entrenched feminism, suggests that something is amiss. Interestingly, that literature is not balanced by a laudatory corpus celebrating the current status of feminism, or its relevance to young women today. That should tell us something. It should mobilize us to action towards dismantling dogmatism, theoretical rigidity, political purism/puritanicalism, an often inward-looking and exclusionary epistemology, and a "feminist stance" that increasingly is being associated with a generational comfort zone.

I say this with caution: the embattled state of feminisms today may partially be of our own making. The virulent assaults by backlash and PC politics notwithstanding, we do need to move past blaming the other and look closely at the politics of tension and difference within and around feminism, and across generations. Three decades of feminist scholarship has produced an inspired, compelling, and sophisticated theoretical, epistemological and historical corrective to Eurocentric male-stream thought. Feminist work has been and remains too important to let it roll off the rails now. In new times, we cannot afford smug complacency and, least of all, maternal chastise and rejection of our daughters.

References

Bauer, D. & Rhoades, K. (1996). The meanings and metaphors of student resistance. In V. Clark, N. Garner, M. Higonnet, M. & K. Katrak (Eds.) *Antifeminism in the academy* (pp. 95–14). New York: Routledge.

Carpenter, M. (1996). Female grotesques in academia: Ageism, antifeminism, and feminists on the faculty. In V. Clark, N. Garner, M. Higonnet, M. & K. Katrak (Eds.) *Antifeminism in the academy* (pp. 141–168). New York: Routledge.

Clark, V., Garner, N., Higonnet, M. & Katrak, K. (Eds.). (1996). *Antifeminism in the academy.* New York: Routledge.

Denfield, R. (1995). *The new victorians.* Sydney: Allen & Unwin.

Fillion, K. (1996). *Lip service: The myth of female virtue in love, sex and friendship.* New York: HarperCollins.

Garner, H. (1995). *The first stone.* Sydney: Allen & Unwin.

Hall, S. (1996). The meaning of new times. In D. Morley (Ed.) *Stuart Hall: Critical dialogues in cultural studies* (pp. 223–236). New York: Routledge.

Hirsch, M. & Keller, E.F. (Eds.). (1990). *Conflicts in feminism.* New York: Routledge.

Luke, C. (1997). Quality assurance and women in higher education. *Journal of Higher Education,* 33, 1–9.

Luke, C. & Gore, J. (1992). Women in the academy: Strategy, struggle, survival. In Luke, C. & J. Gore (Eds.), *Feminisms and critical pedagogy* (pp. 192–210). New York: Routledge.

Luke, C. & Luke, H. (1997). Techno-textuality: Representations of femininity and sexuality. *Media International Australia,* 84, 46–58.

Matthews, J.J. (1994). *Jane Gallop seminar papers.* Humanities Research Center Monograph Series, No. 7. Canberra: Australian National University.

Paglia, C. (1992). *Sex, art, and American culture.* New York: Vintage/Random House.

Tierney, W. & Bensimon, E.M. (1996). *Promotion and tenure: Community and socialization in academe.* Albany: State University of New York Press.

Sommers, C. (1994). *Who stole feminism? How women have betrayed women.*

Wolf, N. (1994). *Fire with Fire.* New York: Fawcett Columbine.

Young, M. (1971). *Knowledge and control.* London: MacMillan Colliers.

2 *Unsettling Academic/Feminist Identity*

Jennifer Gore

Approaching Life History in New Times

The intensification of work so characteristic of our "postmodern condition" has produced new struggles for women (and men) in the academy. I came to academia "accidentally" and certainly much earlier than I had anticipated. I had completed a master's degree in Canada in 1983, for reasons that had more to do with personal relationships and geography than with career aspirations, and returned to Australia fully intending to return to my position as a secondary school physical education teacher. Before the school year commenced, however, I attended a conference at which, serendipitously, I was offered a short-term lecturing contract. In the couple of years which followed, despite having enormous teaching loads—in one semester I had 19 hours of classes on 7 different subjects!—I somehow managed to find time to engage in all kinds of other activities. Yes, I worked hard, but I also managed to play, to read, to cook, to exercise, to have long lunches with friends and extended conversations. Now, post Ph.D., tenure, promotion, research grants, publications, and baby, there seems to be no time. Instead, my life, like that of many colleagues, feels taut, almost to breaking point. It is all too easy, as Liz Ellsworth (1993) put it, to "kill oneself" in the academy. And these pressures seem to be widely experienced (at least where I work), crossing boundaries of seniority, gender, and other markers of social and institutional differentiation. Indeed, the day before I started writing this piece, a young male academic asked me how I keep going, how I maintain the pace.

Answers to such questions are clearly complex. They can be constructed from analyses of the institution and the identities its produces in conjunction with traditional and contemporary discourses about academic work. They can also be constructed from accounts of personal style and life history, of the "discipline" we have learned and the identities we have constructed. And clearly in both of these forms of analysis, and beyond them, cultural factors like gender are embedded. In this brief exploration of shifting academic identity, I focus on aspects of life history. But I do so with more resistances than I could ever have anticipated when I agreed to contribute to this volume.

Life history is not something I am used to writing. Questions of confidence and competence seem to block each new attempt to proceed. The forms of knowledge valued in the academy, for which most of us (academics) have been trained, are not consistent with what I understand to be life history. To the extent that *my* life is the object of analysis here, issues of privacy and disclosure also loom. Elsewhere I have written (Gore, 1993), following Foucault (1983), about the importance of "re-assembling" in examinations of the self. And yet, re-assembling oneself publicly, for an audience, constructs a whole new context. It is not that my experiences, my stories, are particularly precious or secretive. Indeed, it is more a sense that my tales are trivial and unimportant, that my life has been too happy, too easy, compared with the struggles faced by so many others in and outside of the academy. As I attempt to write, I am wrestling with discourses of oppression and struggle which are often used to characterize women's experience, if only as a basis for tales of empowerment or progress. I want to resist those discourses because I believe that mine is a different story. At the same time, I am experiencing a need to conform, to construct myself as part of the collective voice (likely to be) represented in this book (I haven't seen the other contributions), and for whom this book is written. To stand apart from other authors is to risk an incompatibility with this volume and with the "academic woman"/feminist identity that is the focus here. I am deeply aware of how the tales told here and the issues addressed actively construct an identity that, at some level, I seek to convey, as well as an identity, possibly quite different, that readers will discern. These are the brackets I want to place around the work below. I will attempt a closing bracket later.

Attempting Life History

How do I keep going? My mother, like so many mothers, somehow managed always to "keep going." Married at 19, at 23 she had four children under four, including twins and a daughter who suffered brain damage during birth and has never progressed beyond the capacities of an "average" four year old. She returned to teaching when my twin brother and I entered kindergarten and 33 years later is still teaching, as well as continuing the majority of domestic work and "child" care. (My surveyor father was often away on field work.) Little wonder that I have always seen teaching as a noble enterprise. Little wonder that I keep myself going at a pace and with an intensity that is not always good for me or for those around me.

To what extent is this way of being in the world gendered? All I know is that my mother and I are alike in this way. I know women who are not. I know men who are and many who are not. But part of what I have learned about being a woman, and so part of what I bring to my academic work, has come from my mother's tirelessness. Up every day around 5:30 am she still grabs some peace and solitude before others stir. When I was in school she would wake us all if needed, prepare lunches, wash laundry daily without an automatic machine and hang it out to dry, make beds, ensure we were all dressed, teach all day, shop, pay bills, take the washing off the line, fold it, iron, cook, clean, bathe us, help with homework, read stories and put us all to bed. In the morning, not only was everything back in its place, but often there were signs of school work she had completed at night—flash cards made, roll books checked, programs written or, during another phase, essays completed for the upgrading of her teaching qualifications. During her study years, I put on the weekly roast dinner while my mother went to an evening class. To think I thought I was making a real contribution to helping run the household. Little wonder that bed time for us, at least into adolescence, was 7:30 pm.

The pace and intensity that come with contemporary academic work are exacerbated by the administrative responsibilities that many of us take on. Recently, I have been wondering why I let myself get into the position of assistant dean of my faculty. I don't particularly enjoy administrative work, despite the fact that I often find it easier than teaching and writing, and I don't like the ways in which it interferes with my teaching and research. But as a vocal critic of aspects of my faculty and as an advocate of alternatives, I felt some need to put my body where my mouth was. Perhaps I had learned well the feminist message that I was and could be strong, that I could make a difference even, despite the masculine culture of the academy and its particular manifestation at The University of Newcastle. I had learned to speak out, to ensure that "radical" voices are heard.

Funny that I should have that role, that identity as radical, when I have never felt particularly radical. Indeed, I have always felt, despite my commitments, that mine is a rather tenuous relationship with feminism. Born too late to be deeply connected to second wave feminism but before popular articulations of third wave feminism, I have felt that I wasn't quite "in." From the question asked of me at a seminar "How do you rec-oncile wearing lipstick with your work on feminist pedagogy?" to chal-lenges to my current Foucault-based research on power and pedagogy as not "political," and reports that other feminists have characterized me recently and apparently disparagingly as "doing the mothering thing," I have felt that I didn't quite measure up in comparisons with "proper" feminists. (Nonetheless, I am more publicly feminist than any of the other women in my faculty.) At the same time, however, I would argue that some of my effectiveness as a feminist voice in the academy relates to the complexity of my identification as a feminist, to the fact my femi-nism isn't always immediately apparent.

Occasionally I have been asked where my "radicalism"/feminism came from. My answers always relate to the experience of growing up in the '60s and '70s with a sister who was marked, marginalised, and mis-treated by some people and institutions because she was "different." Others saw only an intellectual disability. I saw beyond that. One mo-ment I still recall vividly for its impact on my understanding of Meredith was when I took her to see the movie *Benji*, when we were in our 'teens. I remember looking across at her when Benji the dog had gone missing and seeing tears streaming down her face. I realized then that she felt and understood more than even I had realized. What developed from this experience of growing up with difference was a strong sense of in-justice, insensitivity, indignity. Hence, when first confronted with femi-nist theory, not until my early 20s, the analysis of ways in which women have been/are treated resonated with many of my experiences and ob-servations, including my observation of women playing the major role in caring for people like Meredith.

The pace with which I have risen in the academy has meant that I haven't experienced personally the barriers to promotion and academic success that affect many women. At the same time as I have been rela-tively fortunate, I want to pay tribute to the many women who haven't, whose personal and professional lives have been marked by subtle and/or violent forms of oppression. This is not to suggest that my life is somehow unaffected by sexism, patriarchy, and phallocentrism. Of course it is, but not in ways that have limited my aspirations and accom-plishments. Like most academics, I've worked hard for the position and reputation I have achieved, struggling to stay focused, to take risks, to just get tasks completed. But I've also been surrounded by positive forces and conditions that enabled me to set lofty goals for myself and put into practice ways of meeting those challenges. I had (have) sup-portive parents who encouraged my academic and sporting pursuits, who expected strength and success, who accepted my career moves and supported periods of overseas study. I had teachers (at school and uni-versity) who encouraged and rewarded me. I had partners who encouraged my further study even at the cost of our relationships. I've had fulfilling jobs and opportunities to work with wonderful colleagues and students. I'm in a mutually supportive, respectful, and strong relationship. Mine is a successful story, indeed a joyous story. It is on that solid ground that my identity as an academic has been constructed since my first appointment to a university 13 years ago.

And yet the conditions of my work, of work in the academy for most people, is starting to unsettle the academic identity that I have created for myself and that others create for me—tireless, committed, passionate, enthusiastic, pedantic, consistent, conscientious. Lately, I can't always "deliver" when (or what) I have wanted. Indeed, this piece I am writing is very late. Other demands and commitments have prevented me from giving more time and attention to my life/history. At the same time, of course, time and intensification of work are easy scapegoats for tasks we don't want (or don't know how) to complete: marking students' work, attending meetings, writing life histories.

Some of my own difficulties in meeting the demands of contemporary academic work relate to the birth of my daughter in August of 1995. It seems that there is simultaneously more to do at work and now even less reason to attempt to do it all at the right time and in the right order. Many women's professional lives are marked by these struggles as they attempt to build careers. It so happens (in large part, through the societal conditions that feminism has produced) that I had established a strong career base before establishing a "family" of my own. It is not surprising, then, that Jordan has unsettled my academic identity. Indeed, she has unsettled all aspects of my identity. Desires, pleasures, commitments are different now. From my need to tell the story of her birth over and over in the first few weeks of her life, to balancing the "guilty" pleasures both of escape to the adult world of work and of using the freedom that academic work permits (compared with so many other mothers/parents) of lingering at home to play with my baby or stopping at a playground en route to work, my life is very different now. I am different. For instance, in becoming a mother, I have found new respect for what millions of women accomplish. I have been deeply humbled by what I have experienced, by the common, natural and yet incredible bodily processes of pregnancy, birth, and parenting. In this way, and despite my awareness of their socially constructed nature, I have felt a connection to traditional mothering discourses at the same time as I resist those discourses.

Why does all of this matter? Who I am as a teacher, researcher and/or administrator is very much shaped by my academic and personal identity. Students in a class I teach on "Power and Pedagogy" have told me that they read my speedy entries and exits as a sign that I am busy and that they ought to minimize how much they "bother me" outside of class. This perception "bothers" the nurturing teacher in me, yet pleases the busy researcher/administrator/teacher/mother/partner. My students say they read my enthusiasm as an indicator that there is something important in what I am trying to teach. Even a quite skeptical student said that it makes her "try to figure out what the hell is so important." They tell me that they see the variation in my conduct of classes as a willingness to experiment, and as something they would like to emulate in their own teaching. These perceptions reinforce my passion and commitment for teaching, at the same time as they reinforce the fact that I can continue to get by doing less than I used to, less than I want to, in terms of preparing for classes. They help provide the satisfaction in my work that often I don't feel myself as a result of the corners I cut.

Who I am perceived to be and who I take myself to be as academic, and particularly as "teacher," has far reaching implications. It affects the time and attention I give to other aspects of my work and life. It's not only about short cuts but also about intervening in a life that sometimes feels out of control with how much there is to do. It's about making decisions and choices about what I most value and most want to accomplish. Who I am also affects my effectiveness as teacher/feminist. And it affects my students. That is, my students' informal judgments of me shape not only what I do, but what *they* do, how they respond and react, how they work. Similarly, just as I make all kinds of judgments of students which have consequences for my formal assessments of their work (Canaan, 1997) and for the identities they form, their informal judgments of me shape my practices and identities. Perhaps these influences are all the more powerful within the field of Education where we are direct professional models for students who want to become teachers. In any case, understanding who I am as a teacher and how I have come to be that way, individually and collectively (in multiple collectives), seems to me to be fundamental to working in education.

This brief foray into life history has helped me to articulate issues about teaching and academic work which I may not have addressed otherwise. For instance, this way of thinking about my life and work has caused me to explore, at least briefly, sources and sites of satisfaction and pleasure in my work; how I see myself in relation to other feminists and my fears and hopes for how I am seen by others; and, how I am addressing issues of work intensification and actively reshaping my identity.

Re-assembling

In the "bracketed" section above, much of which I actually wrote first, I have begun with a narrative of hardship despite my desire to avoid self-identification with discourses of oppression. Given that there were no major struggles of my own that I wanted to tell here, I nonetheless wanted to speak from a position that acknowledged the difficulties of women's lives in and outside of the academy. At the same time as I resisted making myself the object of my writing, I have found pleasure and developed understanding through the writing. I enjoyed this forum in which I could make a public tribute to those women whose energy, perseverance and strength have inspired me—most particularly, my mother. Interestingly, I have downplayed the important role of some men in shaping my academic identity through the positions of influence they held and their generosity. From my postgraduate study at the University of British Columbia and the University of Wisconsin–Madison, to the academic positions I have held in Australia, some of my success relates to the sponsorship, assistance, and support these men have given. Most of all, my partner's major role in shaping who I have become/am becoming is absent from this account of my life. Support by men is not a common topic within feminism.

I have also indicated, without much detail, that my path in academia has been relatively smooth, though not without hard work and sacrifices. I have told a successful story and tried to ensure in that telling that I don't appear to be either naive about the role of gender relations in my own life or arrogant about my success. It is interesting that I have felt so uneasy about a rather celebratory account of my life. I have certainly provided more caveats and apologies than I would have liked, given that women so often/too often apologize. However, I see these reflexive moments as consistent with my broader poststructural theoretical approach to ideas rather than with some kind of hyper-femininity. My aim has been to convey some of the complexity surrounding any of these issues, and to problematize "experience," recognizing the discursive construction of both experience and its narration (Scott, 1992).

References

Canaan, J.E. (1997). Examining the examination: Tracing the effects of pedagogic authority on cultural studies lecturers and students. In J.E. Canaan & D. Epstein (Eds.), *A question of discipline: Pedagogy, power and praxis in cultural studies* (pp. 157–177). Boulder, CO: Westview.

Ellsworth, E. (1993). Claiming the tenured body. In D. Wear (Ed.), *The center of the web: Women and solitude* (pp. 63–74). Albany: State University of New York Press.

Foucault, M. (1983). Afterword: The subject and power. In H.L. Dreyfus & P. Rabinow (Eds.), *Michel Foucault: Beyond structuralism and hermeneutics* (2nd ed., pp. 208–226). Chicago: University of Chicago Press.

Gore, J.M. (1993). *The struggle for pedagogies: Critical and feminist discourses as regimes of truth*. New York: Routledge.

Scott, J.W. (1992). Experience. In J. Butler & J.W. Scott (Eds.), *Feminists theorize the political*, pp. 22–40. New York: Routledge.

3 Her-story: Life History as a Strategy of Resistance to Being Constituted Woman in Academe

Kristine S. Kellor

In this chapter, I re-visit and analyze deeply troubling experiences associated with an eighteen-month period during my doctoral studies. For me, this was a time marked by soul wrenching struggles to synthesize and theorize particularly unruly aspects of my dissertation research which I believed needed to be reported and analyzed in a narrative text. I worked diligently to construct the narrative in a voice I recognized as my own. I feared my orals committee might reject my storied thesis which was taking a form not typical of more conventional theses within the fields of Adult Education and Curriculum and Instruction. I suspected some members of my orals committee would declare my thesis a-theoretical and/or un-scholarly. None-the-less, I continued to work on the text, intellectually bolstered and emotionally supported by Sue Middleton's (1993) description of a "theoretical autobiography" which, she says, "rests on the idea that by keeping to the forefront the rich emotional fullness of our own and others' contextualized personal narratives, we can find ways to resist the encroachments and confinements of oppressive institutional and wider political restructuring" (p. 179). I sensed that my dissertation could be read as a theoretical autobiography in which theory, autobiography, and discourse simultaneously complement and resist one another much as described by Shoshana Felman (1993) in *What does a woman want? Reading and sexual difference.*

The form my work was taking felt right and necessary even as it engaged me deeply in intense intellectual, emotional, and psychic conflicts. Although at the time lacking much insight regarding the etiology of my struggles, it is my sense now that these conflicts were strongly energized by my conscious and unconscious efforts to theorize in a storied form the excessiveness of an autobiographic educational case history I had composed during my first semester in graduate school. In this chapter, I describe the case history, discuss the intellectual, emotional, and psychic struggles associated with my analysis of the study and examine the spiritual crisis accompanying my attempts to theorize the excessiveness of the case history. "Excess" as I use it in this chapter refers to an overflow of meaning in representation which is beyond the control of the writer. I describe and discuss excess in more detail later in the chapter.

Storying Unthought Knowns

While attempting to theorize excess, I was unfamiliar with Christopher Bollas's (1987, 1992 & 1995) writings on the "work of unconscious experience." I also did not understand as I do now that I utilized this period to explore and express experiential understandings of what I now think of as embodied theorizing. Deeply engaged in my research, I quite inexplicably found myself re-membering, re-visiting, and re-experiencing—through the lens of my experiences as a woman in academe—my efforts more than twenty five years earlier to work across socially formed difference through feminist, pacifist, anti-war and women's movements activities. My academic research was unconsciously re-connecting me to things I had more than a quarter of a century earlier known and registered in my body but, for which I at the time had not yet had experiences with which to *think* what I unconsciously knew. Bollas (1992) suggests that at such times one is sure that he or she is in possession of critical experiential (unconscious) knowledge for which one does not yet have "the means of thinking" (p. 20). Bollas (1987) calls this knowledge "an unthought known" (p. 277).

Almost two years after I first found myself embroiled in the conflicts I story in this chapter, I read Bollas's (1992) observation: "We all walk about in a metaphysical concrescence of our private idioms, our culture, society, and language, and our era in history" (p. 19). These words provided me with new insights on how I could make sense theoretically of my ten-year practice of utilizing autobiographic narratives in my graduate school papers as testimony to and witness of feminist peacemaking long before I was familiar with theories which now help me understand, explain, and support critical relationships between my work in academe and the life of resistance I had chosen as a young woman. In the autobiographic educational case study written during my first semester of graduate school, I brazenly and, for me at the time, un-problematically described my embodied understandings of the roles of experiential knowledge in working across socially formed differences. I had not yet heard that it was necessary to problematize personal experience. In the semesters following my entrance into graduate school, I became quite proficient at interrogating personal experience as an object of study yet, certain characteristics of experience for me continued to be elusive theoretically. Also, within dominant educational discourses in Western academe, it was my sense that much of what I understood regarding the power of personal experience in working across socially formed difference remained unsayable. Much later I would understand that that which could not be said pertained largely to the work of unconscious experience.

I had much to learn. Several years after writing the case history, and just weeks before completing the writing of my dissertation I read Bollas's (1992) suggestion that "moving through our object world, whether by choice, obligation, or invitational surprise, evokes self states sponsored by the specific objects we encounter" (p. 19). This observation broadened and greatly deepened my understandings of my decision almost ten years earlier to return to the University to "arm myself with theory." This is how I had in 1986 articulated my decision to matriculate in graduate studies at the University of Wisconsin–Madison in the Continuing and Vocational Education Masters Program. This decision was prompted in large part by comments made to me by Nursing School faculty who repeatedly told me that my insights and observations about adult Registered Nurse students' experiences in the traditional undergraduate Nursing Program were "astute" but, lacked a theoretical basis.

I had been working as undergraduate advisor to this cohort of students for seven years. I had come to care deeply about them and their experiences in academe. It seemed imperative that if I were to have my insights valued by the School of Nursing faculty I must take up arms (what I now think of as discursive theory) to defend my everyday and intuitive understandings of experiential knowledge. Although I was not aware of them at the time, today I am highly aware of the contradictions in my use of what is conventionally recognized as a military metaphor. Now I can readily discern how my descriptions of my decision to arm myself with theory might seem to contradict my pacifist beliefs. At the time, this did not occur to me. I was, however, aware that there were strong relationships between academic theories and power relations between faculty and students. I wanted to know more about these relationships. At the time, I had no knowledge of the concept of discursive violence; yet, experientially, I recognized it's effects as I witnessed the painful experiences of Registered Nurse students in the Nursing Program. I believed I must learn to utilize the tools valued by the School of Nursing faculty if I were to successfully defend the value of experiential knowledge in the university education of adult Registered Nurse students. Recognizing in the Registered Nurse students pain similar to that which I had suffered in this same Nursing Program as a returning adult student, I felt passionate and deeply embodied desire and commitment to find ways to intervene in the violence I believed was being inflicted upon this group of women as they attempted to expand their knowledge and practice of professional nursing. My earlier studies of pacifist movements helped me understand the critical importance of having intimate understandings of the working of power if I were to learn to effectively intervene against this violence. I suspect that in rather naively deciding to arm myself with theory, I was acting on things I knew but did not at the time have the experiences to think or express in theoretical terms.

Lost, I Began to Look Around and Listen[1]

In this chapter, I also explore transformative effects my attempts to understand and theorize the excessiveness of the autobiographic educational case history had on my knowledge of identity and subjectivity both as linguistic constructs and as states of being in relationship with self and other. I story intellectual and emotional struggles I experienced while grappling simultaneously first, with resistance associated with several of my here-to-fore un-recognized theoretical blind spots and second, with my attempts to make sense of the questions my dissertation advisor had posed about the excessiveness of the case history. Later, I would understand the necessity of working on these issues at this particular point in my studies. At the time I was engaged in this work, I did not have knowledge of Bollas's concept of the unthought known. I did, however, at this time understand that historically I had needed to autobiographically narrate some experiences and have these stories witnessed by others before I could myself be present to the experiences. Knowing this, in late spring of 1994, I decided to use educational conferences as places where I could share select pieces of my autobiographic narratives. In doing so, I hoped to more publicly explore particular aspects of the experiential basis of my knowledge of self and other which informed my work in academe as student, teacher, researcher, activist, and so forth.

I suspected that most of my, at the time, largely intuitive understandings of critical relationships between the work of the unconscious and experiential knowing were unsayable in Western academe. Having failed to find much educational theory to support my research, I wished to personally discuss my work with educators less directly associated with the institution where I was completing my doctoral studies. My decision to collaboratively explore experiential knowledge and embodied pedagogy at AERA, which many feel is the most alienating of Western educational conferences, was strategic. Co-presenters Chelsea Bailey, Dave Schaafsma, and I had met almost weekly for several months to broadly explore uses and potentials of embodied theorizing in educational settings and more specifically to examine the work of unconscious experience in knowledge of self and other. Although our individual motives for presenting at AERA were complex and diverse, we were united in our desire to use AERA as a venue where we could first, model embodied theorizing and second, begin what we hoped would be ongoing conversations regarding potentials and problematics accompanying the use of autobiographic life writing as a strategy for working across socially formed differences such as race, class, gender, sexual preference, ability, and so forth. Also, personally, for many reasons, some of which I address in this chapter, it felt imperative that I hear myself speak publicly of the power of story in attempts to name and interrupt discursive violence. The papers I presented and discussed at educational conferences during this eleven month period were the beginning of what I believe will be enduring conversations between myself and others about transformative potentials of life history narrative in working with and across socially formed differences.

Severing Critical Connections to Self Experience

Throughout my tenure in graduate school I have, as I intended when matriculating in the Master's Program in Adult Education, armed myself with theory; but, in so doing, I also temporarily severed critical connections to whom I believed myself to be. Particularly painful for me were losses associated with first, the splitting I felt taking place between my mind and body and second, my belief that spirituality and non-cognitive ways of knowing and being were taboo in the academy. I know now that even when not openly stated, these issues were integral to the research I discussed in the conference presentations mentioned above.

In October of 1994, I presented a paper titled "Understanding Self, Understanding Others: Examining 'Experience' Through Discourse Analysis of Autobiographical Narratives Incorporated Into My Graduate School Writings" (Kellor, 1994) at the Research on Women AERA Special Interest Group Conference in St. Paul, Minnesota. The conference theme centered on a discernment process which I later found helped me uncover and understand several intellectual/emotional blind spots which had interfered with my dissertation research and writing. In a call for papers, conference organizers suggested that presenters focus on a discernment process they described as: "Understanding Self, Understanding Others: Observing Others Through Our Individual Lenses." As I engaged with the questions posed by the conference planners: Who am I as a teacher/researcher? Where did my question come from? What do I bring to the question? How do I interpret what I see? How does that interpretation affect my future actions? I kept coming back to two questions: Where did my question come from? What do I bring to the question? These questions resonated with issues I had been struggling with since January of 1994. The responses I gave to the questions also addressed how I know and make theory in academe.

As I addressed these questions, I made some critical discoveries about what I had known first, as a relatively, formally "un-theoried" twenty-one-year-old feminist, pacifist, peacemaker and later what I had known but silenced as a middle aged, feminist, pacifist, peacemaker—now—heavily armed with theory. Theory, which I believe played a major role in subtle forms of academic silencing I experienced as a graduate student. Theory which accounts, in part, for critical absences and omissions I discovered in my doctoral student writings. Theory/discourse which at times continues to silence me through disciplining of my academic body. My analysis of this particular example of discursive silencing and disciplining of bodies in Western academe was productive for many reasons but, especially for the ways it helped me understand personal experience and self as effects of discourse.

Viewed through this lens, it became and remains apparent to me that discursive disciplining of bodies is unavoidable. However, I know now that, while I cannot avoid experiencing myself as an effect of discourse, I *can* alter the meanings of these experiences through the stories I construct. I understand also that I used the conferences to experientially explore—both consciously and unconsciously—relationships between the work of unconscious experience and possibilities for constructing alternate truth stories. I know too that such alternative constructions also have the potential for working in ways which silence and discipline my body both within and outside academe. Yet, I value these alternate stories believing that theory—truth stories—more heavily informed by the work of unconscious experience, posit understandings of self and other which value connectedness and collaboration with those both similar to and unlike oneself.

Advisor's Response to Autobiographic Case History Leaves Me Feeling Dis-associated

When my dissertation proposal was approved, there were two aspects of the proposal that concerned me. First, I was unsure how I could talk about "subjectivity" as Chris Weedon (1987), Judith Butler (1990), and some other feminist-poststructuralists use the term and also defend my use of "Self" as I understood Carl Jung (1968) to use it. I believed there

were critical commonalties between Jung's understanding about the unconscious and Self and some feminist-poststructuralist understandings
of subjectivity but, I was not yet able to clearly articulate the similarities
between them. This, I believed was necessary since I was using subjectivity as a broad theoretical framework for my research. My second concern centered on whether it was safe and/or wise to name spirituality as
a partial explanation for transformative effects of using life stories in education.[2] Trusting I would find a way to deal with these issues, I set them
aside while I worked on other aspects of the dissertation.

Soon after the proposal was accepted, I submitted a draft of a chapter
to my dissertation director. The chapter included the autobiographical
educational case history I had written in 1986 during my first semester
in a Master's Program in Adult Education. I was apprehensive about my
advisor's reaction to the chapter, in part, because in the case history I
had disclosed a great deal about the first thirty-nine years of my life. I
had worked with my advisor for three years, yet she didn't know much
about my personal history. Now, she had my her-story, in her hands. I
was taken off guard by her excited suggestion that I "theorize the excess"
of the case history.

Initially, I had no familiarity with excess in the sense in which I
thought my advisor was using it. I understood things could be excessive
but I had never thought of excess in epistemological terms. As my understandings of excess as a theoretical concept deepened, I began to
suspect that complying with my advisor's request that I theorize the excess would require me to utilize what I by this time thought of as disembodied theory. I feared honoring her suggestion would make me
complicit in my own disappearance. Although I now appreciate how
productive her suggestion was, at the time—alarmed and a bit outraged
that she could so misunderstand me and my work—I believed she was
asking me to deconstruct the very strategy I had used to maintain a
somewhat coherent sense of self as I engaged with disparate academic
discourses, texts, faculty, and peers. Later, Chelsea Bailey and Dave
Schaafsma, with whom I had for several months examined excess as a
theoretical construct, recalled that I had earlier described my reaction to
my advisor's suggestion that I theorize the excess as "a crisis of the personal brought on by a dissolution of the unified subject as articulated by
postmodern theory." While I didn't remember being that poststruc-
turally articulate, I did know that my advisor's suggestion left me feeling
deeply disassociated.

Simmerings

I put my advisor's questions about the excessiveness of the case study
into my "stew pot" along with the concerns I had about theorizing

S/self, subjectivity, and spirituality. While I was grappling with these questions, my adult daughter called and told me she was doing personal work around issues she had with her birth father. She wondered if I would be willing to tell her what I remembered about him before he was imprisoned for returning his Selective Service Student and Fatherhood Deferral Draft Cards. She was an infant when he was imprisoned and had little memory of this time. She told me she realized I might wish to decline her request for information which she said she believed might lead to painful memories for me since her father and I had divorced when my daughter was ten. I told her I would try to help her but wasn't sure how far I was willing to re-visit this period of my life. I also told her I was concerned that I might not be very objective about my memory.

As we spoke, I recalled that I had a box of prison letters in my attic. I told her the letters might provide a way into the questions she was posing. For eighteen months, during her father's incarceration, he and I had exchanged almost daily letters. I was in possession of the majority of the letters we had sent each other during that time; some of my letters to her father did not make it past the prison censors. Many of my letters included stories of our infant daughter's growth and development and discussions regarding our understandings of our parental obligations to her. It was my sense then and now that we used these letters as a way to stay together as a family during his imprisonment. I now understand that we also used the letters as a way to share and reflect on our rapidly changing understandings of self, each other, and those we worked with in the Peace Movement.

Not wishing to violate her father's or my privacy, my daughter suggested and I concurred that, at least initially, I and not she would read the prison letters—both mine to him and his to me. She and I had concerns about her reading letters not addressed to her. I had some qualms also about the ethics of sharing with her content from letters I had originally written to her father. Yet, since he had not taken the letters nor asked that they be destroyed when he and I divided our belongings after our divorce, I believed the letters belonged to me. This belief was bolstered by my memory that a few years earlier when I had offered my ex-husband the letters he declined my offer stating that he wished to have no reminders or textual connections to that dreadful period of his life. Still not totally convinced that the letters were mine to share, but wishing to do what I could to ease my daughter's obvious pain, I began reading the letters. Finding it much too painful to re-read her father's letters to me, I returned them to the attic and read only my letters to him.

My daughter was correct in assuming it might be difficult for me to re-visit the letters. Re-reading them opened a floodgate of memories for me. Mesmerized, I spent the two weeks following her phone call reading almost two hundred letters I had written to her father. Taking notes as I read—some for her and some for me—my reading consumed as much as eight hours a day. As I worked with the letters I had written as a young woman of twenty-one and twenty-two, I could feel something powerful shift within me. I wasn't certain what it was, but I believed it had relevance for my dissertation.

I had been ill with influenza while working with the letters. My illness legitimated to the outside world my need to withdraw from everyday life as I sat in my office reading the letters and giving powerful witness to stories of my life as a twenty-one-year-old feminist peacemaker, mother, and wife of an imprisoned draft resister. I found myself re-visiting, with mind, spirit, and body, twenty-year-old experiences—knowing them again for the first time.

In early February, recovered from my illness—which I had begun to suspect had been not influenza but rather a subtle form of soul-sickness—I returned to the excess question. To move forward with the dissertation writing, I knew I must theorize the excess my advisor had identified in the case study. I had no interest in returning to text books to investigate theoretical understandings of excess. I feared doing so would inhibit or stop the storied writing I was at the time doing on my dissertation. I e-mailed another dissertation advisor asking for advice on how I might approach the excess question in ways which would keep me writing from my body. This advisor had recently written a storied dissertation and I knew he had struggled with similar theoretical issues while constructing and defending his dissertation. In my e-mail, I included the story of having re-read the prison letters. I wrote

> The important thing for the diss. story is that in these letters I discovered that I had written pages and pages about my spiritual, political, and educational beliefs. . . . I was no philosopher, but deeply spiritual with Jung, Watts, T. S. Eliot, Gandhi, and some others as my mentors. . . . Anyway, lots of this stuff [in the prison letters] was incredibly naive and idealistic but truly informed my graduate work in Continuing and Adult Education and later in Curriculum and Instruction in ways I had forgotten (E-mail correspondence, February, 1995).

I had now shared deeply personal information with two of my committee members and felt extremely vulnerable. I also recognized that in sharing these personal stories, I had given them examples of embodied theory. From the feedback they gave me, I sensed that both were supportive of this way of knowing. I began to believe it might be safe to write a dissertation in which I could included Jung (1968); Weedon (1987); Butler (1990); Gandhi (1960); Watts (1951); Ram Dass (1971); Anzaldúa (1987); Fuss (1989); Foucault (1972) and others as sources of my understandings. Still uncertain how to address the questions about excess and the relevance of excess for my expectations regarding novel pedagogical approaches in Adult Education, I was relieved to know that I might find ways to include spirituality and Jung in my dissertation. Expecting to feel up, I was taken off guard when a short time later I entered a period of deep grieving which could not be accounted for solely by current events in my personal life.

Grieving Losses I Could Not Then Name

I knew the grief was associated with my experiences as a woman in academe. Although I couldn't yet name the source of my sadness, I was acutely aware that I was depressed over a loss. Another graduate student who knew me through my e-mail introduction to the Jung-list commented via e-mail on the sadness he picked up in my introduction. He asked if I were a single parent. Surprised to hear he had read sadness in my writing, I contemplated his question. I began to understand that there *was* something big going on inside me that was integrally tied to the prison letters and the analysis I was doing of my graduate school writings. Although I couldn't yet name it, I sensed a deep and familiar knowing rising up in me. I realized that, although I was not at this point a single parent, I was grieving deeply for something that was as dear to me as my own child. I was mourning the loss of a way of knowing I had experienced when I was young and theoretically unsophisticated. I was mourning the fact that instead of simply living in community with others—both like and unlike myself—as I had done in my twenties, I was now in my head theorizing about working across socially formed differences.

Reading the prison letters, I recognized that as a young activist, although lacking formal theory, I knew a great deal about people and nonviolent peacemaking. When I recalled how it felt in multiple contexts to work and live side by side with people unlike myself in terms of race, class, gender, sexual preference, physical and mental ability, age, and so forth, I realized that I had been very wise as a young woman. I had kept my mind, heart, and belly connected as I lived and worked for social change. My grieving, I knew, was connected to my loss of this embodied way of knowing.

Upon transferring to the Curriculum and Instruction Department to begin my doctoral studies, I began studying with faculty and students whose interests centered largely on various forms of structuralism and feminist-poststructuralisms. I found myself in a completely new world. Suddenly the subject was dead, personal experience shunned because it tended to be essentialized, and activism suspect and declared by some in academe to be a form of intellectual vanguardism. I appreciated how these new theoretical paradigms permitted me to go beyond the views of the world offered by Empiricism and Liberal Humanism which had largely informed my previous university studies. I also found that while working within, for me, novel theoretical paradigms, I believed I needed to hide and/or camouflage my understandings about the value of personal experience in education. In examining my graduate writings, I noted with considerable interest that during my early semesters of study in the UW-Madison Curriculum and Instruction Department I abruptly stopped including autobiographic narratives in my graduate school papers. In the Master's Program in Adult Education, I had incorporated life stories into almost every paper. I hadn't realized how radically I had felt silenced by the discourses I was studying until after I worked with the prison letters and remembered the embodied, experiential knowledge I had brought with me when I enrolled in my graduate studies.

Bringing My Body Back to My Work in Academe

I knew I had to bring my body back into my academic work. I suspect that I had known this on intuitive levels when I wrote the case study. I entered the Master's Program in Adult Education with a *storied body*. Adult Education canon privileged experience; naively, in the case study, I flaunted my experience in all its rawness. However, I didn't know then what I know now. Dominant Adult Education canon premises its understandings of experience on a normative, white, middle class, heterosexual man or woman. The life experiences I chronicled in the case study were *not* normal in this context. But, devoid of theory which would help me understand this, I acted in the Adult Education Program as I had acted as a young, un-theoried activist. I used my life experience to give witness to more peaceful ways of being in relationship with self and others.

For several weeks, I continued to grieve the fact that when I entered the Curriculum and Instruction Program I had felt it necessary to abandon and silence myself in order to be consistent with the theory I was studying. Later, I would have words to describe both this loss of self and the silencing. At the time, I had little understanding about relationships between discourses and the governing or disciplining of bodies in academe. I now appreciate the irony in my eventual decision to do research on uses of life story in education; while I was busy separating my mind from my body in order to be consistent with particular academic discourses/theories, my passion for creating cognitive defenses for utilizing embodied theory in education intensified!

A Ritual Flushing

Sometime in late summer, my depression began to lift after my friend Mary and I performed a ceremonial flushing in which I symbolically gave back—and at least temporarily relinquished—culturally, institutionally, and discursively imposed beliefs, attitudes, and ways of being which I no longer wanted to own. I identified and wrote on colorful Post-it notes each worn out and/or restricting discursive belief, attitude, and theory I could think of. Each color represented a specific source of ideological indoctrination. One by one, I deposited the bright, coded Post-it notes into a toilet bowl in the University of Wisconsin-Madison Memorial Library. Enjoying the sound and sight of the notes trapped and swirling madly in the powerful institutional flush, I watched the colorful bits of paper being sucked into the institutional pipeline on their way to the bowels of the municipal septic system. Wanting me to have future access to a visual/kinetic reminder of this powerful purging, my friend silently video-taped the deposition. To date, I have not asked her for the video. I doubt I will ever need a physical reminder of this ritual flushing.

Remarkably, this simple and ironically eloquent ceremony freed me in ways I had not imagined possible. I began to more readily comprehend how and where I had unknowingly abandoned critical parts of myself as I had taken my experiences as a graduate student more seriously—that is to say, after I knew and openly acknowledged I wanted a Ph.D. After performing this celebratory affirmation of self knowing, I felt intellectually, emotionally, physically, and spiritually purged. My energy and curiosity returned and I again took up the questions which had earlier been so troubling to me. Doing so, I experienced alternating waves of disbelief and relief as I began to recognize crucial intellectual and emotional blind spots. Blind spots which both prevented me from seeing inconsistencies and contradictions in my theorizing and more importantly caused me to subtly and not so subtly silence myself. I began to more fully appreciate a former professor's suggestion to the students in his seminar that we be forever mindful of Michel Foucault's observation that "all discourse is dangerous" (comment made by Tom Popkewitz in a Research Paradigm Graduate Seminar, late 1980s).

Pedagogical Implications of Discerning Subjects

As I asked myself: Where do my questions come from? What do I bring to the questions? I realized that my answers to these questions would change as I listened to the stories I told myself and to the stories others told me about what it means to be a woman in the academy. Engaging with these questions helped me understand that my despair over the ways I abandoned and silenced myself when I entered the master's program in adult education intent on arming myself with theory was just the beginning of what I now recognize as forever unstable stories about

S/self, identity, representation, and relations of power in academe. I was intrigued by the productive potentials of such instabilities.

Academic Discourses and Shifting Sands of Identity

As a graduate student, first in the field of adult education and later in curriculum and instruction, I wrote papers in which I theorized using language appropriate to the discourses I was studying. As I situated myself and my writings within diverse paradigms, my sense of personal identity shifted. I believed that it was critical for me to link specific identities with particular texts and discourses. I also discovered that it was impossible to escape particular constitutions of woman within certain discourses. My inability to evade these diverse constructions of woman seemed confusing and unavoidable. Troubled by the shifting sands upon which my identity seemed to be constructed, I decided to focus my doctoral research on the relationships and processes which I believed had lead me to experience my self as an effect of discourse. Through discourse analysis of autobiographic narratives I included in my graduate school papers, I examined both the process of being constituted woman in the academy: how I came to be and know, and the theoretical positionings resulting from these constructions: what I knew and what I could say given the texts and discourses governing the creation of the subject positions I occupied in this context.

Attempting to address my advisor's query about how I came to write an excessive case history within the context of dominant academic educational discourses, I came to understandings about experience as an object of study which required me to look for answers outside my intellect. It became increasingly clear to me that I couldn't address my advisor's questions through my intellect alone. I now understand that I needed to have certain experiences before I could recognize and speak about the "feminine resistance" (Felman, 1993) some read, I suspect autobiographically, in my educational case history .

Initially, I had been surprised that my educational case history occupied such a prominent position in my dissertation research and analysis. Now, I am able to see how the case history represents, politicizes, and historicizes my subtle resistance to being constituted woman in academe. Not always consciously, I engaged in strategic self-naming in the ways I incorporated autobiographic life histories into most of my graduate school papers. In retrospect, it is my sense that I, at the time rather unknowingly, employed autobiographic life writings as oppositional and productive strategies of resistance and self representation. It was my sense then and continues to be now that I used these writings as a way to maintain a somewhat coherent—but, not necessarily historically accurate or true—narrative thread about my self experiences as I discerned that I was being constituted woman in ways I didn't always recognize or appreciate. As I engaged with diverse academic discourses and experienced myself occupying and performing multiple and sometimes contradictory subject positions, I both consciously and unconsciously utilized autobiographic story telling as a way to contextualize and historicize experiences which worked to constitute me woman.

Autobiography as Excess

Writings of Liz Ellsworth (e-mail, 1994); John Fiske (1987 & 1989); Leigh Gilmore (1994); and Peggy Phelan (1993) helped me understand that there is always an overflow of meaning in representation which neither the writer nor the performer can control. Phelan suggests that "Representation follows two laws: it always conveys more than it intends; and it is never totalizing. The 'excess' meaning conveyed by representation creates a supplement that makes multiple and resistant meanings possible" (p. 2). Failing to represent the real exactly, representation produces ruptures and gaps which invite and permit political change. Significant cultural meanings lie in the excesses of representation. Ellsworth suggests that "cultural meanings which exceed legitimated discourses can be rewritten as sites capable of troubling and disrupting those discourses which are intended to control, explain, contain, medicalize, normalize, and educate" (E-mail communication, 1994). As Phelan and Fiske point out, the excess can be taken up in political and social criticism and action.

My interpretations of these works suggested to me that excess is meaning that oversteps the norms of ideological control or the requirements of any specific text. I believe that the case history was excessive, both in how it exceeded the requirements for which it was written and, in the ways I used the document to historicize and contextualize the life experiences I brought to my graduate studies in Adult Education. In analyzing the case study, I have discovered that less than a third of the text directly addresses my educational experiences. Two thirds of the text historicizes and contextualizes the particularities of the educational experiences I narrated in the case history.

Historically, I have used formal education for intellectual gratification, to prepare for employment, and to arm myself with theory. Thus, not surprisingly, the trajectories of my self representations in the case history were not typical developmental ones. Instead, I examined the cultural backgrounds and meanings of my life experiences. In doing so, I told stories which my advisor suggested were "spilling over with theory about the intersections of class, race, gender, sexuality, physical and emotional abuse, religion, and political and social activism" (conversation with Elizabeth Ellsworth, Winter 1994). In addition to the description of my K–12 and college education, I told stories about my experiences with poverty, personal loss and grief, political protest and imprisonment, communal living, single parenting, and growing up in a family of thirteen. These were not common story lines in dominant Adult Education literature describing typical female adult learners.

I storied complex relationships between those in the worlds I occupied. These relationships I knew were critical to my understandings of self and other. "Identity," says Phelan (1993), "is perceptible only through a relation to an other" (p. 13). Although lacking theory with which to express this concept, when I constructed the case history, I suspect that unconsciously and experientially, I already had deep understandings of Phelan's insightful observation. Stories of complicated relationships with diverse people and institutions comprise the bulk of my case history. Phelan suggests that "[c]ultural theory has thus far left unexamined the connection between the psychic theory of the relationship between self and other and the political and epistemological contours of that encounter" (p. 3). While not then knowing how to articulate my understandings of strategic, sometimes transformative, potentials of experiential and psychic knowledge, since my early twenties, I have believed that within the relational connections Phelan speaks of lie powerful potentials for achieving world peace—a peace I believe is necessarily based on universal commitment to nonviolence.

In the case study I storied this idealistic conviction. Shoshana Felman's and Dori Laub's (1992) work on testimony and the crisis of witnessing helps me understand that I offered my life testimony in the case study, not only as a testimony to a private life but also as a point of conflation between text and life. I wonder now if unconsciously I had recognized the potentials the case study offered for testimony about the insanity of war? Perhaps because I came to my beliefs in nonviolence in the sixties, my commitment to pacifism has always been integrally connected to my concerns for the welfare of women. I understand now that my self representations in the case study stemmed from my passionate desire to speak for myself and others who historically have felt themselves silenced by androcentric educational discourses and practices. On some levels, I knew then that in constructing the case study I created a history which exceeded that which was sayable within the context of a conservative, male dominated department at a major university. The case history provided a legitimated avenue for me to theoretically explore multiple subject positions I occupied as a woman in academe. The case history is the story of self in flux. As such, it de-centers the I narrating the story. Carol Steedman's (1987) *Landscape for a good woman* helps me understand that I had strategically, and not fully consciously, utilized the case history as an interpretive device.

The stories in my educational case study historicized the cultural relations and conditions which constituted me "woman" at different points in time. A subtext carried my critique of the descriptions of the normal female adult learner as described in dominant ideology. The autobiographic stories I included in the case study were stories about political and economic struggle and feminist activism; as such, they both exceeded and undercut the story I had been expected to tell. Mine was not a linear, seamless history of normative, female development. The female adult learner in my case study occupied transgressive subject positions. In contextualizing the experiences which constituted these diverse subject positions, I offered story lines which created sites for alternate readings of the text. I had returned to the university to arm myself with theory. I see now how my first attempts to do so rather unwittingly resulted in the creation of excessive and disarming embodied theory.

Theory in the Flesh:
We Enter Academe with Storied Bodies

I included life stories in my academic writing long before I realized that there were complex theories to describe this practice. Bringing my life experiences into educational settings seemed commonsensical. How could I avoid doing so? I had entered academe with a storied body. Hence, it seemed self evident that I would also bring embodied life experiences to the theories I studied. My research has helped me appreciate ways in which dominant educational discourses and practices work to keep minds and bodies disassociated in the processes involved in the construction of theory. I recognize also, that students in Western academe have grown accustomed to and often prefer talking head teaching methods which usually accompany this form of theorizing. The intellect rules—cognitive understanding is prized above other kinds of knowing. I am discovering how comfortable disembodied teaching and learning is for many students—and a good number of faculty as well.

Recently, in designing and facilitating an University of Wisconsin-Madison Educational Policy/Women's Studies course titled "Education and Sex Role Socialization," I instituted pedagogical practices which I believed would work to de-center me in my role as instructor while promoting embodied learning. I found the majority of students in the class confused, resistant, and covertly and overtly angry as they struggled to meet my pedagogical expectations. It soon became apparent to me that I had disrupted familiar and comfortable ways of learning. Within a few weeks, a good number of students seemed to be deeply—often openly—

questioning their historical passivity in the roles they occupied as students.

Embodied Theorizing Invites Crisis

I invited students to bring their lived experiences associated with gender and education to their readings of the assigned texts, to our classroom discussions, to their written assignments, and to other class-related projects. I asked students to engage in their work for the course simultaneously with their bodies, spirits, and minds. During our first class meeting, I announced that there would be no "right answers" in this course; rather, both individually and in collaboration, we would critically examine multiple, at times, conflicting theories about gender, education, and sex role socialization. The latter was a concept I found problematic but felt I must address since it was part of the official course title.

It seems odd to me now that I believed students would eagerly embrace what I understand to be embodied ways of engaging with theory. I now recognize that I had asked students to approach their studies of gender and education in the ways I would have liked to have been asked and/or permitted to work with theory as a student in a similar course. For me, an invitation to engage theory with my lived experiences would have been a welcomed gift. I was soon aware that my somewhat unconventional pedagogical approaches were frightening to many students; the practices I asked them to employ seemed to thrust many students into various states of disequilibrium and crisis in relationship to their participation and learning in the class.

Conclusion:
Illuminating Questions One's Life Addresses

I realized that I, not unlike some other feminists instructors who were also activists during the early years of the Second Wave of the Women's Movement, had greatly disturbed the world views of students who, from my perspective, had in the span of one generation benefited immensely from feminist movements! How, I wondered, was I to deal with the anger, resistance, and discomfort I perceived in myself and many of the students over this and other issues—all of which seemed to be related to certain of my feminist teaching practices? How, I asked myself, might I lessen the pain and confusion I saw registered in the bodies of the thirty some young women and one man enrolled in the class? I have written elsewhere of this struggle and shall not address it further here since other contributors in the anthology have written quite extensively and eloquently of similar struggles in their feminist classrooms.

I do however continue to grapple with these questions and find myself asking similar questions as I work with women enrolled in a continuing education course—"Life writing as spiritual practice"—I am facilitating at a small religious liberal arts college. As I work with life writing with diverse groups of students in different contexts, it becomes clearer to me that to a large extent the questions I explore both in my research on life writing as curriculum and in my attempts to engage students in ways which invite them to embody their understandings of the theories we examine are centered in the questions I believe my life addresses. I believe that recognized or not, this will always be so when theory is engaged with experientially.

I know now that my decision to pursue and complete a doctorate stemmed in part from the conviction that it was imperative that I learn to believe in and value my unique conscious and unconscious experiences of self. I know also the critical importance of learning to speak for and of myself within one of the contexts in which I had felt annihilated and/or asked to abandon experiential knowledge of self and others in the complex worlds I inhabit. Completing and successfully defending my dissertation while editing this anthology was a powerfully informative, deeply embodied experience. As graduate student, I struggled daily in my dissertation writing to find ways to respect and honor my experiential understandings of the role of the unconscious in working across socially formed differences in academe. Feverishly working to de-center the I in ways I hoped would please my orals committee, I found it impossible to escape multiple discursive constructions of self. Attempts to theorize and de-center the authorial I of autobiography kept me firmly planted in what I understood to be my self. In sharp contrast, in my role as co-editor of this anthology of autobiographic narratives of women's experience in academe, I have from the beginning been struck by what seems to be my, Linda Christian-Smith's, and the contributors' seemingly almost ego-less engagement with the discernment process outlined in the prospectus for this anthology. For me, this paradoxical selflessness has been an unexpected pleasure. Not as surprising to me, yet still deeply satisfying, is the knowledge that in engaging deeply with the particularities of our lived experiences of self and other in academe we have paradoxically de-centered the I of our autobiographic texts.

Notes

1. Some text in this chapter was excerpted from papers I presented at conferences in St. Paul, Minnesota (Kellor, October, 1994), San Francisco, California (Kellor, Bailey & Schaafsma, April, 1995), and Monteagle, Tennessee (Kellor, Schaafsma & Trubek, September, 1995). Portions of the chapter were abstracted from my unpublished doctoral dissertation (Kellor, 1996). To minimize the interruptions in

the narrative flow which would necessarily occur were I to follow conventional citation practices, I have elected to not cite passages extracted from the aforementioned texts.

2. Several readers of this chapter as well as readers of my dissertation have commented on my frequent references to, yet superficial textual treatment of, spirituality. While not consciously deciding to avoid a detailed discussion of spirituality in either my dissertation or this chapter, when asked to explore in more detail the role of spirituality in what one reader described as my "self-transformation" I declined. On some levels, I find this ironic since the topic continues to be of immediate and great interest to me. So much so, in fact, that I recently developed, proposed, and facilitate, at a local Catholic liberal arts college, a Continuing Education course for women titled "Life Writing as Spiritual Practice." It is my sense that at this time spirituality is for me too sacred and too tender to be explored openly—and I fear ruthlessly—through what I suspect I think of as the more profane lenses characterizing most research in western academe.

References

Anzaldúa, G. (1987) *Borderlands la frontera: the new mestiza*. San Francisco: Aunt Lute Books.

Bollas, C. (1987). *The shadow of the object: Psychoanalysis of the unthought known*. New York: Columbia University.

Bollas, C. (1992). *Being a character: Psychoanalysis and self experience*. New York: Hill & Wang.

Bollas, C. (1995). *Cracking up: The work of unconscious experience*. New York: Hill & Wang.

Butler, J. (1990). *Gender trouble: Feminism and the subversion of identity*. New York: Routledge.

Felman, S. (1993). *What does a woman want? Reading and sexual difference*. Baltimore: Johns Hopkins University.

Felman, S., & Laub, D. (1992). *Testimony: Crises of witnessing in literature, psychoanalysis, and history*. New York: Routledge.

Fiske, J. (1987). *Television culture*. London: Methuen.

Fiske, J. (1989). *Understanding popular culture*. Boston: Unwin.

Foucault, M. (1972). *The Archaeology of knowledge & the discourse on language*. NY: Pantheon.

Fuss, D. (1989). *Essentially speaking: Feminism, nature & difference*. NY: Routledge.

Gandhi, M. (1960). *All men are brothers: Life & thoughts of Mahatma Gandhi as told in his own words*. (Compiled & edited by Krishna Kriplalani.) NY: Columbia University.

Gilmore, L. (1994). *Autobiographics: A feminist theory of women's self-representation*. Ithaca, NY: Cornell University.

Jung, C. G. (with von Franz, M.-L., Henderson, J. L., Jacobi, J., & Jaffe, A.), (1968). *Man and his symbols*. New York: Dell.

Kellor, K. S. (1994, October). *Understanding self, understanding others: Examining 'experience' through discourse analysis of autobiographical narratives in-*

corporated into my graduate school writings. Paper presented at Research on Women American Educational Research Association Special Interest Group Conference, St. Paul, MN.

Kellor, K. S. (1996). *Autobiographic narrative as curriculum: the work of the unconscious in experiential knowledge, embodied theorizing, and representations of self and other.* Unpublished doctoral dissertation. University of Wisconsin – Madison, WI.

Kellor, K. S., Bailey, C., & Schaafsma, D. (1995, April). *Things we can't say: Stories, gender and excess.* Symposium conducted at American Educational Research Association Conference, San Francisco, CA.

Kellor, K. S., Schaafsma, D., & Trubek, J. (1995, September). *Theorizing the academic body.* Symposium/panel discussion conducted at Journal of Curriculum Theorizing Conference, Monteagle, TN.

Middleton, S. (1993). *Educating feminists: Life histories and pedagogy.* New York: Teachers College, Columbia University.

Phelan, P. (1993). *Unmarked: The politics of performance.* New York: Routledge.

Ram Dass, B. (1971). *Be Here Now.* NY: Crown.

Steedman, C. K. (1987). *Landscape for a good woman: A story of two lives.* New Brunswick, NJ: Rutgers University.

Watts, A. (1951). *The Wisdom of Insecurity,* New York: Vintage.

Weedon, C. (1987). *Feminist practice and poststructuralist theory.* New York: Blackwell.

4 Strangers in a Strange Land: A Woman Studying Women's Literacies

Linda K. Christian-Smith

The title of this chapter reflects my focus on the estrangement that many working class women such as myself experience when they move beyond their class boundaries into the academy where they often conduct research with women. In this chapter I recount and analyze a series of "life" and "research" stories constituting my sixteen years of literacies research with women and the popular fiction they read (Christian-Smith, 1990, 1991, 1993). "Story" refers to a succession of events organized in some coherent manner (Hatch & Wisniewski, 1995, p. 7). These stories represent my reflections on the personal, practical, political and ethical matters when undertaking research with women. These stories also constitute a series of discernment processes through which I examine who I am as a researcher, how my background shapes the focus of my research, the questions I ask, the interpretations I construct and the ways I attempt to translate theory into practice through my involvement with social justice movements. I begin with a description of the intellectual frameworks that shape my personal and professional lives, especially my research.

Research: Frameworks and Frames of Mind

I became interested in methodologies from life history research only recently although the approach itself is over seventy years old. According to an interview with Chinn (in Hatch & Wisniewski, 1995, p. 115), "life history is composed of self-referential stories through which the author-narrator constructs the identity and point(s) of view of a unique individual historically situated in culture, time, and place." These stories are so-cially-situated narratives "in which larger concepts of culture get de-fined and worked out by one individual" (Bloom & Munro in Hatch & Wisniewski, 1995, p. 117). Life history can reveal what it means to oc-cupy particular gender, class, racial, ethnic and sexual positions while providing glimpses of social changes related to these positions.

I find that life history research fits well with several aspects of feminist critical approaches I use emphasizing subjectivities formation and reflexivity. I believe reflexive knowledge not only includes participants' reflections on life experiences, but refers to accounts of the ways researchers' subjectivities shape and are shaped by research and through the research context (Woolgar, 1988). Life history approaches also illuminate the power-knowledge relations between researchers and their participants and the ways written accounts of qualitative research have reduced the complexities of participants' cultures and meanings and obscured the political interests of researchers themselves (Opie, 1992). I agree with Lather's (1986) suggestion that the aim of critical in-quiry is to help participants understand the perspectives that legitimate the dominant orders of society as well as break their hold. I would add that this applies to researchers as well.

Autobiography as a form of life history enables me to account for the interplay between my background, research processes and outcomes. According to Benstock (1988), autobiography is an attempt to re-search one's selves and one's relationship to others and to explore the spaces between inside and outside where difference resides. In autobiography I found an important means for tracing my self-development through conducting research. Writing in one form or another has always been a significant part of my life. In autobiographical writing I produce a series of "life stories" which I regard as discourses to be analyzed or decon-structed. I quite agree with Pearce and Stacey's (1995, p. 27) definition of discourse as "ways of thinking associated with a particular historical moment and legitimated by its ruling institutions." I find in discourse analysis an effective strategy for "reading" and interpreting my life and research stories (Fairclough, 1989; Gee, 1990). Following Gavey's sugges-tions (1989), I look for patterns of power, meaning, contradictions and inconsistencies in written and spoken language. Discourse analysis is an approach that identifies the language processes people use to constitute their own and others' understanding of personal and social phenomena. Because my research is concerned with the formation of women's social subjectivities through popular fiction, my own story in this regard is an important part of the research process. As I will now indicate, much of my thinking has stemmed from my involvement in several important historical moments such as the union movements of the 1950s, the second wave of feminism and the student demonstrations against the Vietnam war, all of which have questioned the dominant social order in the United States.

My Life Stories: Rebel with a Cause

After reading the first draft of this paper, I was struck by how I position myself as a rebel in one way or another. When I was growing up in Northern Minnesota in the late 1940s and early 1950s, there were few books in my Eastern Euroamerican working-class home. My earliest texts were comic books and a few "Little Golden Books" often read to me by family members. I became literate before formal schooling because of Miss Dora Staley, a neighbor who was also an elementary teacher. Miss Dora lived with her mother in a large, elegant home that was unusual for our part of town. Miss Dora was especially popular with the neighborhood children because of the cookies left cooling on the pantry window sill in the summer for us to sneak and the games and books piled in a big basket on her back porch. With Miss Dora's books and coaching, I learned to read before starting school at four years old.

During elementary school my constant companions were library books, Nancy Drew, Archie and Veronica comics and my grandmother's *True Romances* secretly read in my closet. An only child until eight years old, these materials filled the time when friends were not around. Although abundant in religious books, my catholic school library had little for an adventuresome girl such as myself. The public library soon became a part of my world although I was confined to the children's book section which I quickly read. With reading materials always in short supply and in constant trouble for reading adult books, my favorite pastime was to spend hours gazing longingly at the reading materials at the local newsstand. A few doors down, there was a bookstore where the sign "No Children Allowed Without an Adult" confined me mostly to staring through the window.

When I finally entered this bookstore by myself as a teenager with babysitting money in my pocket, I felt like a stranger in paradise. Although this bookstore soon became another favorite haunt, I always felt out-of-place like that child with her face against the glass peering into forbidden territory. For now I was consorting with the likes of Jane Austen, Charles Dickens, George Eliot and Jules Verne, heady company for an unsure girl of my social class. I read a good deal of Charles Dickens and Jane Austen—Dickens spoke of the plight of the dominated classes, something which connected well with the struggles of my family. Austen was my window on privilege and women's subservience despite this. As I searched for good books, I was guided by an image of myself as a girl desiring another life, the life of the mind. This was certainly a different path from my friends, family and for a working class girl of the times.

Being a competent student further estranged me from my immediate social world. Once my family became more prosperous, we relocated to a new home on the edge of town in 1958. This move and starting high school with my sights on college further distanced me from my longtime friends. The price I paid for school success and developing a scholarly frame of mind was not only disconnection from my childhood friends, but much of my blue-collar culture. To be a stand out in segments of the Euroamerican working class, especially if you are a woman, often results in being branded as "uppity," "selfish" and regarding yourself as better than others. My desire for a career rather than boyfriends caused my parents to question my "normality." During high school I underwent a rapid cultural transformation. I did not fit in with the few middle-class students at my school or with my working-class childhood friends. My parents' efforts to acquire the material symbols of what they felt constituted middle-class culture such as newer cars, fashionable clothing and new furniture set us apart from the "old" middle class with their books, knowledge of classical music and garden club luncheons. So despite my wool pleated skirts and Shetland sweaters (the visible markers of middle class teenage femininity), my self-conscious speech and ways marked me as an interloper in this class. My family did not associate with many well-established middle class families because of the realities of my father's job as a steelworker and his fierce trade unionism.

My emerging middle-class subjectivities continually clashed with my working-class heritage. The strong familial trade union tradition had given me a critique of the middle class. From my earliest memories my father's left-leaning CIO steelworkers union had surrounded my life. I developed my activism and probably working class consciousness in the union hall helping to make sandwiches for the strikers and on the picketline marching with my parents and neighbors during the great steel strikes of the 1950s and 1960s. In this tradition, the middle and elite classes represented management, "the enemy." Yet, I felt as if I were living in two separate worlds: the one I was born into, the one my parents yearned for despite their critique and the one I was constructing out of what I thought well-educated women were like. In this, I had few models of an educated woman other than Miss Staley and a few women high school teachers. I groped along the best I could trying to reconcile the opposing forces within me. Upon high school graduation in 1963, I was the only neighborhood girl who was going to college. I had earned a full four-year scholarship. My family was very proud because as a second-generation American, I was the first person on both sides of the family to go to college. I chose education for my major in honor of Miss Staley who had died that year and because that was the only other option readily available to women besides nursing. My parents supported my career choice as it was respectable employment for a young woman until hopefully married with children and would provide "something to fall back on."

Had I attended the university during any other time but the 1960s, I would have quit after the first quarter. Even at a public university like Minnesota, class and gender assumptions permeated the university culture. I found much middle class bias in the assumption that everyone had access to this class's resources and knowledge and willingly shared its perspectives despite the growing numbers of working class students enrolling. This was especially the case in my major fields, English and French. In order to remain in good standing and keep my sights on graduate school, I had to lead a divided life. Although I often felt a great deal of tension, confusion and discomfort in not having women's experiences and that of the working class included in my coursework, I gradually learned to survive in academic environments. I altered my speech, my demeanor and frequently remained silent or carefully articulated my opinions. I was quickly distinguished by my professors as a "serious student" who planned on securing a Ph.D. and having an academic career someday. Yet, the university was merely a means to an end for me: a way to pursue my scholarly interests and a job with dignity and decent pay so that I could be an independent woman in control of her destiny.

While I found the politics of higher education very frustrating, I was clear about my social agenda: the Vietnam War was unjust and all U. S. citizens should have access to the wealth, power and opportunities afforded the few. My heritage of social critique of the corporate sector and the profit mentality made me a strong opponent of the War. Corporate profits were at stake in Southeast Asia and not the political autonomy of the people. I was drawn to the Civil Rights Movement because of the harassment I had experienced as a Polish American, mild in comparison to that of Afroamericans, nonetheless hurtful and disturbing to me. In the 1960s, it was very easy to jettison the "establishment" symbolized by the university. Many of my middle-class acquaintances who took over the administrative buildings and classrooms at Minnesota had family resources to fall back on. My situation was complicated by the fact that I had few financial resources. As a scholarship student I had to tread carefully. Although I daily witnessed the elitism and injustices of the university, it offered the only path to the teaching credential I desired. I became disillusioned with the anti-war movement as it did not provide the hoped-for haven from oppression. Rather, women were often treated as "camp wives" and secretaries. Although I loved to write, I struggled against the denial of credit for position statements and ideas. These circumstances were at odds with the feminist perspectives on women's equality with men that I was developing. Some of this thinking was inherited from my mother, who, in her own way, was a second-wave feminist. She regularly chaffed at my father's insistence that she not work outside of the home and focus her life on home and family. Her outrage at instances of cruelty towards women and unfair treatment and belief that women possessed the intelligence and ability to shape their destinies inspired my work against oppression in any form then and now.

In 1967 I became a certified English and French teacher, gravitating towards young women students like myself long ago, outsiders who desired to control their destinies. I also directed my teaching energies and resources towards children of both genders who by virtue of birth found themselves on the outside looking in at the education they needed and deserved. As in the past, I myself remained an outsider, now within teacher culture as I translated my activism into another realm. My battles to keep students with reading difficulties in their regular classrooms and out of special education often placed me at odds with my colleagues. Once I started working in the field of reading education, I noticed that so many of my students were working class and minorities. I slowly realized that the schools were sorting systems and important sites in maintaining the political and economic status quo, especially through literacy. As the years passed it became increasingly difficult to effectively teach as I saw fit because of my school's practice of tracking students and my own need to simply know more to be a good teacher. In the summer of 1979 I found myself on the other side of the desk, in the heady company of theorists of the sociology of education Basil Bernstein, Pierre Bourdieu, Rachel Sharpe and Michael Young, who spoke in another language, one that would become increasingly familiar as my doctoral studies progressed.

A two-year unpaid leave gave me my formal start on doctoral work in the sociology of curriculum at Wisconsin in 1980. These were difficult times for me: long commutes to the university, working with student teachers, caring for family and declining health. There was also the challenge of learning the new languages of critical theory and various feminist approaches as well as the exhilaration of linking then to my everyday knowledge of schooling and that gained from struggles for social justice. Although I was a mature student with considerable teaching experience, I felt once again like that child of long ago peering into the forbidden territory of the bookstore. With many young students in the doctoral seminar who had been continuously in school and few students like myself, my unsureness was increased. The loss of self was mirrored in a loss of voice during class discussions and in the awkward style of my writing. For the longest time, it was if some other person were writing the essays and dissertation praised by my professors that my English professors of long ago would scarcely recognize as belonging to me. It was not until I wrote my book *Becoming a woman through romance* during the late 1980s that I recaptured the wit, flow and power of my former writing voice with the added edge that four years of graduate school had given me. Yet there was exhilaration and empowerment along with the uncertainty of graduate school. My readings in critical and feminist theory and new research approaches helped me construct social theories and research methodologies that explained and validated so many of my experiences as a woman teacher and activist along with giving me the means to delve more deeply into the meaning of these experiences. When I finished my Ph.D. degree in 1984, I emerged with the theories and research strategies I needed for a more sophisticated analysis of the contradictory positions of schooling, particularly literacy education in western societies. The time in graduate school had also solidified my decision to concentrate on teacher education where I felt that I could do children the best service by preparing more critically-oriented teachers.

I began my career in higher education accompanied by my feminist social reconstruction orientation in 1985. My experiences in higher education certainly mirrors those of other contributors, in particular Luke, Lewis, McCall, and Middleton. While I do not want to retrace their steps, there are some issues that resonate with me strongly. My idea of the critical practitioner was met with much resistance by colleagues and students. I soon encountered resistance to the ideas represented by feminisms, cultural pluralism and critical theory among staff at the two institutions where I have taught. When involved in a controversy regarding the denial of tenure to a male colleague, who was very friendly with my former dean, I found myself and my perspectives "on trial." I was harassed in covert and direct ways: disturbing phone calls and notes, complaints to my former dean about the office schedule I kept, a difficult teaching schedule my first two years, lowered merit pay ratings, attempts to block my tenure and denial of institutional recognition. While the climate in my particular college has vastly improved with several retirements and the hiring of a new dean, who has been very supportive of me and scholarship in general, much damage has been done to myself and others. Although I have finally received the recognition I deserve as a newly endowed professor, the recognition seems hollow. For eight years of battles have dampened my spirits, further weakened my physical condition and kept me at the margins of institutional life to protect myself from further harm. At my present institution, some students have also been especially resistant to the socially transformative content and pedagogies used in my initial teacher certification courses and very vocal about it. Like Lewis, student evaluation comments range from "the best" to "the worst" course taken. However, these circumstances have not deterred me from realizing my vision of a woman faculty person as a change-agent through her positions as teacher-scholar. So much of my joy and reason for remaining in the business of higher education is scholarship, particularly researching with women. Through creating and disseminating knowledge, I hope to effect change for this and the next generation of young women.

This account of aspects of my life story is not intended as a transparent medium, but as a discourse to be analyzed in relation to my research experiences. I now turn to this deconstruction.

Research: The Stories Women Tell

Since 1982 I have been involved in three large scale studies pertaining to the construction of women's social subjectivities, especially gender through reading popular fiction. I conduct all of my research with women because of my desires to understand my own and others' social development as women and how women resist the processes that often defer or eclipse hopes and dreams. I would like to situate the ensuing discussion by providing an account of each study from my own perspectives, which may differ if other points of view, that of participants, were incorporated.

My first study was my doctoral dissertation which featured a close textual analysis of thirty-four teen romance novels popular with young women ages 11–15. These and others were the books that my own students were reading when I entered my graduate program. My students' contradictory responses puzzled me and encouraged me to further investigate teen romance novels. The study's theoretical frameworks and methodologies were drawn from feminist cultural studies, critical theory, political economy and semiotics (Christian-Smith, 1990). I was attracted to these approaches as they provided compelling ways of thinking about social subjectivities formation and the role of popular culture in maintaining prevailing economic conditions that were often not favorable to women. Because a textual analysis alone cannot account for the nuances of interpretations by actual readers, some years later I conducted a companion study with twenty-nine young women readers of teen romance novels ages 11–13 coming from diverse class, race and ethnic backgrounds in three middle level schools. For this reader study, I integrated ethnography and survey research into the theoretical frameworks and research methodologies developed for the first textual study. I was drawn to ethnography as a way to account for young women's understandings of teen romance fiction, especially the presence of oppositional readings. I was also especially interested in the school as the context for situated readings and possible connections between women's present and future lives.

As I was finishing the previous study I became intrigued with the Nancy Drew mystery novels while doing my annual home office cleaning. Behind some books I found the three slim blue-bound novels I had received as a child. Recalling the strong impact these novels had made on me, I wondered if that had been the case with other readers. These wonderings became greatly expanded over the next ten years as I analyzed 100 novels written from 1930–1995, researched the writers of the Nancy Drew mysteries and interviewed related and non-related women readers ages 9–65 from diverse social class and racial backgrounds (Christian-Smith, 1991, 1993, in press 1999). In this study of the Nancy Drew mystery novels, I used several new research methodologies and incorporated new areas of inquiry. These stemmed from my awareness of the limits of previously used methodologies. I now explored the position of the researcher and her impact on the focus and findings of research through the use of life history methodologies in the form of researcher's autobiography and the life narratives of participants. When studying romance fiction, I realized the power of discourse in shaping human subjectivities. My extended reading in the area of discourse theory convinced me that discourse analysis could more fully disclose the nuances of popular fiction's impact on the formation of readers' subjectivities. Interviewing women readers in two families across generations revealed the centrality of women in acquiring literacy and in shaping young women's futures. Adult women's sharing of reading materials with young women was one way of providing them with models of righteous human interactions and as a form of support for young women's aspirations.

With these stories of my research projects in mind, I want to place my research and personal background in relation to the discernment questions from the introduction. Through discourse analysis of my autobiography and research stories, I have identified the following as recurring discourses: gender, class, race, ethnicity, sexuality, estrangement, and empowerment. The discourses available to me as an Eastern Euroamerican woman in the contradictory class locations of working and middle class have strongly shaped who I am as a researcher, what I bring to my research, the questions guiding this research and the interpretation of the data.

My life history provides glimpses of lifelong struggles to obtain access to various gender and class discourses associated with the middle class through which I could realize my dreams for personal and economic independence and the life of the mind. Yet, I also was very critical of the exclusionary practices of this social class. Moreover, I wanted to retain my working class identity which formed the basis of my involvement in social justice movements. My life history also describes the ways my lived experiences of gender, class, and ethnic biases led to my political activism. Formal education provided the theories of feminisms, critical theory, and race and ethnic studies. This education also further distanced me from my heritage and eventually the very institutions in which I worked as I encountered much social bias. The estrangement I felt throughout much of my schooling and teaching career is at the basis of my research. All my scholarship examines why certain groups of women are historically outsiders to wealth and power in the United States and how they attempt to transcend their marginality in that regard.

The decision to study women's popular literacies stems from my life history. My first texts were popular fiction like Nancy Drew, which gave me access to the world beyond my neighborhood and social class. My introduction to the romance genre came from my grandmother's *Modern romance* magazines, a working class genre. I did not read any of the early teen romance fiction writers like Betty Cavanna and Rosamond du Jardin. Rather, I discovered this literary tradition during my doctoral research. Popular fiction coexisted uneasily with the canonical texts my teachers required as preparation for college and later during my undergraduate and graduate studies in English. Popular fiction shaped my social subjectivities by constructing possible worlds in which I could situate myself as powerful, genteel and vulnerable as I became the books' characters in my imagination. Later, as a researcher, I wondered if this fiction had the same impact on others. That all of my research centers around social subjectivities formation in women is also an outcome of my personal and political preoccupations. My interest in young working class women who are often resisters stems from my own feelings of estrangement. While my estrangement was somewhat different due to differences in time and place, I nevertheless have important connections to these women.

When I was growing up, talk shaped the interactions between myself and my female relatives and their friends. Not only did I acquire knowledge through reading, but also through conversations while my mother ironed and I helped my grandmother with the baking. In many segments of the working class, children, especially girls, are also taught through watching adults. I gravitated towards the qualitative research strategies of interviewing and observation because of the importance of talk, listening and watching in my class culture. In my current use of interview methods, I attempt to create a conversation between myself and participants to transcend the "masculine paradigm" of question-and-answer. This has brought many questions from participants in the Nancy Drew study which considerably enriched the findings. I am also concerned with building relationships with participants that are non-hierarchical and based upon mutual respect. I am most at home in participants' kitchens sipping tea or a new coffee I brought along to share. Since childhood, I have been accustomed to "reading across the grain" because my life realities were different from those represented in my books. My early education in working class and gender politics on the picket line, in the union hall and in the kitchen reinforced those literate practices. As an English major, I had to become very adept at textual analysis and am consequently drawn to methodologies such as semiotics and discourse analysis that are sensitive to the ways language empowers and disempowers women. I gradually learned how to deal with the tensions between the "master narratives" of the canon and my critiques of them and to trust my instincts. Because of these oppositional reading practices, I am especially interested in how Afroamerican women in the Nancy Drew study continually " translated" these books as childhood readers to fit their own life histories. I had observed this practice among Afroamerican and Chicana girls in my study of teen romance readers where they critiqued and/or fit themselves into the narrative according to their personal backgrounds. When fifty-four-year-old Afroamerican Louise Jamison reflected on her childhood reading of Nancy Drew, it was in the context of shared reading with the Euroamerican granddaughter of the family for whom Louise's mother cleaned house. Both girls became empowered as they read about a strong and resourceful woman character and became detectives as they acted out scenes from the books. This moment of crossing racial boundaries as each took turns being Nancy Drew and her sidekicks was nevertheless permeated by the larger unequal power relations of gender, class and race played out through Louise and her mother's positions as domestic help. Although Louise's sister Corla was especially critical of the negative and derogatory depictions of Afroamericans in the early Nancy Drew mysteries, she still found the books interesting, educational and worthwhile reading. As a childhood reader of Nancy Drew fiction, I often encountered the gap between Nancy's affluent and expansive world and my own modest circumstances. For the longest time I could not believe that any girl could have these resources and freedom. I continued to read hoping to experience these things myself through the imagination and perhaps in the future.

On Being a Woman Researcher: Some Further Thoughts

My background is a strength and at times a limitation when conducting research with women. Because some of my experiences are similar to

Euroamerican participants, I have to keep in check my tendencies to romanticize and celebrate the resistant practices of working class women, especially when they appear to reproduce dominant patterns of power. This was most pronounced during the Nancy Drew study where I not only shared elements of social class background, but was also a childhood reader of Nancy Drew. Like so many of the senior women, I regarded Nancy as a "free spirit" whose intelligence and strength I admired and strove to emulate. These instances of participants' breaking with dominant views of women as fragile and domestic are thrilling to feminist researchers such as myself. Yet, there is the constant reminder of the discourses of class, race and ethnicity that also shape femininities. For Nancy is a Euroamerican girl of the privileged classes who is also strongly bound to her home. The "revolutionary" aspects of Nancy's character and life are always balanced by her shopping excursions, culinary and sewing expertise and immersion in a teenage heterosexual culture of dances, dating and boyfriends. While Nancy Drew fiction reading may "free" readers to wander further in the world, it also keeps them from wandering too far. Both moments are important to record and analyze as are my reactions and feelings concerning them.

As a woman academic, I am aware of the power differences between myself and participants and how those differences impact on research procedures and the interpretation of the data. As much as I may feel comfortable in a participant's kitchen sipping tea and talking about popular fiction reading, I am shaping the interaction through the questions asked, comments made and my mere presence as a woman who has stepped far beyond the kitchen door. I am also in this kitchen on "business." Research is part of my career, despite my devotion to lofty ideals of creating knowledge and partnerships with women and struggling for change (Lather, 1986). Knowing that I have built my livelihood upon women's knowledge and lives places me uncomfortably in the company of others who have done the same, though perhaps without the intentions of being caring and respectful. These issues are even more evident when conducting research with women whose race and ethnicity I do not share. While spending time with the women of the Louise Jamison and Corla Jefferson families, there were many occasions when differences stemming from culture, power and language emerged which were awkward and difficult to negotiate. By naming and confronting these differences, I am taking necessary steps towards understanding the meaning of these differences and working with and through them. However, I am still a member of a race that has actively oppressed Afroamericans and has privileges based on race for which most Afroamericans must struggle. Dealing with these realities through the writing stemming from my research is ongoing. I believe it goes hand and hand with my gradual coming to terms with being a worker in a "knowledge factory" that has commonalities with other factories here and around the world where women of various backgrounds toil under difficult circumstances. I continue to be guided by these precepts when researching with women: to explore the small and large actions of women that keep them in their places and also have the potential to disrupt these conservative times and offer other ways of being and knowing for women.

References

Benstock, S. (1988). *The private self: Theory and practice of women's autobiography.* Chapel Hill: The University of North Carolina Press.

Bloom, L. R., & Munro, P. (1995). Conflicts of selves: Nonunitary subjectivity in women administrators' life history narratives. In J. A. Hatch & R. Wisniewski (Eds.), *Life history and narrative.*(pp. 99–112). London: The Falmer Press.

Christian-Smith, L. K. (1990). *Becoming a woman through romance.* New York: Routledge.

Christian-Smith, L. K. (in press 1999). More than crime on her mind: Nancy Drew as woman hero. In D. Jones & T. Watkins, (Eds.), *The heroic figure in children's literature.* Hamden, CT: Garland Press.

Christian-Smith, L. K. (1991). Partial and plural visions: Social identities in Nancy Drew mysteries. A paper presented at the Research on Women and Education Conference, November 7–9, 1991, San Jose, CA.

Christian-Smith, L. K. (1993). *Texts of desire: Essays on fiction, femininities and schooling*. London: The Falmer Press.

Fairclough, N. (1989). *Language and power.* London: Longman.

Gavey, N. (1989). Feminist poststructuralism and discourse analysis: Contributions to feminist psychology. *Psychology of Women Quarterly, 13,* 459–475.

Gee J. (1990). *Social linguistics and literacies: Ideology in discourses.* London: Falmer Press.

Hatch, J. A., & Wisniewski, R. (1995). *Life history and narrative.* London: Falmer Press.

Lather, P. (1986). Research as praxis. *Harvard Educational Review, 56,* 257–277.

Longhurst, D. (1989). *Gender, genre and narrative pleasure.* London: Unwin Hyman.

Munro, P. (1993). Continuing dilemmas of life history research: A reflexive attempt of feminist qualitative inquiry. In D. Flinders & G. Mills (Eds.), *Theory and concepts in qualitative research: Perspectives from the field.* (pp., 163–177). New York: Teachers College Press.

Opie, A. (1992). Qualitative research: Appropriation of the 'other' and empowerment. *Feminist Review, 40,* 52–69.

Pearce, L., & Stacey, J. (1995). *Romance revisited.* London: Lawrence & Wishart.

Woolgar, S. (1988). *Science: The very idea.* London: Tavistock.

5 The Backlash Factor: Women, Intellectual Labour and Student Evaluation of Courses and Teaching[1]

Magda Lewis

All teaching is political, even teaching which disclaims its politics. . . . For to teach is to bring others to look at things in new ways, to reorient them to the horizon of their world. That we are changed in the process of education is no mere accident. We teachers want to change our students. And we are certain that the change is for the better.
—Pagano (1990), p. xiii-xiv

If the term "eventful" refers to an experience that is unanticipated and surprising, then most of the time, my experience of the academy is singularly uneventful. Over the years since my first appointment as "regular" faculty, I have learned to recognize the small daily indignities of institutional misogyny[2] to the point where I am no longer surprised by them. There was a time when a colleague's accusations that the courses I teach are an "invasion on the core body of course offerings," left me perplexed and tongue tied for a response. There was a time when I considered it nothing but exceptionally rude when conversations with women colleagues seemed unproblematically to be interrupted by anyone who happened along needing to have something to say. There was a time when colleagues' deliberate steering away of students from courses that had any feminist content (Powell, 1996), their apparent commitment to notions of academic freedom notwithstanding, left me weeping with rage, although never short of students. And there was a time when, the distinctly ambiguous and observably differential application of the processes of peer review for the purposes of tenure and promotion in rank, while, at the time (but no longer), looming large before me, seemed to represent historical residue from another era, or so I thought.

In the academy, the instrumentalities of the ordinary abuses of administrative and collegial power (also known as systemic discrimination) turned to the advancement of personal gain no longer surprise me. Institutional misogyny is one of these instrumentalities; it is a fact of the academy. It functions with precision in the service of a status quo aimed at maintaining "differential social relations of power" (Edelman, 1994). Indeed, what does surprise me is the "endless variety of monotonous similarity," as Gayle Rubin[3] so aptly describes the oppression of women under patriarchy, with which such misogyny is displayed and executed in the academy, whether this be in the realm of practice or theory, private or public, personal or political.

In this chapter, I return to examine yet one more monotonous rendition of patriarchy's capacity for reproducing its power with the force of endless similarity: administrative use of student evaluations of courses and teaching as an instrument of gate keeping across traditional lines of acceptably "bodied" knowledges, for the purposes of renewal of appointment and the granting of tenure and promotion. However, even as I do this I feel a rather weary reluctance to get to the text of this analysis. I note that I do not make this trip happily or with enthusiasm. My spirits for this work are low for good reason. I am exhausted with the questions: Haven't we gone over this before? Didn't we just do this? Hadn't we just begun to think that we might finally be released from this incessant "monotony," gender power in the academy, to finally turn our attention to other things? I am beginning to think that feminist politics, like housework, is never done. Just when it appears some headway might have been made, dust balls begin to gather, first in the corners, then under the furniture and soon we are called back to it again, scrubbing the same floors and polishing the same mantles, gripped by the impossibility of letting it go unattended.

Presently, this "endless variety of monotonous similarity" is gripping me where I live so much of my everyday life: the academy. I am reminded of a casual conversation with Evelyn Fox-Keller a few years ago when she visited my university as a guest speaker. The exact details of the conversation, tellingly, are no longer with me. However, it concerned our delight in sharing with her some apparent gain accomplished for women on our campus around the time of her visit. Apologizing for perhaps dampening our impulse to celebrate too soon, she urged caution. The power of patriarchy, she suggested, is like water. When it is prevented from going in one direction it swells and pours off in another, perhaps altogether unexpected, direction with as much force and power as ever, and perhaps more, because of the advantage of not having been anticipated.

I have carried this thought with me ever since and use it now as a methodological tool for my work. It makes me scrupulously—exhaustingly—attentive to the trajectories of power. It is this attentiveness and scrupulousness which I apply to an examination of one of the processes by which the academy struggles to maintain its own status quo where challenges to this same status quo are equally embedded in the history of the university: that is the use of student evaluations of courses and teaching for the purposes of granting, or not, of renewal, tenure and advancement in rank.

This aspect of institutionalized surveillance and evaluation of our work in the academy is the subject of this paper. Specifically, I urge scrutiny of the processes by which the apparent "objectivity" of student evaluations of courses and teaching are used to hide the limits and constraints on feminist scholarship and, ultimately, on academic freedom. I will suggest that, to the extent that course evaluations are not thus scrutinized for their potential embedded biases, they can become documents of discrimination and administrative weapons by which critical voices might be silenced.

In this discussion I intend to revisit the question of women in the academy not, as I have done in earlier works, from the perspective of woman as student (Lewis & Simon, 1986), or of woman as teacher in the university classroom (Lewis, 1990) but now, from the point of view of woman as intellectual worker: that is, the terms by which women gain, or are denied, access to the full rights and privileges of the academy configured ostensibly by the freedom to think, the freedom to explore previously uncharted intellectual waters, and the freedom to engage with students (and hopefully with colleagues) the fruits of our scholarship.[4]

Typically, in Europe and North America at least, the academy is the last, even if threatened,[5] institution committed, even if only nominally, to the free development and exchanging of ideas: that place where the encouragement of independent thought and the development of new ideas, presumably unfettered by the constraints of economic and social interests, is the stated ideology that configures its practices. That these ideals may not always be present in our experience of the academy is entirely to the point of this paper.

To be sure, the academy is not all of a piece. Within Euro-America traditions the casual irony of the university is that it has been simultaneously a vanguard for progressive change on the one hand and the bastion of conservatism on the other. In this uneasy relationship between rigorous scholarship and the impulse to conserving traditional seats of power/knowledge, the testing and contesting of ideas is not new. Ideological battles have been fought over the production of knowledge configured in the practices of research, scholarship and teaching. Of course, in and of itself, the image of the University as a place of intellectual activity that flourishes most positively when it is most heated with the burning flames of conceptual debate might be seen as indulgence in hopeless romanticism harkening to another time—or perhaps to a time that never was.

Nevertheless, in the North American context at least, more recently the university has seen the struggle for transformation of the very institution itself, as challenge after challenge has come from those for whom the academy was not traditionally intended. This includes women, racial and ethnic minorities, the socially and economically marginal, and those who would challenge the dominant sexual, and mental and manual ability mores. As a personally lived reality, individual members of these groups live the legacy of the history of the academy at the level of the everyday, often as barely perceptible "micro" indignities.

Historically, not only the knowledge that is produced, but the right to battle them has been protected through a system of peer review and ultimately the processes of tenure: a secured space within which the guarantees of freedom of investigation are provided. Yet, while battles for power through the ownership of knowledge have a history that is centuries old, for those of us new to the academy, the reality is that not only heated debate, but processes of measurement and evaluation are used for the purposes of maintaining the status quo embedded within ideological constructs (such as "standards of excellence"), that conform to the conceptual tensions wrought of a "double-cross-reversal" (Lewis, 1993): by which I mean that the concepts by which the terms of rigorous scholarship are established, are precisely the same concepts by which challenges to its logocentrism are deemed inadmissible.

For those who have gone through it, (and some have done so several times in different institutions), it is clear that the achievement of tenure is intended neither to be simple nor gratuitous (nor should it be). Yet, for those who would teach from what many have called "the margins" (Kirby & McKenna, 1989) or "against the grain" (Simon, 1992); those who would challenge the major canons, disciplinary traditions, and teaching methodologies that configure our traditional notions of the university; and those who would confront the ideologies into which our students have been schooled, this process poses a particular challenge. To the extent that feminist teaching crosscuts gender, feminist women scholars present a particular case in point.[6]

Typically, evaluations of performance for the purposes of tenure and promotion have been derived from three sources: teaching, scholarship and service to the community. To be sure the evaluations of scholarship and service to the community have their own complications and problematics in terms of identifying criteria of evaluation and achieving objectivity for the purposes of fair and equal application of those criteria of judgement to all incumbents. However, the question of evaluations of Teaching is even more highly problematic. Since the 1960s it has been generally agreed that students must participate in this process of evaluation in order to ensure, using the language of the 60s, "relevance" in course offerings. The language of the 90s would have us use the more current words: "accountability" or "fiscal responsibility."[7] Specifically, with regard to evaluations of teaching in the academy, there exists a general acceptance of the notion that this can best be judged by those who are the direct participants in and recipients of the teaching and curriculum. Yet, there has been practically no attention paid to the question of what criteria students invoke by which they make their judgements and evaluations.

Were it not the case that student evaluations of course content and teaching are a matter of consideration for renewal of appointment, tenure and promotion—and in the final analysis of who it is that is, and is not, allowed to participate in the labour of knowledge production—it might be possible to imagine a long and perhaps languid examination of how these documents of evaluation are produced and what effect they have in the long run. However, for many scholars and academic workers, an examination and re/visiting of the terms of student evaluations of course content and teaching is already too late.

Mapping the Terrain

Following the long struggles for the admission of women to the academy, feminist women/scholars have turned our critical eye to culture and the social organization of labour, knowledge, power and intimate relations both inside and outside the academy. Indeed, feminist critics of the academy have gone the round with the problematics of exclusionary and one sided curriculum, of disadvantageous hiring practices, of unequal remuneration for our labour, of the "chilly climate" issue, and of blocks to the fruits of our intellectual labour by way of preferential funding for research/conference travel and publication opportunities for non-feminist scholarship. We have known for a long time that in the academy, as in other public as well as private institutions, women generally are expected to do more but are seen to do less; are expected to perform better but are not recognized for what we do; and, in any event, except with a few welcome and notable exceptions, are given less social/scholarly latitude for our work than those whose work springs from traditional, specifically non-feminist, paradigms.

"Hard" evidence of the tenacious grip of discrimination is sometimes difficult to come by. It is not always easy to find those who have left the university (willingly or not) even before they have had an opportunity of engaging a long and satisfying academic career (Aisenberg & Harrington, 1988). It is not easy to document systemic discrimination precisely because the "system" absorbs the conceptual frameworks by which its own hegemony might be uncovered. And finally, it is not easy to document acts of systemic discrimination when those who are the objects of its sting have been taught the processes by which to internalize their own marginalization as personal failure. The singular genius of the workings of hegemony is the way in which it makes us apprehensive to speak the lives we know we have lived.[8]

Unlike acts of personal discrimination, systemic discrimination is such that its dynamics are built into the processes of the institution itself, which is then exacerbated by claims to objectivity. I caution any simple reading of the term "objectivity." In this regard Harraway (1991) states the following:

> All Western cultural narratives about objectivity are allegories of the ideologies of the relations of what we call mind and body, of distance and responsibility, embedded in the science question in feminism. Feminist objectivity is about limited location and situated knowledge, not about transcendence and splitting of subject and object. In this way we might become answerable for what we learn how to see (p. 190).

"Objectivity" as traditionally construed is precisely that process whereby no one is required to take responsibility for anything. The very processes of "objective" investigation—or course evaluations for that matter—work as intellectual blinders which, rather than enhance knowledge, delimits our vision by which we might come to know. The use of "blind" student evaluation of course offerings and of teaching performance is one of these processes and, therefore, serves as a useful case in point.

The typical format for most student evaluations of courses and teaching is a combination of numerical scores given to aspects of the course, its content and the professor's performance in delivering it, coupled with anecdotal commentary. However, it is not obvious how courses aimed at developing in students the capacity for social critique, where this may be a difficult, because real, intellectual journey, can be evaluated within the terms of standard pedagogical parameters. If the aim of a course is to disrupt students' taken for granted assumptions about knowledge and relations of power in order that they may move beyond themselves to new levels of social understanding and commitments to social change, psychic/affective chaos may be a desirable outcome from the perspective of the instructor and yet appear to be a liability within the terms of the evaluation process.

I now turn to an examination of the particular forms student evaluations of teaching take in that space of conjunction between gender and the ideologies of transformative politics, that is, women teaching from a feminist perspective,[9] and suggest some useful ways to read these documents as other than objective judgements of competence and relevance.

In evaluating the very same course I have had students tell me that: it was the absolute worst course they had ever taken and the issues concerning racial discrimination as a function of the curriculum and teaching practices raised in the course (Social Class, Race and Gender in Education, for example) have no place in the classroom. One student declared with apparent exasperation, "why did we talk about racism so much; it has nothing to do with kids in school! Teachers ought not to concern themselves with these social issues that are too large to solve—and can't be solved in any case." On another occasion, another student declared that "school is about teaching kids math not about moral and social issues. Questions of social justice have no place in the classroom."

Or that: the course, its content and my engagement of them was the very best thing they had ever encountered in their *entire* schooling experience and that no other course in *all* of their schooling career has taught them as much as I had done in the 12 week period of the course. One young woman declared with anger and frustration, "why wasn't I taught this stuff before. They have wasted so much of my time; how will I ever catch it up!" Another one wrote:

> I have learned more in this course than I had in my entire schooling. Why did I have to wait so long to get this? Why did "they" save the discussion of these issues until university? This should have been taught in elementary school; this should be a required course for everyone. No one should be allowed to graduate from this (Teacher Preparation) programme without taking this course.

In evaluating the very same course I have had students tell me that: I obviously knew absolutely nothing and was talking off the top of my head. On one occasion, a young man, having been challenged by his student classmates for taking more than his share of classroom time, flew into my office in anger and with a sweeping motion of his arm around my book covered walls declared with passion and dramatics, "I don't have to read all these books to know what's right!"

Or that: I was the most learned scholar they had ever encountered in the academy; that I was their model for what they wanted to be: *A SCHOLAR AND A PROFESSOR!*; that my office (the self same one with the book covered walls) was an oasis and a retreat from the mean and surly halls and classrooms that assault them daily.

In the very same course evaluation I have had students tell me that: I lecture too much; never stop talking; dominate the conversation; and don't practice "child" centered pedagogy.

Or that: I don't lecture enough; give over too much time to whole class and small group discussion; and allow student discussion to dominate the conversation. One student declared that he had come to the class specifically to hear what I had to say and did not want to spend so much time in discussion with students who were just speaking off the top of their heads—especially those who had not done the readings.

In evaluating the very same course I have had students tell me that: I presented a one sided, unbalanced, and biased point of view, that favors women, without regard to the "other side of the story."

Or that: Finally, here was a course that corrected for the one sided, unbalanced and biased point of view that favours men; and here, finally, was a course that countered the seamless ideologies of dominant rhetoric by presenting the other side of the story: a welcome perspective they could add to their current stalk of knowledge.

Of course my first inclination is to want to allow myself the belief that in my classes there are, on the one hand, those "terrible" students who just don't get it, don't want to learn, and are not bright enough to understand the material or, on the other hand, those "wonderful" budding scholars, keen of mind and insight, who will go a long way as a result of their devotion to study under my tutelage.

However, the fact of it is that, in either case, because it has not been sufficiently scrutinized, I have no idea about the terms by which students evaluate my course content and teaching. Nor do I have any idea about how they configure the rationale by which they make either of these judgements.

I am not suggesting that it would be better if such contradictions did not exist. Rather I am making a case for the opposite, that contradictions are the only site of possibility; that place from which social transformation arises. I am suggesting that as a methodology we specifically look to uncover contradictions in our social relations because it is here, in the fissures and crevices between what is and what we desire, between what might be and what never was that the terms of what we can do in the world rests. Sedgewick is informative on this point:

> What you do with contradictions is not straighten them out or pretend to straighten them out, or assume that because you've exposed them that all the bad stuff is going to dissolve—but rather inhabit them and go somewhere. Feel your way around them little by little and see what kinds of power live in those contradictions (Sedgewick & Frank, 1995, p. 33).

The academy, swayed by the weight of empiricism, and fortified by the image of its own power reflected in the mirror of canonical texts which are simultaneously the objects of its protection, stands horrified of the possibility that not singular knowledge, but rather contradiction, is the path to learning; the path to power/knowledge.

In what follows I offer some observations and possible strategies for "reading" such divergent, bipolar and contradictory student evaluations of courses and teaching not as self evident examples of good or bad teaching nor, indeed, as examples of cases of deliberate and intended acts of discrimination, nor even as acts of retribution, although certainly all of these exist in the academy.[10]

To be sure there is a difference between "good" and "bad" teaching from the point of view of the student and the institution. Not everyone has the skills of organization, focus and charisma to capture the imagination of students in conveying even highly interesting material. For such situations most universities provide some instructional development and support. Similarly, it is not an interesting pedagogical/political dilemma to consider the motives of those students who would use course evaluations as an opportunity for overt discrimination, or as an opportunity to repay a bad grade, or as a form of retribution for the professor's insistence that students achieve high academic standards through hard work. There will always be students who resist such encouragements with vehemence and who would use the opportunity of course evaluations as a forum for retaliation.

My interest, rather, is in looking at how we might learn to "read" those course and teaching evaluations that present as contradictory and where students in the same course settle on the bipolar ends of the evaluation scale; those instances where the interesting questions are not about "good" and "bad" teaching nor about overt and deliberate acts of violation, but rather about the larger issues concerning ideology as a function of the social/political positioning of the instructor in relation to the dominant curriculum, the structures of the university as a particular historical/political space and student expectations of the academic body.

The Myth of Objectivity

The ideologies of course evaluation by students, whether of the quantitative or qualitative sort, often have embedded within them the assumptions of objectivity: that of the evaluator and of the process itself. The hegemony of the processes of evaluation is that they are independent, individual statements formed outside of the context of the larger environment of the classroom and the university. It is maintained that they are based on a shared criteria of validity which can be easily ascertained and on which we all agree, that they lend themselves easily to measurement and graphing, that they tell us something, that what they tell us is valuable, and that the terms by which the judgements of the evaluators are arrived at are transparent and reliable precisely as a function of the nature of the evaluation process.

Indeed, if it were the case that the social profile of those in the academy (students, faculty and support staff), was "uncomplicated" by the presence of diverse social, cultural, gender and economic groups—groups carrying differentiated cultural practices, ideas and beliefs, and committed to political agendas not all of a kind—there might be a way to imagine that teaching effectiveness and course content could be measured on a universal scale in the interest of achieving some measure of "objectivity." However, to the extent that the bases on which students judge the work of their professors has not been scrutinized, whatever social, racial, cultural, gender, ideological, political and religious biases, experiences and insights students might bring to the enterprise, is left intact.

However students enter the sphere of influence of our work and scholarship, they do not stand as passive consumers of "schooled knowledge." Neither are they outside the debates which this scholarship engenders. As "apprentices" to the knowledge production enterprise, not only do they actively engage these debates, but bring with them their own experiences, interests (in both senses of that word), perspectives, viewpoints, capacities, and desires (or lack of it) for intellectual vigour and challenge. It is imaginable that, if students spring from a society that displays intolerance for competing ideas, while engaging in practices that reproduce subordinations of gender, social class, race/ethnicity, sexuality and so on, (and there is no reason to believe that they do not) then it might be expected that they will display these same attitudes and participate in these same practices in their academic work as well as in their judgment of the work of the professorate. For some students the aims of social critique and education for critical consciousness, that is the awareness of the social, political, and economic world around us, how it works, why it works that way and what and whose interests it serves, is truly disquieting.

The course I teach in the undergraduate Bachelor of Education programme serves as a useful example. It is a course framed by the concepts of sociology of education, critical pedagogy, feminist theory and cultural studies. It is intended to help education students develop the conceptual frameworks necessary to "see" how, not only individual acts but, significantly, institutional practices and policies work to create and recreate differentiated and, more specifically, unequal opportunities for children in their classrooms. For most of the members of any class in this course, the readings are mostly unfamiliar and often fly in the face of what they have come, over their own experience and prior schooling, to learn about institutionalized education: that success in school is primarily a matter of individual effort; that curriculum is objective, unbiased and conforming to some grander scheme of "really useful knowledge"; that teachers' viewpoints are objective and untouched by the teachers' own social positionings; and that grading and evaluation is a true measure of students' knowledge and ability of some/"thing."

For professors committed to the unveiling of the hegemony that configures the authoritative discourses of traditional disciplines, it is always a risky business to present to students disquieting notions that upset long held beliefs about schooling and knowledge production and, moreover, that call into question students' often firmly held beliefs about who counts in the realm of legitimate authority. It might also be expected that those students who have the most to gain from holding on to dominant ideologies and practices would be the most virulent in opposing ideologies that challenge these dominant social ideas and practices.

Specifically, courses that examine social relations of power and that scrutinize the fundamental bases for the perpetuation of inequality as problematic, also require of students the hard work of analysis and self-reflection. Yet such analysis and self-reflection is not always seen to be a fundamental and necessary part of what is learned and how. There is every reason to believe that course evaluations would register exactly the same dichotomous position from which students operate with a capacity (or not) to engage the necessary self-reflective practice so central to imagining propositions for social change.

The Question of Balance

It is a particularly virulent demonstration of the power of dominant ideology that it can charge one sidedness when encountering social/political/theoretical criticism while failing to see as problematic its own unbalanced representations of human experience and creative energy. In the relentless surveillance of our work, played out in the "politics" of the academy, we know that those of us on the margins have been called upon to justify and clearly articulate our analytical frameworks as a political position even when we (and "they") know that those whose analytical frameworks carry the weight of dominant ideology apparently need no justification and are never required to claim their political spaces or articulate its limitations and intentions. Fortunately, a pedagogy committed to positioning students such that they know what *we* do with what we/they know is integral to critical theory/practice. However, that all pedagogy is thus politically significant is effaced when dominant discourses of power/knowledge are allowed to "pass" unremarked.

Where students have been "schooled" to fear knowledge that might upset certain modernist notions that encourage the widely held belief in singular articulations of knowledge and "objectivity," they actually "see" the presentation of alternate view points as "one sided." At other times, they "see" the presentation of different "ways of seeing," as John Berger (1972), would put it, as biased and lacking objectivity.

Neither knowledge, nor its constitution is a politically free enterprise. Universalizing terminologies canonize the authority of those who have traditionally owned the means of production and distribution of knowledge in Western civilization and thereby hide the deeply political effect of these knowledges: the impulse to conservatism and the maintenance of things as they are. In North America, typically the academy is reproduced in the bodies of faculty, staff, administration, students and knowledges that are, by and large, massively representative of a single minded point of view.

What differentiates traditional educational models from critical ones, as is the case with feminist pedagogy, is that, characteristically, traditional educational models do not articulate their political agenda as part of the justification for the curriculum and methodological approach. Students come to assume, implicitly, that this is so because only critical epistemologies arise from identifiable ideological constructs and that there is no such perspective underlying the "realities" dominant knowledges claim to represent.

Because critical teaching paradigms challenge authoritative knowledges, the dynamics effected by this process in the classroom might not be altogether unexpected. In the critically disquieting classroom, teachers and students are positioned as co-investigators of culture. Indeed, it is necessary to know what "problematics" configure students' everyday lives and what conceptual tools they might be encouraged toward in order to accomplish the conceptual shift from that which is unquestioned to that which is made problematic.

One way to think about pedagogies committed to the development of critical perspectives for the purposes, ultimately, of social transformation, is that it is a process whereby answers are turned into questions. Yet, in a system of schooling where students have experienced the "achievement of answers" as the outcome of "true" education, the turning of answers into question can be, at times, a truly disquieting event.

The tools of critique of critical pedagogy are those concepts which enable students "to see what is hidden" by an examination of "that which is not said." It encourages authentic question asking by an examination of concepts that function hegemonically to maintain things as they are. Pointedly, teaching for social change asks "why this, why here, why now"? Like a culture lens, the tools of critique enable students to see and hear "differently"; to become aware of that which is not made apparent 'at first glance'[11] (Corrigan, 1990).

Culturally, this is a contradictory position for both students and teachers. Through their long history of association with schooling and, ultimately, the academy, students "know" the curriculum and they "know" how schooling is supposed to be constituted. Through this experience, they have come to make certain assumptions not only about its content but, as well, of its processes; they have certain expectations of it (Britzman, 1992). While at times students find the engagement of their critical intellectual capacities challenging and politically motivating, at other times they report feeling discomfort and anger born of threat. At these times the need to hear the "stories" that bring psychic comfort, coded in language that demands to hear the familiar, untroubling/untroubled "other," yet all too familiar, "side of the story," permeate classroom interactions and responses to critical readings.

That this is so, is not entirely a function of ideological debate. Particularly in professional faculties, such as teacher education programmes, students are implicitly beckoned to keep at least one eye on their professional prospects. Some students articulate this instrumentality quite freely as did one student who said to me recently, "Well, I have to worry about getting a job first. How can I take these issues up if I expect to get a job in the school system. It's not going to do me any good, is it?" For others, these contradictions are more sublime and unconscious.

However, the classroom is not all of a piece. Not only social critics and critics of the academy, but some students themselves have challenged the monolithic ideologies that drive much of most university programmes. These students have joined in criticizing its one sided, single storied, and relentlessly white, male, Euro-American-centric bias that does not take into account the "voices" of socially and ideologically marginalized/subordinated groups. This is the other side of teaching and learning from the margins.

As a pedagogical issue, the question of balance is, of course, important. Students ought to be made aware of the whole range of thinking on any particular issue in order that they develop their capacities for critical thinking and informed judgement. Students ought to be taught how to judge the explanatory value of differing, sometimes vastly differing and contradictory, conceptual frameworks. And students ought to be made aware of the debates in the history of ideas and knowledge in order to help demystify claims of objectivity or charges of subjectivity as a function often, not of "good" and "useful" knowledge on the one hand, and "bad" and "useless" knowledge on the other, but rather of the "interests" that knowledge serves.

The implications for the classroom, and ultimately for course/teaching evaluations are significant. Not only what is taught but, specifically, how it is taught becomes a question of ideological debate over which students often come to be solidly divided against one another. They often articulate their opposing ideological positions in the "not enough lecture"/"too much lecture," "not enough critique"/"too much critique," "not enough control"/"too much control" binaries. Teaching methods most suited to canonized knowledge are not the same as those most well suited to education for critical consciousness.

How students judge a course and its instructor, therefore, is as much a function of what any particular student or groups of students want out of their education (the instrumentalities by which they measure their schooling experiences) as it is a function of the teaching skills of the instructor and the interest level of the course content.

By What Terms Authority

For many students, the teacher is not a conduit to knowledge that exists elsewhere: the teacher is an image, a cliché in the sense both of stereotype but also photographic imprinting that freezes knowledge in the seeming evidence of a look, where the image predetermines what the person means to us. . . . The medium is the message, and the image of the professor often matters more than the ideas of the lesson (Polan, 1993, quoted in Weber & Mitchell, 1995, p. 8).

A few years ago, only three weeks into the new semester, a student who had been repeatedly disrupting the class with challenges to the course readings, finally wrote me a fifteen-page-long note. His general claim of the mostly Critical and Feminist well known scholars whose works we were studying was that they were "bad," and that by extension, my presentation of theoretical issues and pedagogical concepts was one sided and biased, in particular in favour of women. The incident arose when a small group of both female and male students confronted this student during class time with the fact that, while he had a right to his opinions, he had not the right to continually disrupt and challenge the course content to the point of stalling the class, as he had done throughout the two previous meetings of three hours each. At the time of the incident we attempted to deal with it collectively and immediately in class through a discussion of questions concerning what constitutes critique, what it means to have voice, what the dynamics of silencing are, and what the gendered, raced and classed face of privilege looks like. During most of this discussion it was my strategy to stay back from what the students themselves needed to say to each other and in order to allow the members of the class to come to terms with the conflict they had uncovered. Most of the students stayed well beyond the end of the class and eventually agreed to come back to the discussion at the next class meeting. However, before the next meeting could take place the student who had been sanctioned by his colleagues presented me with his fifteen page document.

He asked me to consider this document as fulfilment of his "final" course requirement of a term paper! In the end, as it turned out, even this tiny stunning aspect of the lengthy interchange he and I eventually engaged over his document, has served to highlight for me the question of authority in the academy for those whose presence in it is not validated by the long history of the academic body: the body of knowledge and the body of the instructor. I wondered then, and wonder still, by what authority of his own this student imagined that he could write anything resembling a final term paper after only the third week of a twelve week course; and why, by a turn of logic, he felt the need to take the course at all if he believed that he could successfully complete the final assignment after only three weeks.[12] Ultimately I have wondered if the driving force for such intellectual arrogance might have had mostly to do with the relationship in this student's world view between variously positioned embodiments: mine and that which he had come to expect of the academy.

Traditionally and by virtue of the history of their admissions and hiring procedures, universities have engaged in restrictive practices both of the "message" and of the "messenger." Consequently, "university professors," say Weber and Mitchell (1995), "enter a classroom that is already laden with representation, both in their own heads as well as in the heads of their students" (p. 13). These ideas are formed early and hence, neither the meaning of "student" nor that of "teacher" is free of socially laden interpretations, significances and determinations when students and professors enter the classroom.

To believe that, by virtue of the stated hierarchy displayed by lines of authority, institutions escape those deeply embedded social relations of power configured by gender, sexuality, social class, race, ethnicity and so on, is to efface the fact that not only institutional hierarchy but as well social positioning, configure institutional legitimacy.[13] It is an effect of history that in the academy, the voice of authority is distinctly male, white, and privileged. The implications are salient for teachers who do not reflect this social profile and particularly so for those who, at the same time, are committed to the unveiling of the hegemony that configures the authoritative voices/discourses of traditional disciplines. Feminist teachers in these classrooms are confronted with the authority of the traditional canon, both substantively and methodologically, in a context where the authority of hierarchy is viscerally challenged by the authority of gender (Wohlgemut, 1995)

That the social relations of power function to disrupt, indeed, by times turn on its head, taken for granted institutional hierarchies means that not only what is taught but who teaches it comes under a particular sort of scrutiny. For example, viewed with suspicion, women's place in the academy is a terrain which is constantly "under review." The terms by which this "review" is accomplished is the subject of this last section of this chapter.

In their article, "Social Criticism Without Philosophy" Nancy Fraser and Linda Nicholson (1993) state that "while in many societies women possess some or even a great deal of power, women's power is always viewed as illegitimate, disruptive and without authority" (p. 423). It is a common experience, not only for women but for all those from minority target groups to have to repeatedly defend our expertise as a function of the very embodiedness of our presence. It is literally our bodies and the knowledges we "wear" that struggle to claim our expertise in the face of challenges to the basis of our knowledge and to the authority of our voice. This is particularly highlighted by the fact that marginal and differently enrobed voices are not limited by, but rather go beyond traditional disciplinary, methodological and political boundaries.

It would take far more time and space than I have available to me to provide a close analytical reading of the complete text of the previously mentioned student's letter. Suffice it to say that it was startling in its reproduction of gender power and its capacity to assume both authority and control in turning institutional power on its head. However, the following short segment is remarkably illustrative of how gender enters into notions of the authoritative body.

In his letter, this student raises, among a smorgasbord of other issues, his upset with the fact that at the first meeting of the class, I had not shared with the students my first or "given" name. About half way through his fifteen-page "document," he writes: "You somehow managed to omit a detail as humanizing as your first name, introducing yourself as merely Doctor Lewis. I'm sure you've heard the phrase, 'you don't know the first thing about me'? Well, until I read your article I didn't even know your first name. And under present conditions, this phrase carries other particularly significant resonance for me."[14]

What, I wondered, was invested for this student in demanding a particular sort of "familiarity" with me as a prerequisite to our proceeding with the work of the term? What, I wondered, did this student believe about the relationship between us, as constituted by our different institutional positions, that he felt obliged to challenge me for not sharing with him and the other students in the seminar, details such as could be perceived as personal? And by what authority, I wondered, did this student believe that he could position, as a liability, my unwillingness to enter into a particular familiar space which he wished me to enter, and which I wished not to?

A full analysis of the complete incident is not necessary to make the relatively simple, yet overwhelming, point that in the academy women, and other members of socially marginalized groups, are not typically seen as privileged purveyors of knowledge because, historically, we have not occupied the "authoritative," "authorized," literally "entitled," body. Apparently, the "academic body" does not stand singularly apart from students' expectations of it. Hence, if this body is female, or black, or lesbian/gay, or unembellished with the accoutrements of social/economic privilege it will be expected to deliver itself, complicit in and agreeable to its own violation. In turn, what makes incidents such as the one I encountered with this student so powerful in their effectiveness, is precisely the ease with which collective experiences, in their "endless variety" are transposed into individual shortcomings (whether that of the student or that of the instructor—and indeed, perhaps of both) in order that they might be "dealt" with in isolation.

Interestingly, although hardly unexpectedly, the then current administration, to the extent to which it was involved with it, wished to see this incident as one that was isolated and idiosyncratic. Indeed, to the extent that it hadn't happened quite that way before, or since, one might be encouraged to see it that way, but only if one lacked the conceptual capacity, for want of a critical consciousness, to understand the difference between the "private" and the "idiosyncratic": between the endless variety by which social violation is accomplished on the one hand, and the individual circumstances by which we are invited to participate in our own isolation, on the other. It was interesting, for example, in this case that, not only did it take the entire term to arrive at a more or less satisfactory conclusion to the incident, (one with which, in the end, I was, still only marginally satisfied), but that members of the seminar class were explicitly warned by the representative of institutional authority "never again to speak about this incident."

Alas, compliance is often not so easily accomplished. John Berger (1984) suggests that: "When something is termed intolerable, actions must follow. These actions are subject to all vicissitudes of life. But the pure hope resides first and mysteriously in the capacity to name the intolerable as such: and this capacity comes from afar—from the past and from the future" (p. 18). Not unexpectedly the "command" to henceforth remain silent transformed into a "call to arms." The group of students whose challenge of their student colleague precipitated the incident in the first instance completed the course requirement by producing a video document chronicling a range of practices of discrimination in the academy. My own non-compliance with the order has taken a little longer to produce.

It is singularly difficult to document what difference "body" makes because, as is the case with most social science research, in the realm of the social/cultural there is no way of determining whether or not what happens to "me," if I am a "woman," would or would not happen to "me" if I were not a "woman."[15] Incidents such as these cannot be "replicated" under "controlled conditions." And the site of observation cannot be manipulated. Regardless of the "endless variety of monotonous similarity," there are only patterns and, in each instance, one time observations, on which to draw for conceptual understanding. In this regard, as a methodological problematic there is still some important work to be done in how to extrapolate the conceptual knowledges by which to "see" varieties of incidents not as infinite regression into multiplicity, but as different yet shared experiences that become the source of knowledge. "I tell you, it's *queer*, Mrs. Peters. We live close together, and we live far apart. We all go through the same things—it's all just a different kind of the same thing! If it weren't—why do you and I *know*—what we know this minute?" (emphasis added. Glaspell, 1927; see also Heckle, 1980).

From my reading of course evaluations, it is not clear that the judgements students make about the organization and delivery of a particular course, or about the effectiveness of the instructor teaching it, is differentiated from issues of "body"—the body of knowledge and the body of the instructor—such that not only what is taught but who teaches it comes under scrutiny, debate and mistrust.

Conclusion

I have often thought that if it were possible to mandate that everyone, as a prerequisite to becoming a participating member in civil society, be required to read a small collection of essential texts, Virginia Woolf's *A Room of One's Own* ([1929] 1977) would have to be among them. In this book, Woolf is pointedly candid about the situation of women in the academy: that institution by which the boundaries of knowledge production and its distribution is supervised and maintained. Her patient description of the heroine as she moves (or was she removed?) from the riverbank to finally sipping clear broth with her colleagues in the women's college, while the men feasted on pheasant at the men's college, establishes Woolf as a genius in the art of metaphor. While the University has a long association with the development and legitimation of men's knowledge and scholarship, the history of the relationship between women and our legitimate claims to knowledge have been much more tenuous and "thin-brothed." Woolf was neither the first nor the last to point this out, but who has done it more eloquently?

Historically, as an institution, the university was designed exclusively for and by white males of the ruling classes. As a lived reality, individual members of minority and marginal groups, to the extent that we have found our way into the structures of knowledge and power represented by the academy, have lived the legacy of this history at the level of the everyday. What this means, in practical terms, is that while white male heterosexual expertise goes largely without saying it is a common experience for those from minority target groups to have to defend not only our expertise, but our very presence within the academy.

Student evaluations of course content and teaching cannot be taken at face value. In order to make sense of student evaluations we need to know how students configure the terms of their evaluation as a function of their own experiences and interests. As well, we need to know what understandings and experiences of pedagogical strategies students bring to their judgements of teaching and learning. In this regard it cannot be assumed that student perceptions of course content and teaching are free of the very same biases and perspectives that pervade much of the academic enterprise in the larger context. Where there has been no systematic study of how students use teaching evaluations, there is no reason to believe that students' judgements of what happens in a classroom are a function not only of what material an instructor presents and how that presentation is accomplished but also of the authority students are willing to accord to the instructor as a legitimate purveyor of scholarship and knowledge. Not unlike the rest of us, students are not free of biases and prejudices regarding who belongs where on the social/economic/authoritative grid. Gender, race, social class, sexuality, and cultural/political ideologies are factors which influence perceptions of legitimate authority and knowledge.

Given the politics of pedagogy, course evaluations of content and teaching are, at best, an enigma. This is not an invitation to eliminate them altogether. Students need to have the opportunity to voice their experience of what and how they are taught and they need to have the opportunity to reflect on our relations in the classroom. However, I also think, if we are to imagine our work as intellectual labourers and teachers as that of uncovering the fault lines and fissures that bring to the fore, among our students, disagreement and debate over long held ideas, as a prerequisite to learning their lives, we need to see bipolar course evaluations as indication of such learning. We need to understand that a class, multiply divided in debate, including as this debate is carried into course and teaching evaluations, is a learning class. And we need to understand that students, disquieted by what we presume to teach them, are learning students.

Rather than turning into a liability and a mechanism for gatekeeping, the academy needs to authentically embrace its own rhetoric. Intellectual freedom and the debates it engenders ought not to be seen as "schooled exercises." Changing hearts and minds is a matter of concern for both teachers and students. Of teachers it requires deep and authentic—the kind that really matters—commitment to social change coupled with self reflective knowledge. Of the student it requires a willingness to engage new knowledge as a visceral experience that may at times be painful, and that may require that long held beliefs be given up or rethought. Given the enormity of what is required it is no wonder that both teachers and students may, by times, turn, not so quietly, away from what might be on offer. And yet no less is at stake than intellectual freedom, the last stand, in an age of global neo-conservativism, against the erosion of our collective commitment to democratic citizenship.

Notes

1. An earlier draft of this paper was presented at the University of British Columbia in October 1996. I thank all those in attendance and acknowledge the valuable comments on the text.

2. Misogyny is typically defined as the hatred of women. Common usage suggests that this is a gendered concept and that it defines relations between women and men. However, such a narrow definition of the social practices of misogyny fails to take into account that women and men are similarly invited to engage cultural practices that encourage the rights and privileges of the dominant while containing the desires and hopes of subordinate social groups. Not only men, but women as well have the capacity to engage in practices that limit women's possibilities. And not only women, but men as well might find an urgency in transforming social relations of power not only with regard to gender but across a range of socially subordinate groups of people.

3. References for Rubin and O'Brien are not available. Sometimes it happens that flashes of other people's brilliance stay with us even if the exact source has long slipped into "forgotten memory". Such is the case with this statement of Gayle Rubin's. Who, once having heard it, can ever forget this more than perfect, and ever so parsimonious, description of patriarchy: "endless variety of monotonous similarity". "No wonder" as Mary O'Brien once observed, equally as brilliantly, "we, women, are all so tired".

4. I am grateful to Veronica Strong-Boag for pointing out that the question of women in the academy cannot be complete without looking at that largest of female presence in the university embodied in the "support staff." To be sure, it is always the least powerful without whom no institution could function. The colonization of labour has a long and ongoing sordid history. I concur that we need to turn to an examination of the largely invisible and yet personally taxing work of support staff within the academy. In this spirit I acknowledge the work of Pat Deir who is not only invaluable to the work I do, but whose work could never be sufficiently acknowledged so long as institutional hierarchies are held in place.

5. Currently in Ontario, this threat is particularly salient. In the wake of a neo-conservative landslide, universities are threatened with: deregulation of tuition fees; privatization of what, in Canada, has been an entirely publicly funded and collectively articulated system of post secondary education; "rationalisation" of academic departments with business interests for the purposes of gaining finan-

cial support; and the suggestion, that the academy enter the age of "virtuality" through the use of "new" information technologies that prioritize computers at every desk as a substitute for face to face encounters between teachers and students.

6. This group neither includes all women nor only women. However, women in the academy constitute a particular subgroup regardless of our politics, or social/cultural position. Hence all women to some extent, yet of course differently by virtue of our sexuality, race, ethnicity and other social markers, experience the challenge to our status in the academy as a function of being women.

7. For example, currently the functions and social location of universities in Ontario are undergoing review primarily for the purposes of articulating their relationship to business and industry within a global economy. With a shift in emphasis to students' employability skills, public rhetoric is deployed to foreclose thoughtful debate on the place of the university as a site of social critique and knowledge production. That this shift in the language of "education" has taken place in such neo-conservative times is not a surprise. The capacity of governments, through financial and ideological means, to constrain spaces for thoughtful reflection, as well as to limit the possibilities for creative expression, has a long tradition in human history and is intended precisely to serve the cause of those who have the power in the first instance to impose such controls.

8. I want to take care to point out that, while in this regard the history of (mostly white) women in the academy has begun to be written, that of other social minorities still, for the most part, needs to be documented. For the general lack of this documentation, it is not appropriate to make generalizations across categories even if, peripherally, similarities might exist among the experiences of various target groups: women, visible racial/ethnic minorities, and social/cultural and economically subordinate groups. What documentation does exist strongly suggests that, in their relations with both students and colleagues, not only women but other target groups suffer systemically from the application of differential criteria of evaluation with regard to their work in both research and teaching.

9. In my work for this research I have had access to the course and teaching evaluations of a number of individuals who have agreed to share them with me. However, in this instance I will refer to and draw entirely upon my own experience and documentation. I do this specifically to protect the anonymity of colleagues. Yet, I want to state that for many women, feminist, and critical teachers in the academy, the experience of the phenomena which I want to raise here for scrutiny is not an unusual one. Some, besides myself, have written about it (Carpenter, 1996; Nelsen, 1997; Richer & Weir 1995; Mossman, 1995; hooks, 1994; Garber, 1994; Brookes, 1992; The Chilly Climate Collective, 1995; Bannerji, Carty, Dehli, Heald & McKenna, 1991; Ng, 1989; MacDonald, 1989; Aisenberg & Harrington, 1988; and others). These scholars offer a familiar description and further documentation of these experiences.

While for the purposes of this paper I draw entirely upon my own experiences, exactly for the reasons I point out above (that is the ease with which we are encouraged to slip into self blame and ownership of the individualization hegemony encourages), I will try not to take anything I say here personally!

10. In this regard, I note that not every student comes to class with good will. Particularly for women faculty who are declared feminists on campus, there is always the possibility that, motivated by Backlash ideology, a student (or two— or more) appears in class with the expressed intent to harass. On one such occasion in my experience, a young woman approached me rather sadly during the first break in the first class of the term of an advanced undergraduate course. She reported that she thought I should know that there were two young men in the coffee lounge bragging that they had only signed up for the course in order to harass me. Fortunately, I could reassure her that I had already figured this out. I was also able to encourage her to believe that I didn't think they would "last long" in the class when they realized that the apparent pleasures and seductions with which continued harassment might be imbued would be outweighed by the workload which I was sure (based on experience) they were not prepared to do. I was right. However, regardless how prepared we might be in anticipating these incidents they happen regularly. Documentation of them is difficult, policies and their enforcement regarding student conduct are weak and, in any event, do not address most of this sort of classroom harassment.

11. "The second glance 'deranges' (make strange) the taken for granted." (Corrigan, 1990, p. 7)

12. Particularly in a Faculty of Education, this aspect of the incident makes me think we need to explore with much more rigour, than we presently seem to do, questions of what our students (and future teachers) think constitutes learning and what role schooling (the taking of courses) plays in this enterprise.

13. I don't mean to imply by this that professors and teachers in general do not have significant power in how they configure their relations with their students, with their colleagues, with administration, and with staff. It is only my intention to highlight here that, for socially/culturally marginal groups, how these relations are lived in the everyday cannot be seen as a simple equation between institutional position and authority.

14. I need to clarify: Prior to this particular class, I had always introduced myself to students by my two names, "given" and "acquired", leaving it up to them, therefore, to decide how it was they wished to address me. Over the years of teaching, I have found it interesting that some students were sufficiently unsettled by being given this choice to sometimes ask me how I wished to be called, by my first name or by my professional title. As a sociological question, the social implications of entitlement, and the various forms that it takes, has been of interest to me for some time. I had observed, for example, somewhat casually, that there appeared to be a practice on my campus of addressing male professors by their professional titles while women professors appeared far more frequently to be addressed by their given names. This practice seemed to persist not only among students, but indeed in other places where faculty interacted. I was stunned, for example to be present, some time ago, at a meeting of approximately eight people, all faculty, where each of the men were introduced as Dr. Whom Ever and each of the women (of whom of course there were fewer) were introduced by our given names. For some time, prior to the particular course in question, I had been wondering what difference this fact of de/entitlement made. What the inscriber of the letter could not, of course, have known is that, in

fact, on this occasion I had not offered my first name upon introducing myself to the class precisely *because* I wanted to see what difference it would make. The results of course were stunningly interesting.

15. I use the double quotation marks enclosing the word "woman" in order to indicate that I am, of course, not talking about women only nor about women specifically as that term applies to the female gender in its hegemonic formulations. Indeed, how one experiences the other side of institutional "authority" from a point of view where one is assumed to "have it" is a function of how gender, sexuality, race, ethnicity and the cultural markers of social class turn institutional authority on its head.

References

Aisenberg, N., & Harrington, M. (1988). *Women of academe: Outsiders in the sacred grove*. Amherst: University of Massachusetts Press.

Bannerji, H., Carty, L., Dehli, K., Heald, S., & McKenna, K. (1991). *Unsettling relations: The university as a site of feminist struggles*. Toronto: The Women's Press.

Berger, J. (1972). *Ways of seeing*. London: British Broadcasting Corporation and Penguin Books.

Berger, J. (1984). *And our faces, my heart, brief as photos*. New York: Pantheon Books.

Britzman, D. (1992). *Practice makes practice: A critical study of learning to teach*. New York: SUNY.

Brookes, A-B. (1992). *Feminist pedagogy*. Toronto: Garamond.

Carpenter, M. W. (1996). Female grotesque in academia: Ageism, anti feminism, and feminists on the faculty. In V. Clark, S., N. Garner, M. Higonnet & K. H. Katrak (Eds.), *Anti feminism in the academy* (pp. 141–165). New York: Routledge.

Chilly Climate Collective. (Eds.), (1995). *Breaking anonymity: The chilly climate for women faculty*. Waterloo: Wilfred Laurier University Press.

Corrigan, P. (1990). *Social forms/human capacities: essays in authority and difference*. London: Routledge.

Edelman, L. (1994). *Homographesis: Essays in gay literary and cultural theory*. New York: Routledge.

Fraser, N., & Nicholson, L. (1993). Social criticism without philosophy: an encounter between feminism and postmodernism. In T. Docherty, (Ed.), *Postmodernism: a reader*. New York: Columbia University Press.

Garber, L. (Ed.), (1994). *Tilting the tower: Lesbians teaching queer subjects*. New York: Routledge.

Glaspell, S. (1927). *A jury of her peers*. London: Ernest Benn.

Harraway, D. (1991). *Simians, cyborgs, and women: the reinvention of nature*. New York: Routledge.

Heckle, S. (1980). *A jury of her peers*. Film.

hooks, b. (1994). *Teaching to transgress: Education as a practice of freedom*. New York: Routledge.

Kirby, S., & McKenna, K. (1989). *Experience research social change: Methods from the margins*. Toronto: Garamond.

Lewis, M. (1990). Interrupting Patriarchy: Politics, resistance, and transformation in the feminist classroom. *Harvard Educational Review, 60*(4), 467–488.

Lewis, M. (1993). *Without a word: Teaching beyond women's silence.* New York: Routledge.

Lewis, M., & Simon, R. (1986). "A discourse not intended for her": Teaching and learning within patriarchy. *Harvard Educational Review, 56*(4), 457–472.

MacDonald, G. (1989). Feminist teaching techniques for the committed but exhausted. *Atlantis 15*(1), 145–152.

Mossman, M. J. (1995). Gender issues in teaching methods: reflections on shifting the paradigm. *Legal Education Review,* 6(2), 129–152.

Nelsen, R. (Ed.). (1997). *Inside Canadian universities: Another day at the plant.* Kingston: Cedarcreek Publications.

Ng, R. (1989). Sexism, racism, nationalism. *Race, class, gender: Bonds and barriers. Socialist Studies Annual 5.* Toronto: Between the Lines.

Pagano, J. (1990). *Exiles and communities: Teaching in the patriarchal wilderness.* Albany, NY: SUNY Press.

Powell, P. (1996). *The dragon slayers: Three stories from an integrated class.* M.Ed. Thesis, Queen's University, Kingston, Canada.

Richer, S. & Weir, L. (1995). *Beyond political correctness: Toward the inclusive university.* Toronto: University of Toronto Press.

Sedgewick, E., & Frank, A. (1995). *Shame and her sisters.* Raleigh, NC: Duke University Press.

Simon, R. I. (1992). *Teaching against the grain.* Massachusetts: Bergin and Garvey.

Weber, S., & Mitchell, C. (1995). *That's funny you don't look like a teacher.* London: The Falmer Press.

Wohlgemut, S. (1995). *The shame of it all: A study of gendered relations between secondary school teachers and students.* M.Ed. Thesis, Queen's University, Kingston, Canada.

Woolf, V. ([1929] 1977). *A room of one's own.* London: Collins Publishing Group.

6 Can Feminist Voices Survive and Transform the Academy?

Ava L. McCall

It was unlikely that I would become a feminist academic, if one examined my community and family of origin. However, the contradictory family and community voices of my childhood and adolescence strongly influenced me. I heard patriarchal voices early, although "patriarchy" was not part of my vocabulary until I was an adult. Despite my parents' preference for sons, they had five daughters whom they pushed to "make something of yourselves." Regardless of our working class status and the lack of financial resources, my parents were adamant that my sisters and I attend college. Through completing endless financial aid forms, my parents helped us take advantage of available loans, grants, and work study programs in order to attend nearby, affordable colleges or universities. Mother was a "working mother" when most of my friends' mothers worked at home. Rather than working to "have a career," Mother worked to supplement the limited income from the family farm. Amidst all the financial worries, my family and community also spoke in caring voices. My parents were generous with neighbors and extended family members by sharing the resources they had. Such actions seemed to be a way of fulfilling the Christian value of helping others while proving their self-worth and gaining the status they could not earn economically. Other community and family members reciprocated by willingly sharing with us.

College, elementary school teaching, and graduate school also influenced the development of my feminist, scholarly voices. These experiences contributed to my understanding of social and economic inequalities due to gender, race, and class and my naive belief that through teaching, I could lead preservice teachers to a greater awareness of these injustices which we could collaboratively address in our classrooms. I was unprepared for instructional structures and colleagues who helped to maintain the status quo and students' resistance to learning about inequalities. In this chapter, I will describe the various influences on the development of my feminist voices, opportunities to develop these voices, and constraints which impeded speaking with these emerging voices at two institutions of higher education. I will discuss the challenges of developing, integrating, and teaching from a multicultural, social reconstructionist perspective (Sleeter & Grant, 1994); a feminist ethic of care (Puka, 1993); and through engaged pedagogy (hooks, 1994). Finally, I recognize the importance of collective action in order to move toward institutional change to create structures which support faculty who teach, write, and engage in research in feminist, caring voices.

Childhood Patriarchal, Working Class, and Caring Voices: Conservative Soil for Feminist Seeds

Patriarchal voices have always been part of my life. After my parents married, they moved to a small house a stone's throw from my grandparents' house on the 365-acre family farm in southern Indiana, a part of the conservative Midwest in the U.S. My grandparents strongly encouraged my father, their only child, to join them in farming the land my grandfather's father had purchased in the late 19th century. I was my parents' first child and they both looked forward to my arrival and the beginning of another generation of farmers. Since I was born before partners were encouraged to participate in the birthing process, my father sat in the waiting room at the hospital to await the news of my arrival. When a nurse excitedly entered the room to announce, "It's a girl!" my father could not have been more disappointed. He and Mother hoped for a boy, a son who would continue farming the family farm. During the next sixteen years, my parents had four more daughters and each time they were increasingly disappointed to be deprived of the sons they so desired. By the time my youngest sister was born, I, too, had learned males were the preferred sex and spoke openly about our desire for a boy. When my father called during my piano lesson to announce the birth of my youngest sister, I could not hide my disappointment from my piano teacher. Near tears, I lamented, "But we wanted a boy!" Early on I learned the challenges of being a woman in a society which values men, the pressures to become a "good girl" in order to make myself acceptable and prove my worth to others, and messages to devalue myself and other women because somehow we never quite measured up to the male standard.

My early years were filled with my parents' voices lamenting their economic struggles as part of the working class. Having little money seemed to be a source of shame, a sign of personal failure, and a basis for extreme anxiety about survival. My family owned land, affordable through the U.S. government's usurpation of Native Americans' lands which were then sold to European American settlers cheaply. Making a living from that land was difficult. In order to support the family, my mother was forced to work in a factory when I was very young and as a grocery store clerk through most of my childhood and adolescence. These were jobs she did not necessarily enjoy, but did because of our financial need. However, paid labor provided Mother with some economic power within the family. Even though my father's voice was dominant in financial discussions and in most family matters, he could not ignore Mother's voice because she controlled part of the income.

Every spring my father obtained loans to purchase the seeds, fertilizer, and any needed new machinery to plant the season's crops. Throughout the growing season, he kept his eyes on the sky, hoping for the right weather conditions which would lead to a good crop. Then he could pay off the debt and have a profit. Often, this profit was small. Dad became a member of the National Farmers Union and other farming organizations which pressed for governmental assistance to enable family farms to compete with large, corporate farms. It was not until high school economics and family discussions of my attending college that I discovered we could be considered "poor." We had plenty of food which we grew ourselves, my mother sewed many of our clothes, and we lived in a very small, but adequate home. Most others in the community had a similar socioeconomic level. However, the financial insecurity seemed to drive my parents to prove themselves and their worth to others and to impel their daughters to do the same. My sisters and I were expected to work hard and accomplish appropriate goals. As the oldest, I especially understood this message since I was expected to be an example for my younger sisters. It was through achievements that we could earn praise and affirmation from my parents. Gardening, mowing the yard, preparing meals, canning and freezing food from the garden, cleaning the house, helping in the fields, learning to sing and play musical instruments, doing well academically in school, and taking leadership positions in church were accomplishments that led to praise. My parents' voices were not generously laced with praise, but I endeavored to earn as much as I could and avoid their more liberally distributed criticisms.

Although my parents were not generous with praise within the family, they were generous in sharing what resources they had with extended family and community members. They spoke of the importance of caring for others as a way of developing connections and living "Christian values." My mother especially practiced caring in her interactions with neighbors and extended family members. When the garden was producing more vegetables than we could eat, can, or freeze, Mother was constantly taking buckets of the excess produce to neighbors, her sisters, brothers, and cousins or inviting them to help themselves from the garden. Another of Mother's talents was cooking and baking and she generously shared jellies, breads, pies, and cakes with others in the community. Unfortunately, as many women are socialized to do (Card, 1990; Houston, 1990; Puka, 1993), Mother did not balance caring for others with caring for herself. Through caring for others, Mother seemed to look to others to provide the affirmation and care she needed. When she completed a caring act for another, she expected a positive response. If this was not forthcoming, she showed hurt, anger, and resentment.

Developing my socially acceptable patriarchal, caring voices was also encouraged growing up. Our home was always a loud place with arguments, explanations, jokes, and monologues silenced only by my parents' periodic demands for quiet. Attending small, rural schools in which I knew all of the teachers and most other students also made speaking easier in classes. My ease with speech also led to trouble with my teachers when I spoke with and wrote notes to friends during lessons when I was supposed to listen.

Through my parents' help, the encouragement of teachers, and my desire to have a more economically secure life than my parents had and to enjoy how I earned a living which my mother was unable to, I took advantage of available loans, grants, work study, and a position of work in exchange for room and board to attend a junior college a short distance from home. I found it more difficult to speak in classes even though I enjoyed learning and talked easily about my studies with my family. Through attending conservative, mostly European American, Midwestern colleges in the U.S. during the civil rights era, I became aware of the racial discrimination directed against African Americans and the potential power of education to remedy these inequalities. Even though I chose a traditional "women's field," elementary education, the possibility that I could teach for equality became an inspiring purpose for entering this profession. When I graduated from college and began teaching elementary school within a mid-sized, racially diverse city in my home state, I discovered the distinctly different speech of my African American students and their families and the challenges I had with speaking, understanding, and being understood. During these years of elementary teaching, I also began to develop a feminist consciousness which meant my views were often at odds with other teachers, administrators, and parents. I struggled with finding words to speak about the injustices I felt as a European American, working class turned middle-class woman, the injustices I had seen among my African American, poor students, and the overwhelming difficulties I had experienced in teaching and talking with children and families from very different backgrounds.

I turned to graduate school for help in strengthening my feminist voices. I began to discover what bell hooks (1989) described as the multi-dimensional, changing nature of my emerging feminist voices even as I recognized that the university did not affirm all of these voices. During the four years I worked on my doctorate in curriculum and women's studies, I learned the language, theories, and research to help express the strong emotions I felt about the multitude of ways I and other women of all races and classes, people of color, and the poor have been discriminated against in society and in education. These groups have been omitted or misrepresented in the academic disciplines, have the least powerful positions in educational institutions, and have the least space in educational publications. It was also a time of struggle to speak of my experiences in my own voices, my own distinctive expressions as a writer (hooks, 1989). It was a time of struggle to speak of my advocacy of those groups denied power and opportunities to speak within the patriarchal, white supremacist (hooks, 1989) society in the U.S. It was a time of awareness of the connection between developing my voices as well as my understanding of how I thought and who I was. I was another example of what Belenky (1986) and her colleagues found in their research with diverse women in various educational settings. Women's voices are often closely related to the development of their sense of self and mind. Because women live within patriarchy and experience various forms of oppression due to their race, sexual orientation, and class as well as their gender, they are frequently encouraged to develop self-concepts, minds, and voices which support the patriarchal, white supremacist U.S. society (hooks, 1989; Lorde, 1984). Graduate school offered opportunities for me to hear the voices of those who struggled to resist and disrupt patriarchy, compulsory heterosexuality, social class privileges, and white supremacy. These voices gave me courage. As I began writing about my own experiences and oppression and those of the European American working class and middle class women in my research, the power of patriarchy within the graduate school encouraged me to develop only some of my feminist voices. The emotional, personal voices were considered out of place in academia. I was as yet unable to speak in some of my emerging feminist voices, to move outside the frameworks and authorities graduate school had given me (Belenky, Clinchy, Goldberger & Tarule, 1986). After completing graduate school and beginning my work as a feminist teacher educator, the struggle to strengthen and speak with my feminist voices continued.

We Will Let You in, but Do Not Say Anything

Within a few weeks after completing my dissertation, I began my first tenure-track position at a four-year institution of approximately 10,000 students in the Midwestern section of the U.S. The experience of intense thinking and writing about European American working class and middle-class women and student teaching for my dissertation and its acceptance by my doctoral committee had strengthened some of my voices and my abilities as a knower and a writer. In my first faculty position I was hopeful that I could speak, at least about gender issues, and my colleagues and students would listen. My graduate work had significantly increased my understanding of the contradictory nature of educational institutions. They are often structural supports for the continuation of the patriarchal, white supremacist U.S. society as well as sites of resistance, struggle, and change (hooks, 1989). These institutions have been designed and led by elite, European-American men, although women now comprise 53 percent of the student population (Sadker & Sadker, 1994). Feminist academics have also critiqued and, to an extent, modified the curriculum, pedagogy, and structures themselves (Belenky et al., 1986). Becoming part of the faculty at this institution of higher education provided many more opportunities to experience the liberatory and oppressive nature of such institutions and the personal costs of resistance and struggle. These are issues I will address in the following sections.

Surviving Expectations

One of the unstated expectations I quickly discovered through department meetings at my new institution is that new, untenured faculty, who were all women, were expected to listen significantly more than speak. During departmental discussions, a few men and one woman, all senior faculty, dominated most of the discussions, were listened to, and significantly influenced decisions. These senior faculty, primarily men, possessed most of the power to control public talk and decisions within the department. They seldom invited new faculty to offer their ideas. After I voiced an opinion which one of the powerful men in the department vehemently disagreed with during a meeting, I chose to be more cautious about what I said publicly. However, one of my untenured women colleagues was not so easily intimidated and at times engaged in verbal battles with the more powerful men in the department during our meetings.

Another expectation for both new and experienced faculty was that we could handle heavy teaching, supervision, and advisement loads. We each had 12-credit teaching/supervision assignments which often included teaching several different courses. However, mostly junior faculty supervised field experiences or student teachers, consuming significant time traveling to the school sites and attending additional faculty meetings related to supervision. During the first year I taught child development, introduction to teaching, methods for teaching reading, language arts, and social studies, supervised the concurrent field experience for these methods courses, and supervised student teachers. Advising over twenty students was sandwiched in between the teaching and supervision. Since I had not previously taught any of these courses, I worked very long hours preparing to teach each day. To infuse my feminist voices within so many different academic areas was a formidable challenge. The struggle was very real to resist patriarchy, even in small ways.

Yet another expectation was that new assistant professors should publish more than the senior associate or full professors in order to be renewed and eventually tenured at this institution. When my department chair encouraged me to increase the number of conference presentations I had planned and to publish my first year, I silently questioned where the time was going to come from in order to meet this expectation as well as prepare to teach.

Perhaps the most disturbing expectation was that new women faculty would survive with little support. The new women faculty and I quickly discovered we could expect little assistance or encouragement from either the tenured women or men in the department. As is the case with most institutions of higher education (Bentley & Blackburn, 1992), in my department only one of the full professors was a woman, an "honorary male" (hooks, 1989) who actively supported patriarchy and competed with other women and men for the university's limited resources. When one of the departmental student workers was helping an untenured woman colleague prepare for a conference presentation, the female full professor insisted the student worker leave this task to help her prepare for her own conference presentation. It quickly became apparent that surviving the expectations of my position consumed nearly all of my energy, and developing and strengthening my feminist voices received significantly less attention. Speaking, writing, and teaching to create a more just world became an elusive goal. It seemed unlikely that this university would become a site for revolutionary struggle (hooks, 1989) and a place to promote the development of women's minds, self-concepts, and voices (Belenky et al., 1986). In addition, the institution established two policies and practices which subdued even further my feminist voices as well as the voices of other new faculty within the courses they taught.

Renting Textbooks

One institutional policy and practice which I found silencing was the practice of students renting textbooks for multiple sections of the same course. Once new instructors were assigned to teach specific courses, they were then given the textbooks to use. As a new faculty member, I had no voice in the selection of the textbooks I used during my first year. The purpose of the textbook rental policy was to attract more students to this institution with the promise they would spend $55 a semester to rent textbooks rather than $150 a semester to purchase textbooks at other public institutions within the state (School Newspaper, 1989). The textbook rental policy stated: "Basic textbooks adopted for courses are based on a departmental decision and approved by the department chairperson. In cases of multiple sections of courses, the same basic textbook must be used in all sections" (Textbook Rental Service Policy, 1987, p. 1). This policy strengthened the power of departmental members who could influence decisions about course content and textbook selection within the department.

During the first semester, I taught child development and introduction to teaching with these rented textbooks and endeavored to add other readings and information on gender issues which the texts ignored or skimmed. In introduction to teaching, I wanted students to be aware of women's historical struggles for equality in teaching through such voices as Grace Strachan and Margaret Haley (Hoffman, 1981) and make the gender of elementary teachers more of a central focus during our study of many aspects of teaching. This infusion of other materials also had its price. My department chair spoke with me on numerous occasions about the amount of paper I was consuming through these additional readings which strained the department's budget. He complained that I was using more paper than anyone else in the department. Each time the department chair asked to speak with me, I began to feel like a child being called into the principal's office to be punished for misbehavior. These meetings led to increased tension between us as I continued to use additional readings and argued that the department did not need faculty with advanced degrees teaching these courses when we could not make them reflect our intellectual interests and moral commitments. Even though the chair affirmed my right to bring my interests into my teaching, he pressured me to do it without duplicating additional readings.

In preparation for the second semester and the teaching of reading, language arts, and social studies methods, I talked with other faculty who used textbooks in addition to the basic adopted ones. The textbook rental policy offered the possibility for including supplementary textbooks: "If an instructor considers it desirable to supplement the approved basic textbook for a section of a course and if the department chairperson approves, the instructor may recommend, but not require, the purchase of certain supplementary items by students in the section of a course" (Textbook Rental Service Policy, 1987, p. 2). I completed the forms necessary for ordering three supplementary texts which contributed resources and strategies for teaching about family and local history (including women's history) as well as integrating the teaching of poetry with social studies. The chair then circulated my order to the rest of the department ostensibly with the intention of discovering their interest in these texts as well. However, one senior male faculty member who taught another section of this course questioned my use of these texts by writing on my order: "The [copyright] dates [for these supplementary texts] seem a little old. Why are these needed?" The senior woman faculty member affirmed her colleague's right to question my order and also questioned my use of these texts. She wrote: "I agree with _____." No one talked with me about the substance of the texts or asked to review them, but I found their public criticisms of my attempts to integrate other materials with the adopted textbooks chilling. They reflected the broader support for the maintenance of the existing, patriarchal curriculum. However, not all faculty on campus actively supported the textbook rental policy and a few struggled to change it.

Using "Approved" Generic Syllabi

The second policy which also subdued my feminist voices was the development of "approved" generic syllabi for all courses taught in my department. As a new faculty member, I had no voice in the substance of these syllabi even though I was expected to follow them to an extent. I knew other faculty were making modifications in the syllabi and using them as guidelines for their courses. I preferred to create syllabi which honestly reflected the course content I planned to teach and was reluctant to give up my belief that I had the academic freedom to teach what I thought was important. Unfortunately, I discovered the penalty for modifying course content with feminist ideas and documenting these changes publicly in my syllabi. When I prepared my papers formally re-

questing that the institution renew or rehire me during the beginning of
my second year at this institution, I included those syllabi which reflected my intellectual interests to a greater degree, the introduction to
teaching course and social studies methods. Although my department
chair evaluated my syllabi as "carefully conceived and developed" (Department Chair's Evaluation, 10/28/88), the Dean's evaluation warned
me that I was expected to follow the prescribed syllabi.

> Dr. McCall's portfolio documents satisfactory performance in her teaching
> duties. There is, however, one area of concern. While making allowance for
> the issues of individual and academic freedom, it also is recognized the fac-
> ulty are assigned to teach courses which have been designed cooperatively
> by the department to meet specific purposes, which have been approved by
> various curriculum committees, by C.A.A. (Committee on Academic Af-
> fairs), and by C.O.T.E. (Committee on Teacher Education), and which have
> been submitted to NCATE and the state board of education as documenta-
> tion of what we are doing in our program. Dr. McCall must guard lest per-
> sonal biases and assumptions in effect rewrite or, in other ways, alter the
> purpose, content, and direction of the assigned courses (Dean's Evaluation
> 11/4/88).

I interpreted the Dean's evaluation as a reminder that my academic
freedom was overshadowed by the expectation that I teach the "approved" curriculum. If I chose to infuse my feminist voices in my teaching, these voices must be hidden behind closed classroom doors and between the lines of the "approved" course syllabi. This apparent warning
to move my feminist voices underground jarred me into realizing the
obstacles were immense to develop and speak in my feminist voices at
this institution. Patriarchy was supported by people in formal and informal positions of power as well as institutional policies. As Belenky and
her colleagues discovered in their research, when women were not listened to, they frequently became silent. I gave up the struggle to speak
and be heard and began my search for another position.

Opportunities to Develop Feminist, Caring Voices

During my search for a different tenure-track faculty position, I wanted
to find U.S. institutions in which the struggle to resist and change the
patriarchal, white supremacist nature of the university was more evident. I hoped to find institutions which encouraged faculty to develop
and speak in many diverse feminist voices (hooks, 1989). I wanted to
find institutions which were committed to developing the minds, self-
concepts, and voices of women students as well as men students (Belenky et al., 1986). I endeavored to find colleagues with formal power to

hire, retain, tenure, promote, and reward those faculty who struggled to resist all forms of domination and spoke, wrote, and taught to build a more just world.

I agreed to take a position at the second institution after discovering several promising signs that I could develop my feminist voices. This institution was similar to the first institution in size, but was located within another state in the Midwestern section of the U.S. One hopeful indication was the promotion and tenure of one of the women in the department who was a very strong feminist and infused her teaching and writing with gender, race, and class issues. Although she was the only tenured woman in the department, her presence and success offered promise that my feminist voices could develop and be heard. Another hopeful sign was this institution's strong tradition of academic freedom. When faculty were asked to teach specific courses, they were also given the freedom, within broad state and departmental guidelines, to develop the substance of these courses and select the texts to use. A third promising indicator was the description of democratic practices by which the department existed. All faculty were encouraged to have a voice in all decisions including the schedule, curriculum, and programs. Finally, the department showed a commitment to developing their students' voices by including a few students, mostly women, during my interviews. These students participated in asking questions as well as making recommendations about whom should be hired. These promising signs were early indicators of the structures, programs, and colleagues I found at this institution which supported my speaking in caring, feminist voices during the next eight years.

Benefiting from Supportive Colleagues

In addition to the tenured, feminist colleague I met when I took the position at this second institution, another strong feminist was hired in the department at the same time I was hired. These two committed feminist colleagues as well as a growing number of colleagues in my department and college are interested in feminist, multicultural ideas, suggest resources, and discuss ideas with me which have helped me to develop more thoughtful, insightful, multidimensional feminist voices.

Colleagues with formal power to affirm my feminist voices through the renewal, tenure, and promotion process have increased during the past four years. A feminist colleague became the department chair in 1993 and rewards faculty who infuse their teaching, scholarship, and service with feminist, multicultural views. A new dean was hired in 1994 who also supports faculty who speak in feminist, multicultural voices (I was part of the search committee which recommended him and other top candidates to be interviewed). Most tenured members of my department who serve on the departmental personnel committee and evaluate departmental members' teaching, service, and scholarship for renewal, tenure, and promotion are now supportive of feminist, multicultural voices. The members of the college personnel committee change somewhat every year, but overall the committee has become more open to feminist, multicultural approaches in teaching, scholarship, and service. After I was awarded tenure and promoted to associate professor in 1995, I became a member of both departmental and college personnel committees and endeavor to encourage other faculty to speak in feminist, multicultural voices. In addition to supportive colleagues in positions of formal power, two programs at this institution have provided additional impetus to develop my feminist, multicultural, caring voices.

Benefiting from Supportive Programs

One university program which has contributed to my development of multicultural, social reconstructionist (Sleeter & Grant, 1994) content and teaching materials for one of my courses and provided new areas of scholarship has been the faculty development program. After my department chair assisted me in preparing my first proposal, I have been awarded three faculty development grants to study (1) children's literature which raises social problems (such as discrimination due to AIDS, racism, sexism, poverty, and violence) and additional resources which offer social action responses to these problems; (2) Hmong history, culture, and textile art; and (3) Wisconsin Native American history, culture, and textile art. In addition, through the faculty development program, I was given a one-semester sabbatical to prepare to engage in new collaborative action research with an experienced elementary classroom teacher to study what children learn from a multicultural curriculum. This program has strengthened my feminist, multicultural voices in my teaching and research by financially supporting my study of these different topics.

Another aspect of our teacher education program which has encouraged my feminist, multicultural, caring voices was the adoption of the "caring intellectual" as the type of educator we want to develop. This model was adopted as part of the preparation for the National Council for Accreditation of Teacher Education (NCATE) review of our teacher education program during 1996. The model draws on Noddings' (1984) concept of teachers as "one-caring" and explicitly reinforces the value of caring voices among the faculty. The "caring intellectual" model also emphasizes the importance of developing educators who understand diverse groups, analyze stereotypes and prejudices, and value diversity. Even more significantly, the model envisions educators as change agents who are committed to transforming curriculum and teaching practice to create a democratic society. The NCATE review process significantly affirms feminist, multicultural voices among the teacher education faculty, including mine.

Incorporating Feminist, Caring Voices in Teaching

During the past eight years I have developed elements of a multicultural, social reconstructionist approach (Sleeter & Grant, 1994) in my social studies methods course. Social class and race, along with gender, have become significant components of the course. The focus of the course is: (1) to include the experiences and perspectives of women and men from different races and socioeconomic classes; (2) to help students analyze their own experiences for gender, race, or class oppression and address these issues of inequality more broadly; (3) to think critically; (4) to analyze different perspectives; and (5) to encourage social action as a way of moving toward equality (Sleeter & Grant, 1994).

During the course we analyze existing elementary and middle school social studies textbooks and largely discover that European-American wealthy males' experiences and perspectives are emphasized with significantly less attention to working class European-American men as well as women and men from other races (Peterson, 1990; Sleeter & Grant, 1991). We also analyze maps for cultural biases, discuss possible reasons for the biases, and ways we might address these as teachers.

I introduce the students to the life styles and life chances (Banks, 1987) approach to making the social studies curriculum more multicultural which describes aspects of a group's culture as well as the discrimination and oppression this group faces within society. We integrate Banks' ideas for multicultural curriculum with Berman's (1990) conception of social responsibility which encourages students to invest in the well being of others and make a difference in the world. During the course we investigate social issues such as discrimination against those who are HIV-positive or have AIDS, poverty, racism, sexism, and violence through children's literature and consider social action strategies children and youth might use in addressing these issues (see McCall, 1996 for a more complete description).

Additionally, the course focuses on knowledge, curricular resources, and instructional activities in teaching about the history and culture of African American, Native American, and Hmong women and men. Through examining quilts, Hmong textile art (or paj ntaub), and beadwork and ribbonwork on Native American clothing in class, the students have the opportunity to learn more about women's perspectives and contributions to maintaining cultural identity or portraying national or family history. Music, children's literature, and poetry as avenues for learning about different social classes, cultures, and races are explored as well. We reconsider the main ideas and perspectives of traditional teachings about Columbus and Thanksgiving (Rethinking Schools, 1991) in order to review what Native Americans' experiences and perspectives were of these historical events and discuss the current issue of treaty rights for Wisconsin tribes. In addition, we consider ways students can use their power as consumers to patronize businesses which exhibit social justice characteristics such as the advancement of women and people of color to top positions, strong environmental programs, and the disclosure of information about the company's social programs (Dellabough, 1992).

Finally, as the culminating project for the course, students develop a social studies curriculum unit appropriate for elementary or middle-school classes on a topic of their choice. During the past four years, the students have had the opportunity to teach their units in their clinical teaching experience, taken concurrently with social studies methods. The students' cooperating teachers also have a voice in selecting the curriculum unit topic. Even though I have encouraged a multicultural, social reconstructionist approach, I try to give students the freedom to select and deal with any appropriate social studies topic, including those which do not incorporate this approach.

In addition to speaking through many feminist, multicultural voices within the course content, I also incorporate caring voices (Noddings, 1984, 1986, 1992) and elements of hooks' (1994) conception of engaged pedagogy in my teaching. First, Noddings encourages teachers as "one-caring" to *model caring* for students (the "cared-for") in their teaching. One way Noddings (1986) suggests teachers may model caring is through good preparation for teaching. I endeavor to model caring for students through exhaustive preparation for class and the development of rich content and diverse teaching and learning class activities. Through such efforts, I hope to communicate to students I value their time and want to create many opportunities for us to teach and learn together in our class. Another method I use to model caring is by providing additional assistance and support for the students during the main course project. Since students often feel uncertain about the formidable project of developing and teaching a curriculum unit, each semester I hold at least one conference with pairs of students to review rough drafts of their unit, affirm the strengths of the unit, suggest possible improvements they could consider for the final draft, propose resources, and lend materials. Since the students began choosing the curriculum unit topic in collaboration with their cooperating teacher, I also hold a meeting with each pair of students and their cooperating teacher to discuss and decide on a topic. Yet another way I model caring is by addressing students' anxieties about their grades by allowing them to rewrite the journals for the course to earn full credit. Such additional efforts help the students gain competence in responding to course readings through the journals. Finally, I model caring by bringing snacks to class to share during class breaks and encouraging students to contribute food. Since our class sessions are over three hours in length, the students often seem to need the extra nourishment to maintain their energy for the class period and sharing food has appeared to help create community among all of us.

Both Noddings (1984, 1986, 1992) and hooks (1994) emphasize the importance of teachers' *dialogue* with students as an approach that "respects and cares for the souls of our students" (hooks, 1994, p. 13). As part of engaged pedagogy, hooks advocates for active involvement by both the students and teacher, but the teacher must lead the way in taking risks, linking personal experiences with academic readings, and encouraging students to make these personal connections. Additionally, hooks promotes critical thinking as the heart of engaged pedagogy, which is especially important given the discouragement for critical thinking in our anti-intellectual society.

In my teaching, I endeavor to care for students by encouraging dialogue and critical thinking through class discussions and journals. During the first class session, the students and I collaboratively develop class discussion guidelines which begin to establish similar expectations for whole class discussions during the semester. As a form of student involvement in democratic decision-making (Sleeter & Grant, 1994), students use these guidelines to evaluate their participation in the course, a part of the grade for the course. For example, last year, the guidelines we created were:

1. Everyone contributes.
2. Make sincere comments.
3. Stick to the topic.
4. Passing on discussions allowed.
5. One person talks at a time; listen to each other.
6. Learn others' names.
7. Be open to other points of view.
8. Disagree respectfully.
9. Give thinking time.
10. Ask for more discussion time if needed.

In order to encourage all students' voices in whole class discussions, I usually ask the students to discuss readings first in small, cooperative groups. During the small group discussions, the classroom becomes quite noisy with the voices of most students offering many different ideas and responses to the readings. The small group discussions also seem to contribute to students' confidence in their ideas to offer them during the large group discussions. In preparation for class discussions of the readings, I ask students to "talk back" (hooks, 1989) to the readings through journals rather than accept all ideas uncritically. I also invite students to respond to the readings from Elbow's (1973) conception of the "believing game" and "doubting game." When students write from the "believing game," they pretend to believe everything the authors say, try to enter into their point of view and think as they do, and suspend their own judgment. In contrast, when responding from the "doubting game," students doubt the authors' ideas, look for weaknesses and ideas to reject, and question the authors' intentions in the article. As we discuss readings in class, students can refer to their journals as they express what they found valuable from the "believing game" and any weaknesses from the "doubting game." We integrate different views and reactions to form a more collaborative analysis of the readings.

Another aspect of infusing caring within teaching is offering students occasions to *practice caring* (Noddings, 1984, 1986, 1992). In addition to the teacher being "one-caring," the teacher encourages all students to become "one-caring" by structuring opportunities for students to engage in caring actions toward others. One way I encourage caring among students in the course is by asking students to work with a teaching partner during the major course project, developing and teaching a social studies curriculum unit. During the project, the students must share ideas, negotiate schedules, cooperatively search for resources, complete research on the main ideas and concepts, design lessons with diverse teaching and learning activities, select assessment strategies, and create any needed instructional materials. Students must cooperate and help each other in order to complete this project successfully. Often, teaching partners become very close during the semester because of the amount of time they spend together working on the curriculum unit. I also encourage students to show caring for others in the class through community-building activities. During the first class session, the students and I brainstorm activities we might engage in to help create community for learning. Such activities include: work with different people in class and on assignments, share ideas and materials, help others with resources, explain assignments to others, encourage each other, tell others when they have good ideas, and help set up and clean up the classroom. These activities not only are small ways to show caring for others, but also help to develop a cooperative, supportive atmosphere for learning rather than foster competition.

A fourth means of infusing caring within teaching suggested by Noddings (1984, 1986, 1992) is through *confirmation*. Noddings recommends teachers affirm the best in students and attribute the finest possible motives for students' actions as is realistically and ethically possible. Through commenting on students' journals and during class discussions, I strive to affirm the students' voices, their reactions to the readings, and their contributions to our collaborative construction of knowledge. I also ask students regularly to evaluate their own participation and efforts at community building according to the guidelines we developed at the beginning of the semester and confirm students' self-evaluations as much as I ethically can.

Fifth, Noddings (1992) encourages educators to have *continuity* among students and teachers as part of developing caring in teaching. Continuity involves students and teachers working together over an extended period of time in order to develop trusting relationships and create a caring community. During the past four years, I have been part of a program which provides some continuity, especially among the students. In this program a cohort of students complete three education methods courses and a clinical teaching experience together during the same semester. I am part of the three-member faculty team that teaches the courses and supervises the students during their clinical teaching experiences. The students attend classes together three or four days a week and observe, assist, and teach in their clinical placement one day. Along with classroom teachers, the students and university faculty hold informal planning meetings several times during the semester in which we reflect on what the students are learning from their clinical teaching experiences and concerns they have. The students especially develop close relationships because of this program. As a faculty member, I am able to cultivate more personal relationships with the students I supervise as well as have in class and create closer relationships with the other faculty who teach in the program. Even with the limited continuity this program provides, it appears to contribute to students' willingness to speak out more in class and in planning meetings, to feel comfortable making class presentations, and to attempt more challenging teaching activities in their clinical placements.

Until the NCATE review process, caring was not part of the language most faculty used in discussing our teacher preparation program. Higher education has traditionally emphasized the development of students' intellects with significantly less concern for students' overall well-being and development into caring persons (hooks, 1994). The ethos of competition, individualism, and hierarchy of the institution divides students from other students, students from faculty, and faculty from one another. Students compete with each other for grades while faculty compete with one another for small merit pay raises and the few teaching and research awards the institution offers. Professors complain about students' disinterest in learning as students complain about professors' unrealistic expectations. Despite the teacher education program's goal of developing "caring, intellectual" teachers, the university has created a number of constraints to feminist, caring teaching within the institution.

Structural and Internalized Constraints to Feminist, Caring Teaching

Despite my dedication to integrating feminist, caring voices in my teaching, I have struggled with this institution's structural constraints and my own internalized constraints to teach from a feminist ethic of care. This approach to teaching recognizes the importance of teachers receiving care as well as caring for students. When the institution establishes faculty workloads which hinder teachers from developing caring relationships with students and faculty evaluation policies which reflect little care for teachers, my efforts to teach from a feminist ethic of care are diminished.

Struggling with Faculty Workloads

Part of the structural constraints to feminist, caring teaching which the university has created is our workloads, including the number of students the institution requires the faculty to work with each semester and the limited time a teacher has with a class of students. I have found it very difficult to achieve the goal of using engaged pedagogy (hooks, 1994), *modeling caring* and developing *continuity among students and the teacher* as part of caring in teaching (Noddings, 1984, 1986, 1992) with 25 or more students in a class which meets three hours a week for a 14-week semester. With my 12-credit teaching load each semester which includes teaching and working with 50 to 75 students, the goal of developing close, trusting, caring relationships with each student becomes nearly impossible. Faculty who emphasize caring in their teaching at other institutions have also recognized similar difficulties (Thayer-Bacon & Bacon, 1994).

Struggling with the Faculty Evaluation Process

The renewal, tenure, and promotion process is another institutional constraint to feminist, caring teaching due to the lack of institutional caring for faculty communicated through the process. The procedures for faculty evaluations appear to be based on the assumption that faculty are *not* meeting the expectations for teaching, scholarship, and service unless they can document they are accomplishing such achievements. The burden is completely on the faculty to prove to the institution they should be allowed to remain in their positions, be awarded tenure, or awarded promotion.

Because the process by which our teaching is evaluated for renewal, tenure, and promotion relies almost completely on formal student evaluations, this procedure provides another structural constraint to faculty speaking in caring, feminist voices. The student evaluation form rewards faculty whose content and pedagogy match students' expectations and penalizes those who do not. For faculty teaching with feminist, multicultural voices which disrupt the status quo, they often face negative consequences (hooks, 1994). Since most students in our teacher education program are women, soliciting their evaluations of their professors' teaching provides one avenue which affirms women students' voices. Encouraging the development of students' voices, especially women students' voices which are often suppressed within patriarchal societies, is an important goal for liberatory education. However, a majority of students in the U.S., women and men, have been encouraged to develop voices and minds which support the patriarchal, white supremacist society (hooks, 1989; Lorde, 1984). A number of students use the evaluation process to attack me and other teachers who raise gender, race, and class issues as a way to avoid dealing with matters of domination (hooks, 1989). Voicing their resistance may be the result of the conflict between the multicultural, social reconstructionist messages in my teaching and the students' existing knowledge and value system (Dunn, 1987).

During my first four years at this institution, students' evaluations of my teaching were used in the evaluation process to criticize my feminist, multicultural teaching by those faculty and administrators, primarily European American men, who did not value feminist, multicultural voices in teaching and wanted to preserve the patriarchal, white supremacist curriculum of this institution. As with many universities, my teaching, service, and research at the time were evaluated primarily by men (Parson, Sands & Duane, 1992). I was encouraged to soften, minimize, modify, or eliminate the multicultural, social reconstructionist messages of my course by members of personnel committees. Other faculty and administrators told me informally that I should talk less about gender in my course or that I should guard against presenting these messages in an impositional manner. As one European American male colleague asked, "Are you sure you're teaching and not preaching?" My department chair formally evaluated my teaching from my first year with this advice: "She does need to improve her teaching style. Comments from students should be taken seriously in making improvements in the area of teaching" (Department Chair Evaluation 10/29/90). These critical comments were echoed by the dean and vice chancellor. When I inquired about what student comments I should attend to, other faculty and administrators pointed to the complaints about my emphasis on women, Native Americans, and African Americans in my course. Not only did the institution discourage feminist, multicultural teaching through the process by which I was evaluated, but also through establishing institutional norms of a patriarchal, white supremacist curriculum and pedagogy. Students are often socialized to expect all faculty to follow these norms, resist the curriculum and pedagogy of teachers who violate them, and pressure faculty to continue the status quo.

Struggling with Institutional Norms, Students' Expectations, and Resistance

Students rarely expect me to teach from a feminist ethic of care. After I introduce the importance of caring in teaching to students, conflicting expectations emerge between the students and me as to what constitutes caring. While I believe part of caring for students is encouraging their growth and development in order to prepare them for teaching in our diverse society and caring for children from different backgrounds they will likely teach, students expect me to show caring by being warm and completely accepting of their present ideas and perspectives, their contributions to class discussions, and the quality of their work. I find it challenging to balance showing an understanding of where students are in their development, affirming their perspectives as legitimate for their experiences, and encouraging them to understand different perspectives and new knowledge.

Students' expectations for my teaching are often influenced by their backgrounds. Most students in the social studies methods class are European American, working class and middle-class women. Between 15 and 30 percent are working class and middle-class European American men. The majority of students enter the class seriously concerned about becoming good teachers, but with little awareness and experience with diversity, including White privilege and male privilege in U.S. society. The students enter the course with an unstated expectation that the curriculum and classroom will be male-focused. When I consistently emphasize the experiences and perspectives of women of all groups and people of color in the curriculum as a correction to the patriarchal, Eurocentric curriculum they have traditionally encountered in the past in U.S. educational institutions, the students see my emphasis as biased, political, and unfair in its treatment of men.

Students also seem to expect a male-dominated classroom. Although I consciously affirm all voices, when I solicit balanced contributions to class discussions by encouraging quiet students to speak out more and those who tend to be more vocal (who are frequently men) to listen and support the voices of more quiet students, most students are outraged. Many female as well as male students defend male dominance. Some of the quiet students resist speaking more because of their discomfort with expressing themselves in class. Students resist my efforts to have balanced discussions by criticizing my teaching as "biased against men," "letting my personal views cause reverse discrimination," and "sexist toward males."

Students' expectations for feedback on their work also appear violated with my emphasis on not only affirming students' ideas, but also encouraging students to improve the clarity of their writing, include more than one perspective in their curriculum unit, or develop more complete curriculum unit lesson plans. Students seem to perceive my suggestions as uncaring acts and at times have responded by attacking me during our conferences as being unclear, unrealistic, or asking them to do unnecessary "busy work."

Facing my students' resistance to a multicultural curriculum, the inclusion of all students' voices in the classroom, and growth in their thinking, writing, and curriculum development work has been difficult and painful. Others who teach with feminist, critical voices have experienced similar resistance from their students in response to potentially liberatory education (Lather, 1991; Rakow, 1991). Even though I endeavor to show caring for students in my teaching and encourage students' growth, a notable number of students interpret the unsettling curriculum and classroom dynamics as indications of my lack of caring. As Thayer-Bacon and Bacon (1994) discovered, students who prefer to "slide by" do not value caring professors. hooks (1994) also recognized students did not always enjoy her use of engaged pedagogy because they found the courses so challenging and unsettling. Perhaps they might not recognize the benefits of engaged pedagogy until after the semester is over and the course completed. Teaching from a feminist ethic of care encourages caring for and from teachers, students, administrators, families, and community members as it contributes toward creating a more just society. Teachers need to guard against caring for students and others from privileged backgrounds without also encouraging these students to show care for others. Such one-way caring may lead to the students' expectation of always being the recipients of care (Hoagland, 1990). A feminist ethic of care must disrupt the status quo, integrate caring with justice, and spread the caring labor among all members of the educational community.

Such structural constraints as the faculty workload, the teacher evaluation process, and institutional norms which contribute to students' expectations for a patriarchal, white supremacist curriculum and pedagogy and students' resistance to teaching from a feminist ethic of care have been examples of the lack of care I received from the institution. These constraints have diminished my efforts to care for students. In order for me and other faculty to infuse our teaching with feminist, caring voices, we must have some institutional support. Some research affirms my experiences. In a study of high schools with a strong emphasis on caring, administrators showed caring for the staff, encouraged teachers to care for one another, sought to hire teachers committed to caring for students, recognized and supported caring teachers, and were part of a critical mass of teachers and administrators who valued caring (Smith, Purkey & Raywid, 1991). Seldom do faculty in higher education have this institutional support for caring. Not only must teachers in universities have external encouragement to infuse their teaching with feminist, caring voices, they must also care for themselves. Since many women in the U.S. are socialized to devote themselves to caring for others, they have internalized this constraint to caring for themselves.

Balancing Care for Self and Students

Another constraint to teaching from a feminist ethic of care I have struggled with during the past few years is my internalized reluctance to care for myself. I am increasingly recognizing the importance of balancing care for myself with care for students. Growing up and through most of my adult life, I have not learned to care for myself. The socialization in my family, community, and in U.S. society generally to care for others and hope to receive the caring I needed from others was very strong. I am beginning to find this balance. A student wisely reminded me of the importance of caring for myself in a memorable way.

On my bedroom wall is a chalk drawing of a woman sitting alone in the grass looking intently at a shiny object cupped in both hands. Doris, a former student and single parent of three children, drew this picture for me and presented it as a gift several years ago. Doris said she was inspired to create the drawing for me as a reminder to "take care of your inner light." Doris' gift moved me deeply. At the time I was depressed about the recent dissolution of friendships with two women, very anxious about my ability to achieve tenure at my institution, and greatly saddened by the lack of caring responses from students to my efforts to speak in caring, feminist voices in my teaching. I thought I was hiding my depression and anxiety successfully from others, especially students. Doris perceived my needs and responded with care. Although I have not expected to receive such caring responses from most students, I recognized that I was not receiving the caring I needed to maintain my energy for caring for students through teaching.

hooks (1994) recognizes the need for teachers to care for themselves in order to use engaged pedagogy and care for students. "[T]eachers must be actively committed to a process of self-actualization that promotes their own well-being if they are to teach in a manner that empowers students" (p. 15). In Gilligan's research on the importance of caring in women's moral development, she posited the most advanced form of care as one which balances care for self with care for others. Earlier levels involve first, caring for the self as protecting oneself out of a sense of vulnerability and second, caring for others because of the social expectation for caring. For women and other oppressed groups within patriarchal, white supremacist societies, caring for others can be a way of coping with powerlessness by filling privileged groups' expectations, winning their approval, and hopefully participating in their power. Perhaps balancing caring for oneself with caring for others can be a way for women to achieve a level of cognitive liberation from sexist oppression (Puka, 1993). Noddings (1984, 1990, 1991, 1992) emphasizes the importance of students contributing to the caring relationship by recognizing and responding to the teacher's caring and eventually becoming caring persons themselves. Teachers should not remain in the permanent position of providing care for others. However, it is easy to interpret Noddings' ideas as placing the major responsibility for caring on teachers. A feminist ethic of care necessitates the integration of caring and justice in teaching (Card, 1990; Houston, 1990).

Moving Beyond Survival: Toward Collective Feminist, Caring Voices

During the past eight years at two institutions, the main source of support for developing and strengthening my feminist voices has been women colleagues. Although these women did not necessarily agree with all of my ideas and may not have been engaged with feminist research, writing, or teaching themselves, they still encouraged me to speak and listened to at least some of what I had to say. Women colleagues and I have had to develop our own means of support since, as other women professors have faced, we have been excluded from the "old boy network" which has provided knowledge and support helpful for faculty success within the university "system" (Parson, Sands & Duane, 1992). At the first institution, two women colleagues and I provided informal, mostly private support for one another in coping with the oppression and discouragement we felt in our department. We wrote notes of encouragement to one another, met for dinner, and huddled together within the privacy of one of our offices to criticize, complain about, and laugh at the latest sexist, oppressive incident. Since the women in this informal support network were all new, untenured, assistant professors, we had little formal power to help each other develop our voices within our department. However, one of the women did publicly support my efforts to use supplementary textbooks for my social studies methods course. When other colleagues questioned in writing on my textbook order the use of these texts, this supportive colleague wrote on the same order, "Isn't the decision based on the wisdom and preference of the instructor and department head? Long live academic freedom and professionally responsible choices!" Because the institution was so oppressive, one of the women left after one year and I left after the second year. However, new, untenured, women assistant professors joined each year.

At the second institution, the support from women colleagues to develop my feminist voices and mind has been both formal and informal, private and public. The women within my department, college, and in different disciplines within the university who share my interest in equality provide a network of confirmation. Women's networks are often an important means for women to find their work, experience, and support valued (Simeone, 1987). Feminist colleagues have especially been such a network. They have introduced me to people, literature, conferences, and teaching resources which have helped to deepen my thinking about issues of equality to include social class, race, and sexual orientation. These same colleagues have read, affirmed, and critiqued some of my writing and supported my efforts to find publication outlets. We have attended women's studies and education conferences together and offered feedback and encouragement regarding our presentations. We have discussed challenges we face in our teaching.

The more formal, public support for feminist voices and thinking has occurred during department meetings when women colleagues ask me to speak about issues related to my area of expertise when other men who also share this expertise speak. At times, the other women within my department and I have joined together to vote in support of specific decisions we consider important or to vote against those we consider harmful. For example, we have endeavored to hire new department members, female and male, who are knowledgeable of diversity and address educational equity issues in their teaching. Yet another way colleagues have supported me is through offering advice and guidance in preparing renewal, tenure, or promotion papers and in preparing faculty development proposals. I have also formally supported colleagues by observing their teaching and affirming their excellent teaching practices; assisting a department member's preparation of a sabbatical application; nominating a department member for an endowed professorship; sharing syllabi and course materials with colleagues who are teaching the same course; and offering advice in preparing renewal papers. Informally, I have invited new colleagues to my house for meals, dispensed baked gifts to different faculty at holidays, and written encouraging notes. These are small acts which have done little to make the institution more hospitable for feminist, caring voices. For most of my ten years in higher education, I have devoted the majority of my time to surviving and meeting the requirements of tenure by investing enormous amounts of energy in my teaching, research, and writing. I find research and writing very renewing and satisfying and the institution acknowledges these accomplishments, but they have been primarily solitary activities. I recognize the importance of working collaboratively with others who share similar goals in order to make institutional changes.

A weakness of Gilligan's research on caring in women's moral development is its individual focus (Puka, 1993). In order to move beyond caring as individual acts in teaching, we need to have solidarity among those who value caring, feminist voices in their teaching. By engaging in cooperative social action to address institutional structures which impede caring for students as well as faculty, we are more likely to move beyond survival to change the institution. For example, we could consider how the renewal, tenure, and promotion process might be changed to reflect caring for faculty and support for those who teach in feminist, caring voices. We could consider how the academic programs and calendar might be modified to support the development of caring relationships among faculty and students. We could consider additional ways of acknowledging and rewarding faculty for their caring, feminist voices in order to diminish the competition for the few teaching and research awards available through the institution. Without collective action, those who teach in feminist, caring voices will continue to struggle to survive.

References

Banks, J.A. (1987). The social studies, ethnic diversity, and social change. *The Elementary School Journal, 87*(5), 531–543.

Bentley, R. J. & Blackburn, R. T. (1992). Two decades of gains for female faculty? *Teachers College Record, 93*(4), 697–709.

Belenky, M. F., Clinchy, B. M., Goldberger, N. R., & Tarule, J. M. (1986). *Women's ways of knowing.* New York: Basic Books.

Berman, S. (1990). Educating for social responsibility. *Educational Leadership, 48*(2), 75–80.

Card, C. (1990). Caring and evil. *Hypatia, 5*(1), 101–108.

Dellabough, R. (1992). *Students shopping 4 a better world.* New York: Council on Economic Priorities.

Dunn, K. (1987). Feminist teaching: Who are your students? *Women's Studies Quarterly 24*(3–4), 40–46.

Elbow, P. (1973). *Writing without teachers.* New York: Oxford.

Hoagland, S. L. (1990). Some concerns about Nel Noddings' caring. *Hypatia, 5*(1), 109–114.

Hoffman, N. (Ed.). (1981). *Woman's "true" profession: Voices from the history of teaching*. Old Westbury, NY: The Feminist Press.

hooks, b. (1989). *Talking Back: Thinking Feminist, Thinking Black*. Boston: South End Press.

hooks, b. (1994). *Teaching to transgress: Education as the practice of freedom*. New York: Routledge.

Houston, B. (1990). Caring and exploitation. *Hypatia, 5*(1), 115–120.

Lather, P. (1991). *Getting smart: Feminist research and pedagogy with/in the postmodern*. New York: Routledge, Chapman and Hall.

Lorde, A. (1984). *Sister outsider*. Freedom, CA: The Crossing Press.

McCall, A. L. (1996). Making a difference: Integrating social problems and social action in the social studies curriculum. *The Social Studies, 87*(5), 203–209.

Noddings, N. (1984). *Caring: A feminine approach to ethics & moral development*. Berkeley: University of California Press.

Noddings, N. (1986). Fidelity in teaching, teacher education, and research for teaching. *Harvard Educational Review, 56*(4), 496–510.

Noddings, N. (1990). A response. *Hypatia, 5*(1), 120–126.

Noddings, N. (1991). Caring and continuity in education. *Scandinavian Journal of Educational Research, 35*(1), 3–12.

Noddings, N. (1992). *The challenge to care in schools: an alternative approach to education*. New York: Teachers College Press.

Parson, L. A., Sands, R. G., & Duane, J. (1992). The campus climate for women faculty at a public university. *Initiatives, 54*(1), 19–27.

Peterson, B. (March/April, 1990). What are our children learning? *Rethinking Schools, 4*(3), 18–19.

Puka, B. (1993). The liberation of caring: A different voice for Gilligan's "different voice." In M.. J. Larrabee (Ed.), *An ethic of care: Feminist and interdisciplinary perspectives*. New York: Routledge.

Rakow, L. F. (1991). Gender and race in the classroom: Teaching way out of line. *Feminist Teacher, 6*(1), 10–13.

Rethinking Schools, (1991). *Rethinking Columbus*. Milwaukee: Rethinking Schools.

Sadker, M. & Sadker, D. (1994). *Failing at fairness: How our schools cheat girls*. New York: Simon & Schuster.

Simeone, A. (1987). *Academic women: Working towards equality*. South Hadley, MA: Bergin & Garvey.

Sleeter, C. E. & Grant, C. A. (1991). Race, class, gender, and disability in current textbooks. In M.W. Apple & L.K. Christian-Smith (Eds.). *The politics of the textbook* (pp. 78–101). New York: Routledge.

Sleeter, C. E. & Grant, C. A. (1994). *Making choices for multicultural education: Five approaches to race, class, and gender (2nd ed.)*. Columbus: Merrill.

Smith, B., Purkey, S. & Raywid, M. A. (1991, April). *Caring teachers and caring schools*. Paper presented at the annual meeting of the American Educational Research Association, Chicago, Illinois.

Thayer-Bacon, B. & Bacon, C. S. (1994). *Caring in the college/university classroom*. Unpublished manuscript, Bowling Green State University, Bowling Green, Ohio.

7 Deconstructing Feminist Pedagogy: Seeing That Which Is Ordinarily Obscured by the Familiar[1]

Janice Jipson & Petra Munro

In-sight

To look back on one's teaching can be a painful process. Questions from the past re-appear and linger, opaque and unresolved, intermittently penetrating our conversations as we talk about our present situations. We agonize once more with being positioned as experts in the academy, our identities as women excluding us as creators of knowledge and leaving us with traditional roles of reproduction and facilitation. We struggle yet again with how to support and encourage our graduate students and younger colleagues without assuming the inherently condescending and controlling roles of the men-tor. We talk of power, of nurturance, of being connected teachers in dis-connected worlds. We ramble. We commiserate. We complain. We disagree. We tell stories.

To be human is to be in a story. To be human means not being able to step outside of or to step back from one's story to capture or recapture what has transpired. To look back at our course entitled Women & Teaching: The Role of Nurturing in Education[2] is necessarily fraught with contradictions. Yet, to re-interpret the events which transpired in that curricular moment seems as inevitable as it is impossible. Our original impulse as we began this project was to believe that we might be able, due to the distance of time, to reconstruct the events and get it right this time. We hoped to understand the students' reactions to our project of engaging feminist pedagogy as a way to validate women's experiences while simultaneously retheorizing "curriculum" based on those experiences.

Our original interpretations (Jipson & Munro, 1993) addressed much of the current critique of feminist and emancipatory pedagogies (Gore, 1993; Orner, 1992). Yet to "trash" feminist pedagogy as reifying a unitary self, as reproducing the very hierarchies we are striving to critique, and as engaging in the very essentialisms we struggle to avoid, is to engage in a deconstructive discourse which situates us again in a binary quandary of having gotten it right or wrong. More importantly, we wish to avoid a critique which assumes a rational understanding of events. To assume a linearity of events that we might reconstruct would be to construct merely another fiction.

Our desire to review the events of several years ago speaks to the ongoing problematic of teaching, writing and reading from a feminist, poststructuralist perspective in which one struggles to name the subject "woman" while simultaneously disrupting it. How this process can translate to pedagogy without reproducing another naturalizing discourse is the heart of this project. Our acknowledgment that translation is a fiction underlies all that follows.

Reflecting on shared memories of the teachers as mothers seminar we co-taught over 5 years ago, our conversation returns to the familiar analyses of our feminist pedagogies, of our current struggle to "stay real" and to provide environments that validate our students, and us, too. And once again we puzzle, re-analyze, re-consider what had happened in that first seminar when we had hoped we could together really "practice" a feminist pedagogy. There were differences between us, however, from the beginning—even in how we remembered the title of the course with Petra calling it "The Role of Nurturance in Education" and Jan remembering it as the "Teachers as Mothers" seminar.

We questioned the oppression of nurturance—how had our dreams of supporting and facilitating our students, of being the midwife that Belenky et al. (1986) describe, turned into a nightmare of rejection—their rejection of our stories and our attempts to be the good mother and our own rejection of their needs. We questioned the irony of empowerment—how did our desire to validate the lives of women teachers through the use of feminist pedagogy lead to an environment in which our own students found themselves undermined, oppressed by theory that did not speak to their personal understandings of their worlds.

Re-viewing

We found ourselves returning to a discussion of the course. Petra recalled that she had fantasized about examining issues relevant to women teachers:

I wrote in my journal that I envisioned a space where our hopes, fears, experiences would be heard and accepted. A space in which we could rid ourselves of the self-consciousness inevitably brought on by the presence of men. What would it be like to have my voice represent me, not a projection of what I thought was acceptable or needed? Where I would not be tempted or distracted to appeal to the approving nods and confirming glances of the male gaze.

I imagined intense discussion over feminist readings. What was the relationship of feminist theory to our personal lives and experiences? If theory and practice/reality really were dialectical mutually informing, wouldn't it be wonderful to have a course in which women conducted life histories and looked at the usefulness of feminist theory in understanding their lives? I hoped that by looking at our everyday lives as teachers we would also come to understand our oppression and work together to explore ways in which we could create change or at least support one another (journal entry 4/90).

In deciding to co-teach a graduate seminar on the role of nurturance in education, we actively chose to explore our own understanding of feminist pedagogy and to pursue our desire to hear how other women think about their teaching. Through our personal recollections of our experiences as teachers and through ongoing interpretations of the seminar experience, we hoped to explore how feminist pedagogy might be practiced in teaching about feminist theory and to examine the issues and questions concerning feminist pedagogy which might emerge from a seminar focused on issues of teaching.

We wished to develop curriculum that would reflect the experiences of women that have been ignored or marginalized in educational literature. We were also concerned with the commonly employed rituals and methods of teaching which positioned the teacher as expert with expected and prescribed roles to enact, roles which privileged particular ways of knowing and, thus sometimes, limited student participation.

In re-forming our teaching practices, we planned to implement pedagogical strategies consistent with those advocated by feminist educators. We hoped to create an environment where students are confirmed as knowers, classrooms are viewed as communities of learners, personal knowledge is legitimated, and multiple ways of knowing are acknowledged and encouraged (Belenky, et al., 1986; Grumet, 1988). We also embraced Carol Shrewsbury's (1987) concept of a feminist pedagogy which envisions "a classroom characterized as persons connected in a net of relationships with people who care about each other's learning as well as their own." Resonating with the ideas of critical feminist theorists, we also hoped to empower our students to critically examine their work and begin to view themselves as agents for social change (Ellsworth, 1989; Lather, 1992; Weiler, 1988).

Conscious of the impositional nature of theory and the textual dominance of male experience, we decided to feature the stories and voices of women as the texts for the course. The required texts included works of fiction such as Buchi Emecheta's *Joys of Motherhood,* Doris Lessing's *The Fifth Child,* Toni Morrison's *Beloved,* Tillie Olsen's *I Stand Here Ironing,* and a selection from Louise Erdrich's *Beet Queen.* The fiction was paired with formal essays on feminist theory compiled in a xeroxed packet, the contents ranging from liberal to post-modern perspectives and including writers such as Shulamith Firestone, and Madeline Grumet. To make the stories and voices of actual women teachers an integral part of the curriculum, we also included selections from the biographies of women teachers and asked participants in the seminar to complete life histories of each other. We were excited by our creation of what we believed was a truly feminist reading list, an ideal syllabus.

The seminar had included 18 female students enrolled in masters and doctoral programs in curriculum and instruction with focuses on early childhood, elementary, secondary and special education. Although we had originally planned to limit enrollment to 10 doctoral students, we found ourselves responding to the strong interest expressed by varied students in our university. Eventually, we permitted everyone to register for the seminar, perhaps smugly pleased that "our topic" had generated such widespread enthusiasm. We argued to ourselves that we were practicing inclusion, fostering diversity even as we acknowledged the unwieldy size of the group.

When the class began, we had defined our roles as facilitators but also identified ourselves as teacher-researchers considering questions about how curriculum emerges in a graduate course created within a feminist framework. We saw the highly personal and political nature of the topic as presenting an ideal opportunity to explore the creation of an interactive and collegial classroom environment. We also saw the opportunity to examine how we could empower participants to question those institutions and conventions that define their lives. Our own reflections and our experiences as participants were seen by us as providing a base in practice as we reconceptualized the notion of "feminist seminar" and attempted to enact personal aims through a teaching methodology that acknowledged relational and connected forms of knowing.

Almost from the very beginning, the course did not go as we had expected. Several students appeared never to read the assigned material and most did not integrate the fictional texts into their discussions, their writing or their presentations. Jan's reaction to their neglect of the fiction was one of disappointment.

> I sensed rejection of the "lovely stories" I had so carefully collected. I resented the lack of student effort to share their own experiences or to relate

them to the fictional material. I also felt guilty—my disappointment and resentment certainly were inappropriate responses for the "good mother/teacher" I tried to be. To me, the actual teaching of the course did feel like mothering—the kind of mothering that involves nagging your kids to clean their rooms, or do the dishes or vacuum the floor, to stop fighting and get to work (10/90).

Petra was also frustrated with what was happening in the class:

Based on other experiences in courses addressing feminist issues, I believed that both the theoretical and fictional readings would prompt discussion of our situations as teachers and would empower us in a system that consistently belittles us. Rather than being empowered, however, several students found the readings by feminists disturbing because of what they felt were their essentialist and exclusionary perspectives. They felt manipulated by feminists' claim to have "the" right answers.

We had assumed the readings would provide a common text from which we could explore our experiences. For the students, however, it seemed the text should *be* their experiences.

Reflecting back on the class, Petra observed:

I recognize that my affinity to the written word is perhaps part of my discomfort in connecting with my real life experiences. It is easier for me to abstract experiences through readings than to discuss the "real thing." My assumption that the students in the class would be stimulated by the readings, would find them thought provoking, and would use them as a catalyst for discussion proved to be wrong. Instead, students seemed to feel that the readings dismissed their personal experiences, and elevated the author's ideas above the student's experiences. From the students' perspective, in placing so much emphasis on the readings we were, in effect, discrediting their experiences. Although several students commented on the usefulness of the readings in their journals, the predominant feeling was that the readings were irrelevant.

For some students, many of the readings seemed distant, cold and rational. We sensed that the strong resistance to the readings had to do with their focus on feminist theory. Not only did students have diverse definitions of feminism, but they appeared to oppose the theory because it was abstract, not necessarily because it was feminist. They questioned what, for them, was the obvious contradiction of feminists who wrote about caring and nurturance yet did so in a detached, impersonal and theoretical manner which reified male ways of thinking and knowing. By imposing feminist theory on them, were we asking them to subsume their own life experiences, in direct contrast to our intention to value the personal? Were we trying to force a fit which, for some students, didn't work?

We continually struggled to understand the role of the readings in the awkward class discussions where the majority of students did not participate. Students' journals revealed that some of the tensions during the class discussions might have resulted from the explicit focus in the class on "mothering" and "nurturing", a focus that some felt was talked about but was not delivered. One student suggested that participants in the class perhaps had inappropriate expectations because they wanted something that was not being offered such as a "love object" in the teachers or a opportunity for group therapy.

Several students resisted feminist theory because they felt that feminists were taking the language and the hierarchical structure of the patriarchal perspective and applying it to women. For others in the class, feminism seemed an alien thing, that only "others" embraced. Feminists were perceived as radicals, either men-haters or, on the other extreme, wanting to be just like men. In the eyes of the students, the fiction and feminist theory were relevant only to the curriculum, not to their personal experience. We sensed that some women in the class perhaps feared they must give up their femininity in order to become feminists.

We wondered if there was a romantic expectation or illusion that we would sit around with tea and cookies and support, nurture, and accept each other unconditionally. That was not our intent. We sought a balance between the personal, the theory and the fiction. Were some students interested only in fictionalizing their lives? If we were to be responsive to the needs and interests of the students and not impose our own hidden curriculum, did that mean we needed to throw out the theory, shed what they perceived as protective theoretical armor? If the classroom was to be truly nurturant we asked, didn't that mean allowing for different needs and experiences, including our own? We felt stuck in the constant dilemma of having to recognize, understand and acknowledge the different processes, needs and expectations of the class while also acknowledging our own needs and expectations as teachers.

Seminar activities had been planned to promote dialogue and interaction. By juxtaposing women's fiction and life history with feminist theory we had hoped to create a textual dissonance within the class, thereby encouraging the questioning of taken-for-granted assumptions about teaching and about text. The readings themselves (fiction, biography, theory) and the informal seminar discussion format were chosen to provide a context in which the participants could examine their personal experiences as teaches and mothers. We wanted seminar participants to re-interpret their lives as teachers through their exploration of shared concerns and personal connections. We wanted them to discover, with us, the multiple genres through which women told their stories and wrote their theories.

But what actually happened was entirely different. Petra recalled:

As the class ended I couldn't help but feel that we had somehow failed. Where was the stimulating dialogue about the meaning of post modernism for our classroom teaching? Where were the attempts to figure out whether there was such a thing as feminist theory? Where was the search through fiction for the meaning of our lives? These intense debates did not take place. The connections that I had hoped to form between feminism, fiction, theory, and our personal lives had not occurred. Had I fictionalized feminist theory in my need to place everything in nice little boxes? Was it my own need to remain grounded in the corridors of patriarchal thought which resulted in my clinging to theory? What were my real motivations for using feminist theory? How was it that I remained blind to the needs and desires of our students? Why couldn't I see that feminist theory fulfills certain needs for me, but not for others?

And Jan recalled writing in her journal after the class was over:

Had I fictionalized my own role as teacher? What did it really mean to be caring, connected, nurturant? Some in the class had asserted that to be cared for was to be challenged and corrected. Others desired, even expected, gentleness and unconditional acceptance. Our concerns with nurturance seemed to revolve around how each of us defined and misinterpreted each other's acts based on our own experiences and definitions. In my eagerness to employ a feminist pedagogy of nurture and care, I had failed to notice the expressed needs of my students and had been, in fact, uncaring. The fiction I had created did not represent the experiences of the class. Was I "writing" my life as a teacher as I thought it "should" be—as Ruddick, and Belenky and Grumet would have it? Was I trying to enact their text? (6–90)

In reality, the actual seminar curriculum was not dictated by our "perfect" syllabus which sought to integrate theory, personal experience, and works of fiction. Multiple and sometimes contradictory realities were created right in our classroom as we tried to negotiate, express, demand, and defend the different needs and expectations which we brought. For most of the students, theoretical readings were not helpful in making sense of their lives. Why did we have such a hard time accepting this?
Petra puzzled:

Was I so socialized into academia after two years of graduate school that I no longer felt secure enough to venture my own thoughts without validating them immediately with parentheses? Had feminist theory become my patriarchal surrogate? Or was my need for theory, for intellectual validation, a continual acting out against the role of nurturer, which my experience taught me was of little value.

And Jan recalled:

I had positioned myself as a participant in the seminar with personal experience to share as a woman and a teacher. But I also entered with a deliberate agenda, to examine my own personal questions about mothering, nurturance and teaching. As I analyzed my attempts during the seminar to nurture and provide facilitation, I found that my romanticized role of mother-teacher did not adequately account for the resistance that emerged within the seminar environment, a passive resistance, initially directed toward the fictional texts.

I faced the contradictions of my initial assumptions. Conflict, dissent and resistance seemed an inevitable part of teaching, perhaps essential to the learning process. To be a mother was not enough. As I struggled to create a new definition of myself as a teacher and to further understand how feminist pedagogy might work, I asked myself, in a feminist pedagogy which valorizes connectedness and relationship, must curriculum be based primarily on the needs of the students? The implications of a student-centered, emergent curriculum for teachers with definite agendas for social change became an increasingly important issue for me. I went on to wonder how a curriculum might emerge that meets the interests and needs of all participants, teachers and students? Unless we acknowledge the needs of teachers as well as students, we succumb to the traditional feminine role of denying ourselves in enacting our roles as nurturers.

Petra also reflected back on the class:

I am confused about my role as teacher. I have always resonated strongly with the role of teacher as social change agent. Yet now I question, "What right do I have to impose my vision of social change?" Am I assuming that I can "raise the consciousness of my students?" Is that my responsibility? If I am truly a feminist, how does this role as social change agent conflict with accepting the multiple realities present in any classroom? Was a ten week university course in which students met once a week the appropriate space for this intensive process? More importantly, can the necessary trust for sharing personal lives be developed within the bureaucratic dimensions and constraints of a university? Finally, how do I resolve the curricular tensions in which students relativized theory and fiction by making their own lives the central text of the class? Whose fictions do I choose as I prepare to teach my next class. Who do I allow to write the text?

We were left with confusion and dissonance which, in theory, was what we strove to achieve. We agreed that real learning occurred when students faced the disequillibrium between their own beliefs and assumptions and those of "new" knowledge. However, in our fictionalized world of the perfect syllabus, the ideal seminar, and the nurturant teacher, confusion and dissonance did not fit in with out initial conceptions of a "caring" feminist pedagogy.

Re-membering

And so nearly four years later we continue to try to make sense of that teaching experience and the many experiences which we have since had, experiences which seem, in some ways, facsimiles of the first. Students who reject our readings, resist our theory, assert their right to give their own interpretation to their lives. We e-mail, we fax, we spend Saturday mornings on the phone, in deep conversation. We remember, we speculate, we talk. Acknowledging the rights of students to construct their own experiences, valorizing the presence of an emerging curriculum in our own classrooms, and puzzling over why, at times, we still feel disappointed, rejected, confused.

Surfacing in our conversation, perhaps exposed by the similar recurring dilemmas we each faced in our separate universities, were ever shifting understandings of what had happened in that class and how it had impacted our continually emerging understanding of the place of feminist pedagogy in teacher education. Nurturance, oppression, silence, voice—were the very concepts we had been analyzing part of the essentialism we wished to critique? Consideration of the oppression of nurturance and the irony of empowerment were not new for us. We recognized how they still hung over our work and how they still obscured our understanding of our own teaching.

As we talked, we began to consider the perspective of several of the students, that the lens for the understanding of our own teaching, and thus of feminist pedagogy, was through our past experience and that the only understanding which we could construct for a feminist pedagogy in education was our own, as we lived it in our teaching lives. We asked each other: Which of the feminist issues were our issues? How had they connected for us in our practice of teacher education? Could our experiences enlarge other educators' understandings of their daily lives as teachers?

Our students were correct. Women's life experience, itself, must also, always be the text. The call to examine our own life experience also echoed from our reading, from Linda Nicholson (1990), from Liz Ellsworth (1989), and, most recently, from Sue Middleton (1993), who suggests we "make visible and explore the aspects of our own life histories that impact on our teaching . . . to analyze the relationships between our individual biographies, historical events, and the broader power relationships that have shaped and constrained our possibilities and perspectives as educators" (p. 17).

As we examined the notion of a feminist pedagogy grounded in our personal experience; of our experience as text; and of our students' resistance which forced us to put them at the center of our curriculum, we affirmed the centrality of our experiences in the constructing of our own feminist pedagogy and in our understanding of its significance in teacher education as an alternative to more traditional models of teaching. We found we shared with Maxine Greene (1988) her quest to "single out the determinates in my life, the seductions as well as the controls . . . the dialectic: the recognition of the determinates and of the inevitable tension between the desire to *be* and the forces that condition from within and without" (p. 4).

Jan: I can clearly remember my first formal introduction to feminist ideas. It was 1963 and I was a seventeen year old college freshman at the University of Wisconsin. A boy I was dating asked me if I had ever read Betty Friedan's (1963) *The Feminine Mystique.* I feigned sophistication and said, "of course" . . . mentally adding the book to the growing list of things I had missed during my northern Wisconsin childhood, classical music, impressionist paintings, Marxism, and now feminism.

I discovered later that my fortunate, yet perhaps intuitive, early exploration of issues from the women's movement was articulated in arguments with my junior high school friends about how lucky I was that my mother was a teacher and didn't have to stay at home and do farm work. I felt truly unique in rural Wisconsin in the 1950s to have not only a mother who worked outside the home throughout my childhood but also aunts and great aunts who were teachers and a great grandmother who had been a missionary. The fact that my maternal relatives worked out of financial necessity to support families where the fathers were most often absent was not part of my initial analysis. I can remember, however, declaring to my friends when my first daughter was born in 1971 that of course I would keep working, it was a family tradition *and* a financial necessity.

By 1973, with degrees in literature and psychology and two very young daughters, I had developed a strong interest in gender differences and in the writings of authors such as Doris Lessing and Jean Rhys and I had begun to label myself as a feminist. My professional life had veered from that of the school psychologist and had curled comfortably around college teaching and early childhood education, a field that seemed to more readily accommodate my interest in my own two children. Fiction, story telling, mothering, all seemed to fit. I recognize now that I had constructed for myself an identity of nurturance, mirroring, in my own generation, the grandmother who had cared for me, told me stories, met my needs while my own mother worked.

I now identify myself as a middle aged, Euro-American woman who is beginning to understand her intense and tangled connections to her working class, fundamentalist family. I also identify as an early childhood teacher educator and as a mother who is, rather ironically in this world of multiple levels of reproduction, the mother of an early child-hood teacher. I recognize that I have identified primarily with a mater-nal, nurturant role for most of my life and acknowledge that I became interested in early childhood education when my daughters were born, perhaps because of my intense personal involvement with mothering. Or, as a colleague recently suggested, perhaps my need to nurture really revealed a desire to be nurtured myself.

It was after several years as an early childhood educator, however, and despite my obsession with the idea of teacher as mother, that I began to formally examine the sources of my attachment to the idea of mothering and nurturance and their connections to teaching (Jipson, 1992a & 1992b, Jipson & Munro, 1993; Jipson, Munro, Victor, Froude Jones, & Freed-Rowland, 1995). My initial explorations into the literature of femi-nist theory were in response to a need to legitimize my self-claimed identification as a teacher-mother. Since the very beginning of my teaching career I had been struggling to develop a teaching process that was empowering for both my students and myself. I can remember my first year of college teaching, collecting course evaluations, and reading, to my temporary dismay, that "Jan is not like a teacher, she's more like a real person." A colleague helped me to see the affirmation in that iden-tity that I had intuitively projected onto the teaching role.

Later, in my examination of curriculum development at the graduate level, I formally explored feminist pedagogy. As I read the ideas of Be-lenky, et al. (1986), Shrewsbury (1987) and Grumet (1988), I saw myself very much as the mother-teacher, hoping to support my students think-ing, but not, as Belenky, et al. (1986), warns, doing the students' thinking for them or expecting them to think as I do.

Teaching has always focused, for me, on the relationships that exist between teachers and students in the classroom. My emphasis has been on nurturing these relationships through my commitment and belief in the interconnectedness of people, ideas, and experiences. I have tried to provide my students with opportunities to focus on their own experiences as teachers and mothers in relationship to the formal theories and pedagogies which they study. Most of all, I have attempted to explore mother-teacher relationships for myself, perhaps to better understand the conflicts I experience within these roles. From my ro-mantic attraction to the metaphor of teacher as mother, I find myself now sliding toward an acknowledgment of the potentially oppressive nature of nurturance. I observe my young adult daughters struggling to resist my seemingly instinctive protectiveness as I question whether they have money for rent or feel safe on the streets. I more readily rec-ognize similar reactions to my students as I catch myself worrying about them, their problems, their futures. More frequently I can step back, accept the possibilities of a more separate self, and explore the promises of self nurturing.

Petra: I did not want to be a teacher. Teaching was women's work. Teaching a graduate seminar which took as its central metaphor the term nurturing was necessarily an ambivalent endeavor. Unlike Jan, my own story was one of continual rejection of the maternal, that which was not valued. My own story of becoming a teacher was shaped by the metaphor of "activist." The irony of taking up the masculine narrative of "activist" remained blurred. Teaching was a political project in which I hoped to "raise the consciousness" of young students regarding issues of oppression, imperialism and racism. What surprised me as a graduate student was that my own teaching techniques as a high school teacher: creating a student centered classroom, acknowledging student voices, teaching history from multiple perspectives, and repositioning myself as a co-learner acquired a name, feminist pedagogy. That it was feminist, did not shock or surprise me, that it was associated with caring or nurturing frightened me. What did caring and nurturing, things associated with women, have to do with my teaching? This naming created a category with which I could not identify. It was a language that did not speak me.

My interest in teaching about feminist pedagogy arose primarily from my indignation that a profession which is predominately female did not reflect women teachers' experiences in its professional literature. Women's experiences and voices were still being silenced. I had hoped that graduate school would provide the opportunity for teachers to share their personal experiences of teaching in an attempt to make some sense of them. As I wandered through my first year of graduate courses we read what all the experts had to say. I learned curriculum theory, statistics, and kept wondering when there would be a course that would talk about my interests, reflect my experiences, I felt like an outsider in 'women's true profession'. In all of the talk about teachers, why weren't my experiences as a woman social studies teacher represented? Many courses did contain readings from feminists, but, as usual, they were done the last two weeks along with the other token pieces. It was hard to believe that in the halls of higher education the experiences of women were still being excluded, that the male experience was still accepted as the norm.

Valerie Walkerdine (1990) reminds us that under the guise of progressive education where teachers become facilitators, women teachers as were "caught, trapped inside a concept of nurturing which held them responsible for the freeing of each little individual, and therefore for the management of an idealist dream, an impossible fiction. Does feminist pedagogy reposition women teachers for erasure in which we are to "empower others," thus giving up our own power? In creating a space for validating and acknowledging multiple voices, what happens to our own voice? When all voices are equal, even those of the oppressors, are we in fact required to allow the racist, sexist voices, have we lost our voice yet again??

The Oppression of Nurturance

Jan: I still read Grumet, Greene, Noddings, Belenky and her colleagues. Having experienced the validation that comes from finding one's own ideas represented as someone else's theory, I was startled, upon a recent re-reading, to recognize the conflicts in their words, conflicts between caring for self and caring for others. Re-reading heightened my awareness of the complexity and confusion sometimes inherent in the multiple and demanding roles assumed by teachers, the press to be both nurturer and manager. Finally, I recognize in their writings and in my own work both the assertion and denial of an essentialized role for women as teachers/mothers.

My attraction to various concepts of feminism, I suppose, is also to their partial acknowledgment of these same inescapable personal issues that periodically surface from my working class childhood into my academic life—control, the fear of loosing my job and invoking financial chaos, the need for connection in an unfamiliar world, the search to locate my own voice in places where alien-seeming languages are spoken, the struggle against oppression in its not always subtle, institutional forms. I question, again, my complicity.

Many feminist writers have discussed the centrality of nurturance in women's lives. Valerie Polakow has discussed the "cult of American motherhood and the ideology of care" (p. 29) extensively in her book, *Lives on the Edge: Single Mothers and Their Children in the Other America* (1993). Linda Alcoff, in "Cultural Feminism Versus Poststructuralism" (1989) presents arguments by Echols, Eisenstein, and others against a cultural feminism which invokes "universalizing conceptions of woman and mother in an essentialist way" (p. 303) and are characterized by a "belief in women's innate peacefulness and ability to nurture." According to cultural feminists, she reports, the problem is one in which women are defined by men resulting in "a distortion and devaluation of feminine characteristics which can be corrected by a more accurate feminist description and appraisal," thus construing "woman's passivity as her peacefulness, her sentimentality as her proclivity to nurture, her subjectiveness as her advanced self awareness, and so forth" (p. 297).

Arguing that "under conditions of oppression and restrictions on free-dom of movement, women . . . have developed strengths and attributes that should be correctly credited, valued and promoted" (p. 304), Alcoff asserts that "what we should not promote, however, are restrictive con-ditions that gave rise to those attributes; forced parenting, lack of physi-cal autonomy, dependency for survival on mediation skills" (p. 304). She questions, "What conditions do we want to promote: A freedom of movement such that we can compete in the capitalist world alongside men? A continued restriction to child-centered activities?" (p. 304). She goes on to write "There is no essential core 'natural' to us" (p. 305). She opens a door to possibility.

Ironically, not surprisingly, perhaps appropriately, as I re-read Alcoff's words, a disembodied advertisement on my television sounds, "You made her stop crying." "Of course," is the reply in a very young voice, "I'm her mommy." I turn, catching a glimpse of a young girl clutching her doll to her chest and immediately I understand Alcoff's point. I recall the words of Georgia Savage in *The House Tibet* (1989): "Life's perilous for girls, isn't it? . . . a girl's whole life is war. She can't even walk around after dark in her home town. And if she does and gets bashed and raped or tortured to death or something, some sodding old judge will say she asked for it" (p. 220). The next day, my daughter calls, tells of a rapist on her campus and of the young woman blamed for using illegal mace to scare him away. She ends by saying it was in the parking ramp across from where she works. Frightening juxtapositions—the warmth and safety of my grandmother's lap fades into distant memory.

Maxine Greene (1993a) writes, "We can only understand through the play of our own assumptions, our own pre-judgments, our own memo-ries. . . . We can only attend from own interpretive communities" (p. 15). She reminds me that the communities that have been created for women, those in which we continue to work, and the experiences we have been allowed to have are what determine the meaning we are able to make from our experiences and the actions we are able to take.

I think again about the doll advertisement on the television and I am reminded of Tillie Olsen, whose stories speak to me across my own ex-perience. She writes, in *Tell Me A Riddle* (1961):

> She was two. Old enough for nursery school they said and I did not know then what I know now—the fatigue of the long day, and the lacerations of group life in the kinds of nurseries that are only parking places for children. Except that it would have made no difference if I had known. It was the only place there was. It was the only way we could be together, the only way I could hold a job.

As a mother, I intuitively understand Olsen's experiences. I reflect again on my life's history as one of continual struggles to define myself, sometimes it seems, in spite of my own early experience. I think about my present identity as an academic woman, question its differences from that of being the mother or early childhood teacher that I was raised to be, and try to figure out what it is that academic women are supposed to be. I recall no early stories of academic women to whom I could relate, no comforting novels of successful women professors with children of their own. The stories I read told of other women's lives, lives outside the ordinary . . . I recognized that somehow the stories of pain and loss seemed the most real. But I also began to understand why the fictional mothers in the teacher as mother course, the mothers of *Beloved* and the *Fifth Child*, were not the "good mothers" destined to live happily ever after which my students admired. The mothers in the novels we had selected reminded us all, instead, of trauma, of the reality of mothers struggling to survive.

Petra: But to me, teaching is also a trauma. It requires the abandonment of completion and closure, a resistance to the myth of progress or the romanticization of the past. As I reflect back on the course, I realize that my enactment of my feminist pedagogy which maintains that we could connect to some past lineage of our foremothers faltered, not because it sought connection, but because we assumed that connection would be experienced in the same way by all of the students in the class. My expectations were grounded in my assumption that all the women in the class had experienced the trauma of motherhood and teaching as I had. It became evident that we each had not only experienced this differently, but named it differently also.

Jan: And as I indulge in my other, more personal life, reading the fictions that also tell my story, I think of E. Annie Proulx writing in her novel *Postcards* (1992):

> [S]he went dizzy with power for the first time in her adult life . . . She had never guessed at the pleasure of choosing which turns and roads to take, where to stop. Did men, she wondered, have this feeling of lightness, of wiping out all troubles when they got into their cars or trucks? Their faces did not show any special pleasure when they drove. Men understood nothing of the profound sameness, week after week, after month of the same narrow rooms, treading the same worn footpaths to the clothesline, the garden. You soon knew it all by heart. Your mind closed to the problems of cracked glass, feeling for pennies in linty coat pockets, sour milk. You couldn't get away from troubles. They came dragging into the mirror with you, fanning over the snow, filled the dirty sink. Men couldn't imagine women's lives. They seemed to believe, as in a religion, that women were numbed by an instinctive craving to fill the wet mouths of babies, predestined to choose always the petty points of life on which to hang their atten-

tion until at last all ended and began with the orifices of the body (pp. 126–7).

Proulx's character Jewell Blood reminds me of myself. Each day, entering my classroom, I struggle with fitting myself into that mythical appropriate persona. I question why my transition to academe has been so hard, knowing that it in some way I was taught to believe I am not 'supposed' to be there, sensing a message from my past that I, too, should have focused on being a mother. And so with a deliberately calm (numb? passive?), self contained (isolated?) and facilitative (nurturant? sentimental?) manner I begin to teach. Sometimes I find security in my academic self, my carefully worked lectures and writings but I sense, always, that if my real personal voice were heard I would risk sounding like Jewell Blood, raw, tired, perhaps even vague or muddled . . . or motherly . . . not unexpected, perhaps, at home with my children or in a child care center but incomprehensible in the academy.

So which, I ask myself, is the real oppression? And I am reminded, again, of the oppression of nurturance, the boundaries of our lives. We begin from the position of women, after all.

Petra:. And as always, I begin with theory. Reducing critiques of feminist pedagogy to reproducing essentialist narratives which reinscribe oppressive discourses like caring and nurturing merely implicates us in maintaining the very notions of a static, unitary self. Like Judith Butler (1990), I am unsettled by those works which have sought to elaborate a feminist epistemological position from maternal identification or a maternal discourse which evolved from the point of view of that identification because it tends to reinforce precisely the heterosexist framework that carves genders into masculine and feminine. Were the students' rejections of feminism actually a rejection of *theory*, of the abstract knowledge that must be acquired to maintain the illusion of entry into the fathers' world? Or was their rejection a resistance to our *imposition* of feminist theory, pedagogy and fiction? Did their resistance serve to make clear the erroneous nature of our assumptions that we could enact a feminist pedagogy without hearing *their stories*. And, how did our own expectations distort our ability to understand the complex and multiple readings students would bring to the class?

Does our own critique of feminist pedagogy as essentialist support the very ideologies we question, those which refuse to acknowledge our voices? In reproducing dualistic understandings of gender, of class, of theory, are we limiting ourselves to reconstituting the myth of woman, therein appropriating the argument of an essentialist discourse which positions women as part of the system, thus giving power to men

(Hekman, 1990)? Was the apparent student resistance to "feminism" their intuitive strategy for disrupting a pedagogy which did not take seriously their personal experiences? Are we as teachers guilty of this? In participating in the agendas of nurturing and enigmas of empowerment are we further obscuring the possibilities which make our lives real?

The Irony of Empowerment

In a culture that idealizes Motherhood but holds real mothers in contempt, women know only too well how near impossible it is to enact Mother but elicit the respect accorded to Father (Griffin, 1992, p. 35).

We are confronted again and again with our ambivalence toward embracing the metaphor of "mother." As teachers, this ambivalence seems warranted given the fact that we are the abandoned daughters. Where is our mother? Alone in what Joanne Pagano (1990) calls the "patriarchal wilderness," we find ourselves in a place which demands our silence, which denies the stories of our experience, which negates even those cautiously constructed theories we offer as gifts of peace. But for us to imagine any other story for our lives is also to "risk essence," to have our real being silenced once again. Is there any doubt that we will abandon our "true stories" about the mother as easily as she has abandoned us, thus ensuring our silent survival in the world of academe, telling stories (theories?) not of our making? And still we continue to ask, why has she not saved us, sacrificed all for us? Why is she not here with us when we have come all this way?

Perhaps our goal in teaching the mothering seminar was to create a space in which a reconciliation could take place. We would present the story of the mother, we would be the healers, empowering our students to reclaim their many stories, and their many theories, and their many selves. And yet, the mothers of Doris Lessing's *The Fifth Child* or Toni Morrison's *Beloved* or Buchi Emichita's *The Joys of Motherhood* resist easy identification, as do we. Students in the seminar responded with shock to these "bad mothers," mothers who abandoned their children and who murdered their children, even as they responded with dismay to our own failure to give them the nurturant seminar for which they longed, the barely remembered fairy tales at their grandmother's knee. They could not accept that in the context of oppressive institutions like slavery or schools, love takes on new meanings. They could not easily understand that in contemporary suburban society, to uncover the fictions of the big house, happy home, loving children, and safe, warm grandmotherly lap requires that we make our lives real and that this act requires brave acts of naming and of uncovering. Unlike traditional plots which assume that acts of love, caring, and nurturance are unaffected by the economic, political and social forces of the times, the stories we chose and the stories we lived portrayed confusion and complexity beyond the reproductive simplicity of caring and connection. In constructing together the story of our shared experience, we neglected to anticipate a happy ending, an answer to the questions we raised, a sudden climax that would allow resolution. In reality, the stories we read and the stories we told each other about theory and ourselves rejected the myth of returning back to a true maternal self, to the mothers of our childhood dreams and offered, instead, a challenge to re-invent ourselves again and again in an ever shifting, ever changing reality.

Notes

1. Maxine Greene, in the *Dialectic of Freedom* (1988) uses this phrase to refer to Merleau-Ponty's exploration of possibility.
2. Women & Teaching: The Role of Nurturing in Education was designed as a doctoral seminar for students at the University of Oregon. The seminar focused on the roles of women teachers with a particular emphasis on the relational aspects of teaching.

References

Alcoff, L. (1989). Cultural feminism versus poststructuralism: the identity crisis in feminist theory. In M. Malson, J. O'Barr, S. Westphal-Wihl, & M. Wyer (Eds.), *Feminist theory in practice and process* (pp. 295–327). Chicago: University of Chicago Press.

Belenky, M., Clinchy, B.M., Goldberger, N.R., & Tarule, J.M. (1986). *Women's ways of knowing: the development of self voice and mind.* New York: Basic Books.

Butler, J. (1990). *Gender Trouble.* New York: Routledge.

Edgerton, S. (1993, October). *Remembering the mother tongue(s): Toni Morrison, Julia Dash, and the language of pedagogy.* Paper presented at the annual Conference on Curriculum Theory and Practice, Dayton, OH.

Ellsworth, E. (1989). Why doesn't this feel empowering: Working through the repressive myths of critical pedagogy. *Harvard Educational Review 59*(3), 297–324.

Emechita, B. (1979). *The joys of motherhood.* New York: George Braziller.

Erdrich, L. (1985). The Beet Queen. In *The gray wolf annual two: Short stories by women.* St. Paul: MN: Graywolf Press.

Firestone, S. (1970). *The dialectic of sex.* New York: Bantam.

Friedan, B. (1963). *The feminine mystique.* New York: Norton.

Gore, J. (1993). *The struggle for pedagogies.* New York: Routledge.

Greene, M.(1988). *The dialectic of freedom.* New York: Teachers College Press.

Greene, M. (1993a). *Friendship, imagination and the caring community*, Unpublished manuscript.

Greene, M. (1993b). *Narratives and awakenings: Discovering the situated self.* Unpublished manuscript.

Griffin, G. (1992). *Calling: Essays on teaching in the mother tongue.* (p.35). Pasadena, CA: Trilogy Books.

Grumet, M. (1988). *Bitter milk: Women and teaching.* Amherst: The University of Massachusetts Press.

Hekman, S. (1990). *Gender and knowledge: Elements of a postmodern feminism.* Boston: Northeastern University Press.

Jipson, J. (1992a). Midwife and mother: Multiple reflections on curriculum, connections, and change. *Journal of Curriculum Theorizing, 10*(1), 89–116.

Jipson, J. (1992b). What's feminist pedagogy got to do with early childhood practice? In S. Kessler. & B. Swadener, (Eds.), *Reconceptualizing Early Childhood Education.* (pp.149–164). New York: Teachers College Press.

Jipson, J. and Munro, P. (1993). What's real: Fictions of the maternal, *Journal of Curriculum Theorizing, 10*(2), pp.7–28.

Jipson, J., Munro, P., Victor, S., Froude Jones, K., & Freed-Rowland, G. (1995). *Repositioning feminism and education: Perspectives on educating for social change.* Westport, CT: Bergin & Garvey.

Lather, P. (1992). *Getting smart.* New York: Routledge.

Lessing, D. (1988). *The fifth child.* New York: Random House.

Middleton, S. (1993). *Educating feminists: Life histories and pedagogy.* New York: Teachers College Press.

Morrison, T. (1987). *Beloved.* New York: New American Library.

Nicholson, L. (1990). *Feminism/postmodernism.* New York: Routledge.

Noddings, N. (1984). *Caring: A feminist approach to ethics and moral education.* Berkeley: The University of California Press.

Olsen, T. (1961). *Tell me a riddle.* Philadelphia: Lippincott.

Olsen, T. (1980). As I stand there ironing. In J. Mazow, J., *The woman who lost her names.* San Francisco: Harper & Row.

Orner, M. (1992). Interrupting the calls for student voice in "liberate" education: A feminist poststructuralist perspective. In C. Luke and J. Gore (Eds.), *Feminisms and critical pedagogies,* (pp. 74–89). New York: Routledge.

Pagano, J. (1990). *Exiles and communities: Teaching in the patriarchal wilderness.* New York: SUNY Press.

Polakow, V. (1993). *Lives on the edge: Single mothers and their children in the other America.* Chicago: University of Chicago Press.

Proulx, E. A. (1992). *Postcards.* New York: Collier.

Ruddick, S. (1989). *Maternal thinking: Toward a politics of peace.* Boston, MA: Beacon Press.

Savage, G. (1989). *The house Tibet.* New York: Penguin.

Shrewsbury, C. (1987). What is feminist pedagogy? *Women's Studies Quarterly, 15*(3&4), pp. 6–14.

Walkerdine, V. (1990). *Schoolgirl fictions.* London: Verso.

Weiler, K. (1988). *Women teaching for change: Gender, class and power.* New York: Bergin & Garvey.

8 Asian Women Leaders of Higher Education: Stories of Strength and Self Discovery

Lori M. Ideta & Joanne E. Cooper

Stereotypes of Asian Americans abound. If not being noted for their docileness and passivity (Nakanishi, 1993), they are touted as the model minority (Chun, 1995; Escueta & O'Brien, 1995). This latter generalization has evolved partially because students of certain ethnicities within the category of "Asian American" pursue higher education in substantial numbers (Escueta & O'Brien, 1995). When one examines Asian representation in roles other than that of student, however, the numbers decrease dramatically (Carter & Wilson, 1995; OWHE/ACE, 1995).

Nakanishi (1993) asserts that the representation and administrative experiences of Asian Pacific Americans in higher education's faculty and administrative ranks have not received "sufficient policy or programmatic attention," (p. 57). Suzuki (1994) calls for more qualitative studies conducted on smaller sample groups and using techniques such as in-depth interviews to understand the nature of the "glass ceiling" that Asian Americans "apparently encounter as they try to move upward to the higher levels of administration" in postsecondary education (pp. 278–281). For Asian American women, encounters with this glass ceiling are frequent. Research on women in higher education (Aisenberg & Harrington, 1986) and on women leaders (Astin & Leland, 1991) has urged us to move beyond mere facts and figures and has emphasized the need for the study of the lives of individual women "as a means of understanding the antecedents of activism and passion—the driving forces in leadership behavior" (Astin & Leland, 1991, p. 160). Asian American women stand at the crossroads of our understanding of women and leadership. Through their perspectives at the boundaries of culture and organization, they bring new understandings of leadership and of individual transformation.

Little is known about the experiences of Asian women in higher education either as students or as they begin to move into the ranks of faculty and administrative positions. What pressures do they encounter and how do they respond to these stresses?

In response to the concern over the low representation of Asian American leaders and in an effort to understand the lives of diverse women in higher education, to uncover the driving forces behind their work as leaders, we examined the lives of four Asian American women administrators. Research on these minority leaders furthers the past work on women in the academy discussed above, by breaking silences and giving voice to the tensions that these women experience in their work settings. This process, according to Aisenberg & Harrington (1988), is the key to creating a countersystem of social order in the academy that "opposes excessive hierarchy and exclusivity in holding of authority . . . that incorporates diversity, spreads authority through processes of cooperation, resists centrality . . . and protects individuality," (p. 136).

This study examined the lives of Asian (Chinese, Filipino, and Japanese) American women who were all senior-level leaders of postsecondary education. They were from varying states, varying institutions, and varying institutional types. Personal experience methods (Clandinin & Connelly, 1994) were used to elicit these women's stories and through them, the narrative understanding of their professional practices. The narratives in this chapter were collaboratively constructed with the study's participants. Each narrative was co-authored by the researcher and the individual whose story was being written. Through a feminist-cultural lens, we offer the critical events in these women's lives which have led to their ability to survive and to work in their institutions of higher education. The results of this study refute the commonly held misconceptions of Asians as a "model minority" which will become the focus of this chapter.

Misconceptions of the Asian "Model Minority"

Asians have long been touted as the "model minority," (Chun, 1995; Suzuki, 1995; Sue & Okazaki, 1995). As such, Asian Americans are considered successes in all that they pursue, especially in the realm of academia. Nakanishi (1993) explores three basic misconceptions which arise out of society's stereotypical view of Asian Pacific Americans.

The first misconception is closely tied to the assumption that Asian Pacific Americans are "especially successful and talented in academics," (p. 52). The reality, however, is vastly different. Nakanishi (1993) asserts that Asian Pacific Americans, like other minority groups and women in general, decline substantially in numbers as one moves up the academic ladder from high school graduation through college, graduate school and into the ranks of faculty and administrators.

The second misconception is that Asian Pacific Americans do not face discrimination or unfair employment practices in higher education institutions. Nakanishi claims that this view combines two widely accepted but false notions. The first is the claim that Asian Pacific Americans have been fully accepted into American life and no longer encounter either overt or covert racial discrimination in their social and professional interactions. The second notion is that colleges and universities are unique places of employment which are "somehow more tolerant, more enlightened, more objective, and more open to new ideas" and are "free of bias and subjectivity," (pp. 53–54). Nakanishi asserts that one manner in which this biased treatment emerges is in the negative reactions to and evaluations of multicultural work conducted by ethnic minorities.

The third misconception is that Asian Pacific Americans who encounter problems in their employment or promotion are more inclined than any other minority group to walk away and not contest unfair denial of tenure or promotion. This misconception is fueled by the stereotype that Asian Pacific Americans are "passive, docile, and are expected to quietly fade away" when conflict arises (p. 55).

The results of our study generated evidence to refute the second misconception, and provided support to refute the third stereotype, held of Asian Americans by society. In contrast to Nakanishi's (1993) focus on Asian Pacific Americans, this study focused on Asian women of Chinese, Filipino, and Japanese ethnicities. Through the methodology of narrative these women revealed stories of both the adversity and support they have faced and continue to encounter as professional women in a field dominated by White males.

The Power of Narrative

Scholars of narrative inquiry such as Clandinin & Connelly (1992), Elbaz (1991), and Grossman, (1987) assert that story is an important component of understanding teacher's conceptions of their professional and personal lives. However, few narrative studies have focused on administrators at any educational level.

One of the main rationales for using narrative in examining the lives of women higher education leaders is that narrative is viewed as an "especially appropriate form of women's knowing and expression" (Belenky, Clinchy, Goldberger, & Tarule, 1986; Carter, 1993; Helle, 1991). Carter (1993) asserts that we must "dignify the stories of women's work so that we will not degrade what they do" (p. 11).

Heilbrun (1988) states, "Few studies of the last twenty years, and, of course, even fewer in earlier years, have concerned themselves with women's biographies or autobiographies" (p. 29). To Heilbrun, women's access to narratives is more than a matter of having the right to tell one's story. Rather, she views the ability and the right of women to talk about their lives, as central to issues of power and control.

In order for women to gain control of their stories and of their own lives, they must recognize the fact that they have the right to tell their own stories. This means breaking away from the long-accepted standard of men narrating both men's and women's stories. Weiland (1994) states, "In (Heilbrun's) view, the stories of women needed to be freed of their dependence on the forms of male narrative, biography being then an epistemological project formed primarily by gender, and, hence, promoting redefinition of what is worth knowing about lives" (p. 104). In the case of Asian women, their stories have been doubly silenced, both as females and as Asians.

Lessons from the Third Wave of Feminism

Collins (1991) asserts that people of color, especially women of color, have always been expected to put their concerns into the language and structure of the dominant group. This, she states, changes the meaning of what she and others have to say. In the Third Wave of feminism, Collins, and other Black feminist writers, such as Audre Lorde (1995), are finding their own approaches to writing and their own voices in telling their stories.

There have been three "waves" of feminism used to illustrate the evolution of feminist theory and contribute critical information to our understanding of society's views of women and women's views of themselves. The First Wave began in the 1700s and ended when women secured the right to vote in 1920. The Second Wave emerged on the heels of World War II and flourished during the 1960s. Although these two waves of feminism enhanced our thinking and improved the lives of women, the Third Wave of feminism has attacked previous feminist thought and writings as being too White, too middle-class (Nicholson, 1990), and too universalizing of all women's experiences (Kelly, Burton, & Regan, 1994). In addition, the philosophies and writings of the movements have also silenced women of color who have been left out of the arena of mainstream feminism since its inception (Collins, 1991). Current feminist scholars are calling for research that attends to participants' ethnicity, class, color, etc., in addition to issues of gender (Frankenberg, 1993; Lorde, 1995; Collins, 1991). Where the prime targets of feminist critiques were once male-dominated narratives emerging within male-dominated disciplines, now feminist criticism has turned on its own narratives.

Collins (1991) further asserts that we need to reconceptualize people who have multiple identities. She urges us to stop conceptualizing, for example, gender first, then adding race, then adding, religion, etc. Rather, Collins states that she sees all facets of identity as interlocking and interactive. The three constructions of race, class, and gender are, for women of color, an umbrella of dominance (hooks, 1989; Smith, 1987). One construction cannot exist without the other. The theory that all characteristics are interlocking rather than additive is reaffirmed in the findings of this study and moves us away from defining people through separate and fractured identities.

The narratives that follow reveal interlocking and interactive identities that serve to refute the current misconceptions of Asian American women.

Snap-Shots of the Women's Narratives

The most dominant theme which emerged from this study was the participants' ability to become stronger when confronted by discriminating situations. Rather than responding with passivity, these women used their experiences as springboards for more determined action and as sources of strength, growth, and deeper understanding. Their experiences help correct two of the misconceptions explored by Nakanishi (1993): that Asian Pacific Americans do not face discrimination or unfair employment practices in higher education, and that when they encounter discrimination, they are more likely to respond passively, to "quietly fade away" in the face of conflict.

The four Asian women whose narratives follow recalled incidents in which they faced racism or sexism in their places of employment. These women's written narratives give us insight into the discrimination they have endured and their struggles to respond in ways that address the conflicting demands placed on them by their own sense of identity, their workplace, and their family expectations.

The narratives of Jane and Ayla shed light on the misconception that Asians do not face discrimination. In fact, as Asian women, even in senior-level positions, these administrators continue to encounter both racist and sexist situations in the world of higher education. The larger question is how to respond to these situations. Here the narratives of Sally and Audrey address the additional misconception that Asians (and perhaps most especially Asian women) confront these situations with passivity and without contesting unfair treatment.

Discrimination in Institutions of Higher Education

Jane. Jane's experiences as a Chinese immigrant in a predominantly White state underscore the ignorance and insensitivity Asian Americans have encountered. Although much of the discrimination she faces is subtle rather than blatant, it is nevertheless pervasive and debilitating. Unfortunately, it comes from both the White community and from other minorities who erroneously assume that Asians are not "real minorities" and have therefore experienced few barriers to their success. Jane's response has been to make the work of equal opportunity her life's work.

Jane is the sixth daughter and eighth of ten children of Chinese immigrants. Jane and her siblings were born and raised in a predominantly White state and in conditions which would be described today as urban poverty. Jane was discouraged by her family to pursue a college degree as girls of her generation were expected to marry and bear many sons. Despite the lack of support she received, Jane went on to a local college where she was the only student of color. On her first night in the dormitories, Jane was overwhelmed with visitors who "came down to my dorm room to look at 'the Chinaman' because they had never seen one before."

Jane went on to secure a teaching position at the college level while working on her doctoral studies. She reflects on the unreasonable work load expectations she was handed by her superiors in her days as a fledgling faculty member. She also recalls the denial of her request for an extension to complete her dissertation which was posed as an ultimatum for her to retain her job. Jane later learned that such extensions had been granted to her White, male colleagues and, although with less frequency, to her White, female colleagues.

Jane asserts that both positive and negative interactions with family and community as well as the larger society have strengthened her ability to withstand the many forms of criticisms and judgmental reactions that seem to be part and parcel of working in the areas of civil rights, EEO and diversity. Today, Jane serves as the Director of the Center for Multicultural Affairs of a large, public research university. While she feels she is able to handle the "invisible" or "colorblind" treatment; the neglectful, often insensitive and patronizing behaviors; and the frequent "drill" questions (Where did you come from? No, where did you *really* come from? Where/How/When did you learn to speak English so well?);

she does not deny the emotions that arise when these situations occur. Perhaps the most difficult to address and ultimately the most damaging to one's sense of self is that of being denied opportunities for personal and professional growth and development because of one's race, ethnicity, or gender, because of assumptions about one's worthiness, or whether "someone like her" could succeed.

Jane finds being a female Asian American has its own specific challenges. While she has not been subjected very often to overt discrimination, nor have there been many refusals to interact or work with her, it is not always possible to ignore subtle signals which indicate that while one may not be openly excluded, neither are there the indicators that one is included. This seems to be an especially universal perception among people of color. Moreover, Asian Americans in positions like hers may also be questioned by people representing other racial/ethnic groups since there is the assumption that as "model minorities," Asian American are not "real" minorities.

Jane has amassed her encounters with discrimination and used them as the driving force behind her life's work. Of her dedication to issues of equity Jane says "There are days when I wonder, 'What am I doing? Are we doing the right thing? Are we headed toward our goals? Are we using the right map or blueprint? Are we using the right tools and methods? Well, there *are* no maps. [There are] no blueprints."

The lack of a guide or how-to handbook for creating the desired university community does not deter Jane. She persists in working in an unpopular area that is fraught with resistance referred by some as "Just another P.C. bandwagon." Jane knows there are no easy answers, but perhaps that is the challenge that motivates her. She shares, "I humorously use phrases like 'Chinese water torture' as a description of my persistence—I keep at it until what needs to happen, happens."

Ayla. As an immigrant to the United States, Ayla categorizes the discrimination she has faced in two ways. First, there are those who see her as downtrodden and want to champion her causes in order to help out the poor minority woman. Second, are those who have real questions about her ability because she is Filipino and wonder subtly if she is able do the job. Ayla faces both these challenges with a determination to be heard and to be respected for her abilities.

The second daughter, and youngest child of an English father and a Malay-Chinese mother, Ayla was born and raised in the Philippines. Ayla's immersion into the all-girls' schools she attended as a child was critical in empowering her as a young woman. Ayla went on to receive her college degrees in the United States. Currently, Ayla serves as the faculty developer for a public research institution.

Ayla has found that her ethnicity, rather than her status as a woman administrator, seems to cloud the judgment of some of those with whom she works. Ayla believes that those members of the dominant ethnic class are often unaware that they approach her and other ethnic minority administrators in these disturbing and disrespectful ways. She says, "(There are those that say), 'I want to be the one to help this minority rise to glory,' and there are those who look at you and (think) maybe you can't handle the job." She admits that these actions are very subtle, "but it comes through in the oddest ways."

Although mainly confronted by ethnic bias, Ayla does not deny that gender has certainly been an issue for many women in the academy. She feels fortunate to be in the field of education, where women are better represented than in other professions. She admits that if she is experiencing discrimination in a field populated by a large number of females, she shudders to imagine the experiences of women in fields largely dominated by men. Her negative experiences are common to many women. She tells a tale of being ignored at meetings only to witness that when a male reiterated her already stated idea or question, he received affirmation or credit for his contribution. To deal with these events, this leader has learned to speak up and repeatedly say, "I think I said that ten minutes ago." Over the course of her career she has learned this and other strategies for gaining voice and "establishing equity" in those meetings and in her life. These approaches have earned Ayla the reputation of being "tough." Despite the struggles, Ayla continues to champion for equity issues for women and ethnic minorities, particularly those of Filipino ancestry.

Contemplating retirement, Ayla is only now able to say that she is "comfortable" with who she is as a woman and as an administrator. When questioned about this process of self discovery and acceptance she revealed, "You get better at it. You get better at it with everyday experience."

Not Going Quietly

Next the narratives of Sally and Audrey illuminate the ways in which Asian women have responded to discrimination when they have encountered it. These responses are a complex blend of strategies arising out of their status as women, their cultural heritage as Asians, the particular workplace pressures they face in their institutional settings and their own individual leadership styles. In general, these responses begin to undermine the myth that Asians do not challenge the status quo when they encounter racism. As Asian women, they describe the layered oppressions of racism and sexism, often responding with renewed determination to stand up, speak out, and fight for the right to their own identity in the academy. For Sally, this response includes careful reflection on who she is as a woman and how this might affect her future career plans. For Audrey it is a fighting stance, one in which she fiercely defends her staff, whom she describes as "family."

Sally. Sally has encountered prejudice from the minority as well as the White community. As a woman of mixed Asian race, Sally spans the boundaries between White and Asian communities as well as between Filipino and Japanese communities. In addition, her work takes her into the interstices between public K–12 education and higher education, a space where she encounters additional pressures to meet the expectations of each institution's organizational culture. For Sally, at this particular juncture in her life, these expectations have centered more on her role as a woman than on her ethnicity. Her response has been to reflect carefully on her own identity and her subsequent professional goals. Surviving as a woman in a "man's game" and whether this requires more conformity than she is willing to give have been constant questions for Sally.

Currently, Sally serves as Director of Articulated Curricula for a community college. Sally realizes that although she views herself as a competent *person*, others see her as a *woman*. Perhaps still competent, but nevertheless, a woman. Her male colleagues to whom she relates so well, do not include her when they venture out to the golf course or local bars to conduct business. She has come to endure the reality that her acceptance of diversity is not always a two way street. Her gender and her mix of ethnicities are often boundaries she faces within her institution. The culture of the community college in which Sally works is one dominated by White males. Despite the large number of ethnic minorities in her community, Sally believes that the institution is prejudiced against people of color. Being born and raised in the community, and being of Filipino/Japanese ancestry, Sally realizes that she has many strikes against her.

Recently, Sally has spent a great deal of time reflecting on her path as articulation coordinator. She always aspired to rise up the bureaucratic ladder and be a top level administrator. Now, she is questioning this long held dream. Sally is questioning if upward mobility is still really what she desires. Her identity has always rested on the title of her position. Now, she realizes that her identity is centered around her family—her husband, son, grandmother, mother, father, and siblings. She finds herself enjoying her role as nurturer to her family and co-workers. Perhaps, she says, expanding herself horizontally in her position is actually more appealing. She elaborates, "Even though I don't have everything sorted out,

I'm getting to like who I am. I'm getting to see that indeed Sally is a woman, that has definite woman needs and issues that have to be addressed in this lifetime as a woman. And never mind playing this man's role or this man's game, because you're always going to lose because you're not yourself."

Sally is now at a crossroads. She wonders if her long-held need for security means she will conform to the norms of the institution or if she has the energy to continue being unique. She feels the tension between climbing the career ladder and being nurturing in the workplace. She wonders how she can successfully explore herself as a woman and still survive the male game of higher education. Sally shares, "It is truly a man's game . . . and what I'm learning is how to survive as a woman by playing a game that's more aligned with my identity as a woman and being appreciated and still survive . . . "

Audrey. Early in her career Audrey faced triple layered discrimination due to her young age, her gender, and her ethnicity. Her response was not one of passivity, as described by the myth Nakanishi (1993) discusses, but one of fierce and determined resistance. She continues to be true to her values in the face of administrative requests to "drop the matter," submitting rebuttals, and going to bat for employees as well as standing up for herself as she encounters racist or sexist attitudes. These actions certainly belie the misconception that Asians will not contest unfair treatment, but instead are likely to "quietly fade away."

The personification of the Asian American stereotype, Audrey is not. While school teachers expected Audrey to have high test scores to be placed in the honors program, she did not. While society expected Audrey to excel in mathematics and be able to attend UCLA, she did not. And while higher administration expected Audrey to be quiet, complacent, and submissive, Audrey is not.

Audrey was born into a highly conservative Republican family in California. She was raised in a Black ghetto in which she witnessed tremendous racial discrimination of her neighbors and friends while, as an Asian child, she was viewed as a member of the "model minority" and expected to succeed in the academic realm. Audrey has battled the stereotypes of racism her entire life. Her experiences as a higher education administrator have not been any different. She shares, "People have found it easy to dump on me—easy to jump to conclusions—to blame before fact-finding. Is it because I was a comparatively young Asian woman?"

Audrey currently serves as the Dean of Student Development at a public community college where she actively works to promote equity issues. When Audrey's institution recently undertook a new evaluation system, Audrey's composure was tested to its limits. Audrey described the results of her evaluation as a "scathing attack." Some of the comments received read, "She is racially biased against Whites, she only hires minorities." "She comes to our office and only greets Blacks and Asian Americans." "She is intolerant." "She is pushy." "She has embarrassed me." These painful comments were amidst other comments which read, "She's a role model." "She's a visible leader." "She's a student advocate." The president of the faculty senate also wrote, "I don't know much about her, but rumor has it that she doesn't get along with her staff." He submitted this statement despite the fact that he had met with one of Audrey's staff members and she reportedly told him, "No, (Audrey) gets along well with all of us, that's not a problem." The same faculty senate president also wrote, "(Audrey) tends to appear at various functions." Audrey explains that she often organizes numerous functions on campus and thus, "shows up" to direct, emcee or oversee them.

In response to her evaluation, Audrey submitted a five page rebuttal requesting further clarification on several points. She shares that the administration refused to respond. She says, "The chancellor came up and told me, 'You know you're wonderful. You know we think you're doing a great job. Drop the issue. Don't push this any further.'" The administration then sent Audrey a three line memo stating that her comments were received and were on file. She immediately wrote back stating, ". . . you're finished with it, I am too. Now, please give me a letter of recommendation. I need to move on." Audrey reports she has yet to receive a response from the administration.

Audrey reflects:

> One of the biggest lessons I learned from this is that when you avail yourself to staff, the more out there you are, the more vulnerable you are . . . The more you put yourself out there, the more you become like family . . . you're still in a leadership role and so they expect you're going to be that close to everybody. So I walk a very dangerous tight rope because of that, you know?

Audrey is currently working at maintaining harmony amongst her staff. Although she would like to be personally connected to each one, it is difficult as her staff has grown from ten employees to seventy.

Despite the difficulties, Audrey still holds to her values of equity and equal opportunity for all. She continues to work fiercely for diversity issues and to speak for those who do not have a voice in the bureaucracy of education. Audrey believes this dedication comes from a lifetime of what she calls a "second class nature" which she has had to combat her entire life.

Audrey perseveres despite her internal war. She attempts to mentor her staff by facilitating their networking and appointing them to committees in her place. Audrey considers mentoring those to come after her as critical. She asserts, "I have to do that because if I don't replace myself, then I didn't create anything." She explains that she has witnessed too many social movements and programs fall to pieces when great leaders do not take the time to nurture others to take their places. She states, "If you don't take the time to grow your own, then it won't happen."

Discussion

Collectively, these women represent various ethnicities within the broad category of *Asian American*. Through the revelation of critical incidents in their lives, we have learned that their experiences with racism have differed and have been painful. Instead of displaying the stereotypical characteristics others expected of Asian women (i.e., docileness, passivity, silence), especially during challenging times, these women became stronger and more determined to prove those who held those misperceptions of them wrong.

Most of these women were able to single out a series of incidents over their lifetimes in which they were confronted by racial or gender discrimination. Rather than becoming disempowered by these experiences, the women grew more determined in their goals for success. For some of the women, their choice to work in the field of education or to work for equity issues, was the direct result of the critical encounters they had with racism. In many ways, the racism these women faced early in their lives became one of the most compelling findings of the study because of its impact on the participants' identity formation.

The participants of this study faced sexism in one form or another. The individual details of how the women responded to these incidents vary as greatly as the occurrences themselves. However, the common thread which ties them all together is that all the women took the anger, shame, resentment, or bitterness which resulted from these run-ins and became strengthened to counter any wrong impressions of them. Instead of losing faith in other women when they experienced greater discrimination from females than males, they assumed a larger role in fostering young women.

Given the stories of racism and sexism encountered by the participants of this study, there is evidence to refute the second misconception of Asian Americans as reported by Nakanishi (1993) that Asian Pacific Americans do not face discrimination in American higher education institutions. These narratives support Nakanishi's assertion that Asian Pacific Americans have not been fully accepted into American life and that they continue to encounter discrimination. The fact that numerous incidents of discrimination occurred within these women's work environments refutes the stereotype that colleges and universities are more tolerant and more enlightened than other institutions (Nakanishi, 1993, p. 54). Audrey's experiences of facing greater discrimination because she assertively works for equity issues, further supports Nakanishi's assertion that ethnic minorities and women who pursue scholarship concerning multicultural issues, often receive hostile reactions to and evaluations of their work (p. 54).

The women's anti-stereotypical response of transforming the negativity of discriminating situations into catalysts of strength can be traced, for some women, to their families' responses to their complaints. When some of the women attempted to speak with their families about their encounters with discrimination, they received responses stating that these encounters were "no big deal," or that they should simply ignore them. For these women, the internalization of grief and the response of determination may have been the only possible response because nothing less was expected of them. They were expected to be strong. Not all of the women in this study reported this type of message from their families, yet they all reported more determination in response to discriminating situations. This determination provides evidence to refute the third commonly held misconception as reported by Nakanishi (1993), that Asian Pacific Americans who encounter problems in their employment are more inclined to walk away from the situation in a passive manner (p. 55).

Asian women leaders seem to live within the confines of powerful paradoxes. As Asian females they struggle in organizations which define leaders as primarily male and White. In addition, organizations simultaneously reward leaders for behaviors such as fortitude, courage, and heroism (Morgan, 1986), while punishing women for displaying these behaviors because they are considered to be gender inappropriate. Asian women face compounding cultural demands that increase this tension between their roles as women and their roles as leaders. The participants of this study were both rewarded and admonished in their organizations for the same behaviors. Behaviors which are typical of leaders (displays of power, authority, and fortitude) are considered atypical for women and doubly atypical for Asian women. As Bloom and Munro (1995) assert "Our very understandings of terms like power and authority are located in and dependent on gendered understandings in which male behavior is constituted in opposition to female behavior (Butler, 1990). To be female is to not have authority. Thus, to be a female administrator is necessarily a contradiction in terms" (p. 104).

For Asian women, this becomes a double contradiction, given the standard of cultural expectations that Asian women are to be more compliant or subservient in their behavior. These contradictory expectations manifest themselves both at home and at work, creating a kind of schizophrenic existence in which some women reported being subservient at home and assertive in the workplace. Yet, even when the women display power and authority in their workplaces, they work against the contradictory cultural stereotypes of what it means to be a woman, and what it means to be an Asian woman in our society.

Compounding these dilemmas are cultural expectations that Asian women should succeed outside the home in order to bring honor to the family. Here, family expectations presume these women to display courage and fortitude when they face discrimination in their professional lives. Thus, they are confronted with multiple paradoxical demands in the workplace as women leaders and as Asian women. To be an Asian woman demands that one be, if anything, less assertive than one's White counterparts. To be Asian also demands that one display courage in the face of adversity, so as not to bring shame to the family name. These conflicting and contradictory demands create what Bloom & Munro (1995) define as "nonunitary" or fractured selves (p. 107).

Summary

Through the mutual construction of written narratives, four senior-level Asian women leaders gave voice to their experiences as ethnic minorities and as females in the predominantly White male arena of postsecondary education. They were also given the space to reflect on how their gender and ethnicity have become lenses through which they perceive the world. Evidence emerged from this process to refute common misconceptions of Asian Americans. The women of this study faced sexism and racism in their careers as higher education leaders. The painful and often subtle stories they shared are powerful evidence to refute the myth that Asian Americans do not face discrimination in institutions of postsecondary education (Nakanishi, 1993). The manner in which these women were able to transform these sexist and racist encounters into catalysts for greater strength, determination, and advocacy stands as evidence to contradict the misconception that Asian Americans would be more apt to passively walk away from such problems (Nakanishi, 1993).

The time is right for the stereotypical perceptions of Asians to change. As we enter a new century, society is faced with a diversification previously unknown to the world. Third Wave conceptions speak a truth that can no longer be ignored. Women are already the majority gender on campuses of higher education. By the turn of the century, it is estimated that the Asian American population will be ten million strong (Hsia, 1988). It is logical to then assume that Asian American women will soon become a significant presence on campuses in roles other than that of student. Although our study was conducted on a small sample, it is our hope that it creates a deeper and greater understanding of the struggles and strengths of Asian women. For the discrimination that this population encounters in the world of higher education is tremendous, but so are the contributions they have to offer.

End Note Reflections

The coming together of two women authors from diverse backgrounds served to strengthen this study. Joanne is an established professor of higher education with expertise in the area of narrative inquiry. She was raised in a White, middle-class environment in Oregon. Lori is a recent Ed.D. graduate and is a new professional in the area of student affairs administration. She is the fourth-generation of her Japanese-American family to call Hawai'i home. With an innate understanding of Asian culture, Lori was able to gain deeper insights into what the project participants were relaying through their interviews and narratives. She was also able to feel the tensions the women experienced between family and work and understood the very natural tendency to create family in the workplace. In addition, Lori's own family background, where her mother was the breadwinner and her father the househusband, has led her to an interest in women and leadership. She first saw women take a leadership role in her own life at a very young age. Her mother has served as a model of what strong women can do when they are determined to do what they must. For her, the words of Eleanor Roosevelt ring true, "You must do the thing you think you cannot do." Thus, in studying Asian American women leaders of higher education, Lori was able to bring to the study all that she was and all that she represented. Standpoint epistemology informs us that a person occupying the same space in society as her participants is a definite strength. Joanne's abilities, because of her location outside of the culture and background of the participants of the study, were equally valuable. While delineating themes from the interviews and narratives, Joanne was quick to discover ones which were so second-nature to Lori that they were not visible. For example, in analyzing the women's narratives, Joanne immediately recognized the importance of the women's philosophy of bringing the concept of family into their work environments. Joanne had unearthed a concept deserving of attention and exploration which was so commonplace for Lori that she was unable to recognize it as a theme in the study.

As a young professional in an area nearly void of senior-level Asian women administrators, Lori quickly became an admirer of the project participants. Joanne helped to temper Lori's tendency to revere the women in the study, which arose naturally from her strong Asian cultural value to respect one's elders. Together they successfully negotiated the balance between celebrating the successes of the participants and presenting a clear picture of their lives and struggles.

Writing together has helped both Lori and Joanne to "work the hyphens" of othering, as described by Michelle Fine (1994). As an Asian American, Lori brought knowledge of her culture to this work. As a Caucasian American with eighteen years of experience in institutions of higher education, Joanne contributed knowledge of mainstream culture, as well as knowledge of academic cultures. Both women function simultaneously as insiders and outsiders to the cultures and issues addressed in this study. While functioning as insider/outsider to Asian cultural values and the culture of higher education, both women function as insiders to the understandings of what it is to be female. Thus, they simultaneously worked the hyphens of their mutual existences, forming at times a balanced equation, at other times highlighting the knowledge and strengths of one particular author. Through this work we seek to uncover ourselves and our own investments, rather than "burying the contradictions that percolate at the Self-Other hyphen" (Fine, 1994, p. 70). With Fine, we believe our work breathes "a renewed sense of possibility" into the work of Asian/Caucasian, advisor/student, administrator/faculty, local/mainland, female/female, bonds, dichotomies and contradictions that percolate at our own personal hyphen.

References

Aisenberg, N., & Harrington, M. (1986). *Women of academe: Outsiders in the sacred grove.* Amherst: University of Massachusetts Press.

Astin, H. S., & Leland, C. (1991). *Women of influence, women of vision: A cross generational study of leaders and social change.* San Francisco: Jossey-Bass, Inc. Publishers.

Belenky, M. J., Clinchy, B. M., Goldberger, N. R., & Tarule, J. M. (1986). *Women's ways of knowing.* New York: Basic Books.

Bloom, L., & Munro, P. (1995). Conflicts of selves: Nonunitary subjectivity in women administrators' life history narratives. In J. A. Hatch & R. Wisniewski (Eds.), *Life history and narrative* (pp. 99–112).

Bordo, S. (1990). Feminism, postmodernism, and gender-skepticism. In L. J. Nicholson (Ed.), *Feminism/Postmodernism* (pp. 133–56). New York: Routledge.

Carter, D. J., & Wilson, R. (1995). *Thirteenth Annual Status Report on Minorities in Higher Education.* Washington, DC, American Council on Education.

Carter, K. (1993, Jan.–Feb.). The place of story in the study of teaching and teacher education. *Educational Researcher,* 5–12.

Chun, K. T. (1995). The myth of Asian American success and its educational ramifications. In D. T. Nakanishi & T. Y. Nishida (Eds.), *The Asian American educational experience* (pp. 95–112). New York: Routledge.

Clandinin, D. J. & Connelly, F. M. (1992). Teacher as curriculum maker. In P. Jackson (Ed.), *Handbook of research on curriculum* (pp. 363–401). New York: Macmillan.

Clandinin, D. J & Connelly, F. M. (1994). In N. K. Denzin & Y. S. Lincoln (Eds.), *Personal experience methods. Handbook of qualitative research* (pp. 413–427). Thousand Oaks: Sage Publications, Inc.

Collins, P. H. (1991). *Black feminist thought: Knowledge, consciousness, and the politics of empowerment.* New York: Routledge.

Cooper, J. E. & Heck, R. H. (1993). Using narrative in the study of school administration. *International Journal of Qualitative Studies in Education.*

Elbaz, F. (1991). Research on teacher's knowledge: The evolution of a discourse. *Journal of Curriculum Studies, 23,* 1–19.

Escueta, E., & O'Brien, E. (1995). Asian Americans in higher education: Trends and issues. In D. T. Nakanishi & T. Y. Nishida (Eds.), *The Asian American educational experience* (pp. 259–272). New York: Routledge.

Fine, M. (1994). Working the hyphens: Reinventing self and other in qualitative research. In N. K. Denzin & Y. S. Lincoln (Eds.), *Handbook of qualitative research.* (pp. 70–82). Thousand Oaks: Sage Publications.

Frankenberg, R. (1993). *The social construction of whiteness: White women, race matters.* Minneapolis: University of Minnesota Press.

Grossman, P. (1987). *A tale of two teachers: The role of subject matter orientation in teaching.* Paper presented at the Annual Meeting of the American Educational Research Association, Washington, DC.

Heilbrun, C. G. (1988). *Writing a woman's life.* New York: W. W. Norton.

Helle, A. P. (1991). Reading women's autobiographies: A map of reconstructed knowing. In C. Witherell & N. Noddings (Eds.), *Stories lives tell: Narrative and dialogue in education* (pp. 48–66). New York: Teachers College Press.

hooks, B. (1989). *Talking back: Thinking feminist, thinking black.* Boston: South End Press.

Hsia, J. (1988). *Asian Americans in higher education and at work.* New Jersey: Lawrence Erlbaum Assoc.

Kelly, L., Burton, S. & Regan, L. (1994). Researching women's lives or studying women's oppression? Reflections on what constitutes feminist research. In M. Maynard & J. Purvis (Eds.), *Researching women's lives from a feminist perspective* (pp. 27–48). Bristol: Taylor & Francis.

Lorde, A. (1995). Age, race, class, and sex: Women redefining difference. In M. L. Andersen & P. H. Collins (Eds.), *Race, class, and gender: An anthology, second edition* (pp. 532–540). Belmont, CA: Wadsworth.

Miles, M .B. & Huberman, A. M. (1984). *Qualitative data analysis: A sourcebook of new methods.* Beverly Hills: Sage Publications.

Morgan, G. (1986). *Images of Organization.* Newbury Park, Sage Publications.

Nakanishi, D. T. (1993, Spring). Asian Pacific Americans in higher education: Faculty and administrative representation and tenure. *New directions for teaching and learning, 53,* 51–59. San Francisco: Jossey-Bass Publishers.

Nicholson, L. J. (Ed.). (1990). *Feminism/Postmodernism.* New York: Routledge.
Office of Women in Higher Education. American Council on Education. (1995). *Women presidents in U.S. colleges and universities.* Washington, DC: OWHE.
Smith, D. E. (1987). *The everyday world as problematic: A feminist sociology.* Boston: Northeastern University Press.
Sue, S. & Okazaki, S. (1995). Asian American educational achievements: A phenomenon in search of an explanation. In D. T. Nakanishi & T.Y. Nishida (Eds.), *The Asian American educational experience* (pp. 133–145). New York: Routledge.
Suzuki, B. H. (1994). Higher education issues in the Asian American community. In M. J. Justiz, R. Wilson & L. G. Bjork (Eds.), *Minorities in higher education* (pp. 258–285). American Council on Education. Oryx Press.
Suzuki, B. H. (1995). Education and the socialization of Asian Americans: A revolutionist analysis of the "model minority" thesis. In D. T. Nakanishi and T. Y. Nishida (Eds.), *The Asian American educational experience* (pp. 113–132). New York: Routledge.
Tripp, D. (1994). Teachers' lives, critical incidents, and professional practice. *Qualitative Studies in Education, 7*(1), 65–76.
Weiland, S. (1994, Summer). Writing the academic life: Faculty careers in narrative perspective. *The Review of Higher Education, 17*(4), 395–422.

9 Dancing on the Sharp Edge of the Sword: Women Faculty of Color in White Academe

Frances V. Rains

She is pushed,
pulled,
her identity defined, used, and constructed from outside her,
her work suspect,
her authority questioned,
her very essence simultaneously in demand and repulsed,
as she struggles to maintain who she is,
to keep ever present why she came,
to keep her spirit strong,
to resist oppressive forces,
All while she is asked to dance faster.

Dancing on the sharp edge of the sword is a high price to pay to be on "equal footing" with those whose feet have never come close to the blade, never cut their feet and had to keep moving while bleeding. (Rains, 1996b, p. 1)

When I was a doctoral student at a predominantly White university, I was both curious and concerned for what my own future might be like in academe, given my experiences as a woman of color[1] in graduate school up to that point. Although I was at a large school of education (approx. 100 faculty), during my masters and doctorate, only one of my classes had been taught by a professor of color. The students of color[2] that I knew at the graduate level in the department, I could count on two fingers. In almost every class, I was the only student of color. When I taught undergraduate classes, I was often the first person of color my White students had ever spoken with or seen "up close." The students often had such a limited understanding of "diversity" in their own world that someone of a "different" religion, meaning someone that was not Baptist, Methodist, or Protestant (e.g., "Catholic") was considered to be "diverse." These students often discussed "race" in terms of Blacks and Whites. To have a non-Black, woman of color as their instructor really challenged their perceptions of "diversity" and "race." I wondered what it was like for women faculty of color. Was it like this for them?

During my graduate course work, the vast majority of the theorists we studied were White, and most were male. While some of these White theorists theorized about people of color, they frequently did so from their locations (via race, class, and gender) as privileged individuals. Their locations, values, or ways of thinking from such positions were rarely brought into view. For example, as I examined studies conducted by White researchers regarding the societal patterns, cultural, educational and linguistic issues of various Native Nations in the United States, it was clear to me, as a First American[3] woman, that their work often misunderstood or misinterpreted what they observed. From my vantage point, the White generated theories did not necessarily adequately explain phenomena related to the lives of people of color.

What few theorists of color I had studied, on the other hand, brought with them a different set of lenses with which to view people of color. Theorizing from the "inside out" these scholars often offered different definitions, and explanations that provided insights in the lives of people of color that White theorists had missed (Reyes & Halcón, 1990). However, the works of these scholars of color were often criticized as "weak" by my predominantly White peers. The most common argument used to dissuade and devalue the work of theorists of color was often grounded in the theorists being the same race as the people they were studying (e.g., Black-on-Black research, Brown-on-Brown research), hence, inherently biased. "The assumption is that minority researchers cannot be objective in their analyses of those problems which are so close to their life experiences" (Reyes & Halcón, 1990, p. 76). Yet, *White* researchers had been conducting studies on *White* concerns (i.e., White-on-White research) for almost 100 years and I had not heard of these researchers being dismissed as being biased, nor weak merely because they were White (Rains, 1995).

My concern grew for how the status quo played out. My peers would be some of the future movers and shakers in the academic world. If my White peers could assume that the caliber and integrity of theorists of color were flawed when they studied concerns of people of color, then what would happen when I, as a future researcher of color, attempted to do research related to people of color? After all, would I not have similar peers if my career path led me to a research institution?

Given my concerns, and my experiences, along with a supportive committee, I launched into a rather unique study. This study was grounded almost exclusively upon the theoretical works of women scholars of color, without dependence upon comparisons to White theories, and without the necessity of relying upon White theorists for their "expert" or "authoritative" theoretical perspectives regarding people of color. This study offered me an opportunity to discern what the future might hold in store for a woman of color like myself, in the academy.

It is this ethnographic study (Rains, 1995) that informs this chapter. This chapter briefly describes the study and highlights how for some women faculty of color in the academy, their professional lives are laden with contradictions and tensions, along with resistive responses to their circumstances which resemble a life of having to constantly dance on the sharp edge of the sword.

Within the Walls of the Ivory Tower

Academe has long been the bastion of White males. It is true that the civil rights movement and subsequent legislation cracked open the door, making it possible for more White women, and some men and women scholars of color to gain entry into the ivory tower (e.g., Caplan, 1994; Washington & Harvey, 1989). Yet, despite the rhetoric within the halls of academe about their interest in, and dedication to, ethnic diversity, institutions of higher education have only reluctantly opened their doors to scholars of color (Farmer, 1993). This has occurred more often by force than by voluntary initiation. The force has materialized by way of " . . . the courts, by Congress, by presidential executive orders, and by citizen and student demonstrations, by people of color in the cities and on the campuses" (Wilson, 1989, p. 88). Three decades later, the number of faculty of color are " . . . still alarmingly small" (PBS, 1997). For example, Touchton & Davis (1991) note that of the 12,000 doctoral degrees awarded to women in 1985, women of color received only 11 percent. They continue:

> Black women received 5%, Hispanic women 2%, Asian women 3%, and American Indian women less than 1%. . . . Since 1900 the number of women faculty has grown substantially. . . . The greatest increases in the number and proportion of women faculty have come at the rank of assistant professor. . . . [where] women constituted the following proportions of total full-time assistant professors: White women, 31%; Black women, 3%; Asian

women, 1%; and Hispanic and American Indian women, less than 1% combined. . . . Of the 53,608 tenured women faculty in 1985, 3,790 were Black (7%), 1,078 were Hispanic (2%), 1,344 were Asian/Pacific (3%), and 138 (less than 1%) were American Indians. (p.14–15)

More recently, Bernstein and Cock (1994) have examined the demographic trends for women in the academy. While they do not specify information on various groups of women of color, they do indicate that overall improvements have been slow.

The proportion of faculty members who were White women jumped from 24 per cent to 28 per cent between 1981 and 1991, while the proportion of non-White women rose from 3 per cent to just 4 percent during the same time period. Clearly, we must be careful not to claim success in achieving a measure of sex equity for *all* women, when the figures for women of color tell a very different story. (emphasis original; p. B2)

It is a glimpse into this "story" that women faculty of color, by their location in White academe, offers to reveal in this chapter.

Views from Within

Fifteen women faculty of color at Everwhite University [pseudonym], a large public research university within a day's drive of the Great Lakes, participated in this study. Everwhite University is located in Heartland, a Midwestern city of just under 100,000, with a predominantly White community. There are between 30,000 and 40,000 predominantly White students enrolled, and approximately 1,500 faculty at Everwhite University, with less than 350 of the faculty being female.

All three ranks of the professoriate were represented by the women in this study, with the majority of the 15 being either at the assistant or associate level. Their ages ranged from the late thirties to the mid-sixties. Ethnically the women of color identified as Chicana, Hispanic, African American and bi-racial.[4] The participants also varied in their marital and family status as well as in their sexual orientation. The women who were in relationships had all been with their respective partners for over seven years. Several of the women were divorced, some having teenaged children at home.

All faculty are busy, yet these participants graciously allowed a series of four interviews each, on their backgrounds, research, teaching, and collegial situations, respectively. While interviews offered substantive data collection, as Ely (1990), LeCompte & Preissle (1993), Guba & Lincoln (1985), and Merriam (1988) discuss, shadowing and observations were performed, and artifacts and documents were also collected and examined.

Conceptual Framework

Oppressed groups are frequently placed in the situation of being listened to only if we frame our ideas in the language that is familiar to and comfortable for a dominant group. This requirement often changes the meaning of our ideas and works to elevate the ideas of dominant groups. (Hill Collins, 1991, p. xiii)

This study positioned women of color at the heart of the analysis as a means of bringing volume to voices seldom heard in the academy and illuminating their perspectives on faculty life in the ivory tower. The conceptual framework that undergirds this study was based upon the theoretical works of women scholars of color (e.g., Allen, 1988; Anzaldúa, 1990; Bannerji, Carty, Dehli, Heald, & McKenna, 1992; Chan & Wang, 1991; Davis, 1983; DuBois & Ruiz, 1990; Green, 1990; Hill Collins, 1986, 1990, 1991; King, 1990; King, 1991; Pollard, 1990; Reyes, 1994, b; Trinh, 1990; Williams, 1991a) as a means of not merely giving voice to the ideas that many scholars of color find important, but also drawing upon these theoretical works as a means of conducting research. In reviewing these works, consistently, three themes emerged. The themes, invisibility, multiple oppression, and resistance, grounded in this literature, formed the conceptual framework of this study.

The first of these, invisibility, brings to light the absence of women of color in much of the research literature. Anzaldúa (1983, 1990), DuBois & Ruiz (1990), Harrison, (1993), Lewis, (1990), and Trihn (1989) assert that much of mainstream research has overlooked the lives of women of color. There appears to be an assumption that the experiences, concerns, and issues of women of color falls under one of two headings—either "people of color" or "women." These scholars argue that this assumption is problematic. Upon examining the literature on "people of color," the focus of most of the analyses about people of color emphasize the experiences of men. Such scholars as Dill (1987), Hull & Smith (1982), and Yamada (1983) further contend that women of color are not only absent from the analyses of people of color, they are also absent from analyses on "women," which have focused upon White women. Even the term "women" has been appropriated by many Whites and scholars to exclusively mean "White" women (hooks, 1981) as the key phrase "women and minorities" indicates. Being subsumed under the headings of "people" of color or "women" makes invisible the issues, experiences, or perspectives of women of color.

The theme of multiple oppression concentrates on how various forms of oppression (e.g., racism, sexism and classism) intersect in the lives of women of color. Women scholars of color (e. g., Butler, 1989; Hill Collins, 1991; King, 1990; Lewis, 1990; Pollard, 1997) stress the need to recognize the often subtle, yet complex ways that multiple oppression may interact, not as separate variables but as intertwined, dynamic components that bear upon the lives of women of color. These scholars point out that women of color do not exist in a vacuum but live in a society where they are often oppressed via their economic conditions, their ethnicity/race, as well as their gender, in varying combinations and degrees. Zinn, Cannon, Higginbotham, and Dill (1990) assert "scholarship that overlooks the diversity of women's experiences cannot reveal the magnitude, complexity, or interdependence of systems of oppression. Such work underestimates the obstacles to be confronted and helps little in developing practical strategies to overcome the. . . . barriers that. . . . women [of color] inevitably confront" (p. 36). An analysis that examines only one of these oppressive forces as it impacts women of color may fail to reveal the complexities that daily pervade the experiences, perspectives and issues within the lives of many of these women.

The theme of resistance stresses how women of color have not always been passive victims in their circumstances as marginalized members of society (e.g., Davis, 1983; Green, 1992; Hill Collins, 1991; hooks, 1981; Pollard, 1990; Trask, 1993). Many women of color have adapted their roles and resisted multiple oppression either directly or indirectly throughout this country's history. Resistance might take a subtle form such as refusing to give eye contact to an oppressor, or it might be as bold as refusing to give up one's seat on a bus, thereby birthing an entire movement (Rains, 1995). Yet, rarely are women of color presented as people capable of adapting to or resisting the forces of oppression (Davis 1983; hooks, 1981; Lorde, 1984; Rains, 1997). While it is true that oftentimes these acts of resistance, in particular the subtle acts, were not able to liberate these women from the oppressive forces and conditions under which many lived, such acts remain notable in the way that they shed light on intricate and multifaceted roles many women of color have led and continue to lead. These scholars argue that recognition of how women of color have resisted oppressive forces is essential to an examination of women of color—their lives, roles, experiences, and issues.

Many studies about people of color have been grounded in the works of White theorists. Yet, many women scholars of color have been deconstructing and critiquing such studies for almost thirty years now.[5] During this period of time the themes—invisibility, multiple oppression, and resistance—have consistently been gaining strength. Using these themes to form the conceptual framework of the study offered different voices to emerge, while also responding to the concerns that Hill Collins (1991) posed, by allowing these voices to be heard without pressure to change their meaning for purposes of a more palatable translation.

The study from which this chapter is drawn examined the areas of collegiality, teaching and research, and is much more detailed and comprehensive than the pages of a chapter will permit. Therefore, the area of collegiality which helps form the professional climate for most academics will be highlighted to bring to light certain issues in the professional lives of some women faculty of color.

Now You See Me, Now You Don't

Based on the review of the literature, invisibility was conceptualized as a unidimensional phenomenon related to the absence of the experiences and perspectives of women of color. By grounding this research in the works of women scholars of color, my intent was to respond to this phenomenon by making their work "visible." However, the issues that emerged in this study reveal that invisibility is dynamic and encompasses more than the concept of unacknowledged presence of women of color.

Many of the participants at Everwhite University raised issues of invisibility during early interviews. In fact, these women not only encountered an "*imposed* invisibility" but they also encountered a more often occurring phenomenon of a "*designated* visibility." These contradictory, socially constructed phenomena coexisted in the lives of many of the participants in ways that daily tested their perseverance in the academy and challenged their ability to maintain their footing on the sharp edge of the sword.

On the one hand, the small numbers of women of color in the academy, compounded by the expectations of others, create situations where the women are neither seen nor heard (e.g., Caplan, 1994; Carty, 1992; Farmer, 1993). I call this phenomenon "*imposed* invisibility" in the sense that it is socially constructed and "imposed" upon those whose presence can be ignored.

The discussion of "imposed invisibility" emerged in the conversations of the majority of the participants. It occurred in both social and political interactions with their White colleagues in their departments and across campus.

Dr. June Jackson,[6] for example, in her mid-forties, in the School of Social Sciences, described how "imposed invisibility" affected some of her social interactions with colleagues. She relates,[7]

—I'm the first minority person to be in this department in all its years [approx. 150 years] on this campus! Initially, there was some curiosity. But no one talked to me. They stared a lot. I don't even think they knew they were doing it!!

Do you know in all the years I have been here, I have never been invited to a colleague's house or to any social situation outside of this office. That never happens to the White faculty. There was a new White woman last year that joined our department. She had three invitations within the first two weeks!! There are still very few people that will ever talk with me. In the hallways, they, —some will *deliberately* look down [when she is walking by]. It's so strange. It's like I am part of the wall, —like I am not here at all. . . .

She was stunned by the apparent contrast in how the new White female colleague was welcomed into the department, while she remained invisible to many of her colleagues.

Another participant, Dr. Barbara Woods, also encountered similar experiences with "imposed invisibility." Dr. Woods is in her early fifties. Her department, in the College of Arts and Letters, has other faculty of color there. Like Dr. Jackson, she remarked about how she felt invisible socially. She described the following, "Well —there have been, —I can go into somebody's office and have an hour long, detailed conversation with them and we leave on very friendly terms, —you know? And I can see that person the next day on campus, or in the grocery store —and I don't exist!!!" When I pressed her on the point, she continued,

Let's put it this way —if there were two Whites and that happened, and the one being ignored stopped and tapped the first person on the shoulder and said something like, "Hey!" or and addressed them, you know like, "are you just going to walk right by me and not say hi?" The other person would probably turn and extend themselves, "oh, I didn't see you" or "I didn't mean to . . ." —something like that. Now, if I did that, and stopped a White person, and said, "are you just going to walk right by me without saying hi?" —Well! *That's considered confrontational.* They would pull back and there would be a tone to the voice, not a friendly tone and —well —okay, I just thought of an example!! I've known this person for a while academically, we've been on several committees together, a White woman, and we've always been on friendly terms —and the other day, I saw her walk by, and I stuck out my arm and tapped her on the shoulder as we passed. She turned and, —and she stepped back when she saw me, and said, "Yes???" Very business-like, not, "hi, how are you" or "Oh, I didn't see you" or anything!!! What happened was that it set the tone, I became very business-like and said, "We haven't had a meeting for a while . . ." And I think she got a little embarrassed, —and I, —it made me realize I was "just a Black" to her. I thought I had a friendly colleague here, and I misjudged it and the whole thing became uncomfortable!

These examples bring to light some of the ways "imposed invisibility" affects the social aspects of collegiality, in the lives of women faculty of color in this study.

Another way to conceptualize "imposed invisibility" is to consider how it functions politically in committees. For example, Dr. Lydia Brown, also in her early fifties, is in a department in the College of Arts and Letters that has about an equal number of White male and White female faculty. She is one of several faculty of color in her department. She responded this way to the question of the impact, if any, of invisibility upon her academic life.

> Yes, —yes, it's had an impact. Well, it happens for me —I tend to be very, very articulate. I tend to wait before, to get the lay of the land before I say what I'm going to say, in any given meeting or whatever. I find I usually come up with the idea that turns the discussion to a higher and more substantive level —*and what happens is that then the men in the room pick up the point and bat it around.* And *credit* for initiating the discussion will *always* go to the man who picked up *my* comment, *rephrased it and ran with it!!! Happens all the time! Happens — all —the —time!!!* [sighs heavily]

For Dr. Brown, her experience with "imposed invisibility" is in how her ideas are appropriated by her White colleagues in the political arena.

Dr. Leona Lewis has had similar experiences. Dr. Lewis is in her early sixties, in the School of Social Sciences. She, like several other participants, is the only faculty of color in her department. She described her experiences with "imposed invisibility" this way,

> I've had a couple of things that I don't like that have happened . . . —I have expressed an opinion that I have documented. I don't usually just talk off the top of my head!! *And that was ignored. That happens a lot!!!* That has happened to me here, and that has happened to me at University "Z" [a previous academic position] —in that, *I'd* say something and then *everybody would ignore what I said.* And then, say a month later, on the same discussion, *a WHITE PERSON would say what I had said!!! And they'd say, "OH, GREAT IDEA!!"* [to the white person]. But the thing is —*I let them know!!!* I say, *"wait! Ho! Ho! Ho! Ho!* [tapping on the table with her finger] I said, *"I said that a month —ago!!!!! I said the exact same thing. And you didn't' think anything of it!!* And everybody sloughed over it!!! I don't let them forget!! You know, I'm not going to let it get by with that!!!!! *And that happens an awful lot to me!!!*

In this example by Dr. Lewis, it is the appropriation of her ideas by her white colleagues, that sustains her invisibility. It is only through her persistence that she is able to reclaim the idea that she set forth. But it is often at the cost of being seen as "pushy."

Nor is imposed invisibility at the political level something limited to African American women faculty. This was also raised by Dr. Zapata as problematic. Dr. Ruby Zapata, in the School of Social Sciences, is in her late forties. She remarked,

> For me, it just blends —I mean, sometimes, having an idea at a meeting, and voicing it, I'm trying to get them to think about something I think is important —and —discussion occurs, and usually a White male will ponder it,

even a White female —and the White male takes the idea, like —well, and makes a statement, it's like *he's paraphrasing what I just said,* — as if it's *his* thought!! *It's almost like he has to translate my idea to the White folks!! Then, everyone's looking at him!!! There's agreement, and then it's his!!! And after that, I don't exist!!* It gets tiring, but —my focus is usually on getting it accomplished no matter what you have to go through to get it. Cause usually for me, it's around the student [issues that relate to them] So, you know — [voice trails off]

In the area of collegiality, many of these participants encountered the phenomenon of "imposed invisibility." This occurred in social situations with their peers, both within the department and across campus. Further, this occurred in departmental meetings with their colleagues.

On the other hand, these women faculty of color also described an often occurring phenomenon, which I call "designated visibility." I posit that this is another socially-constructed phenomenon, where women of color are often tokenized for what their racial presence represents or they are "on display" in ways that their White colleagues are not (e.g., Caplan, 1994; Patai, 1991; Williams, 1991). These women raise as problematic the way their visibility is constructed and used by those around them.

For many of the participants, their experiences regarding imposed invisibility were exceeded by their experiences with "designated visibility." There was the sense by majority of the participants that their individuality was often ignored, their identity was tokenized. "Designated visibility" emerged in the discussions participants had regarding their collegial interactions, but it also extended to commentary related to service issues and time commitments.

The participants' explanation of the first aspect of "designated visibility" emerged out the discussions on invisibility. Many described a sort of "selective" process of visibility, that is, they would remain invisible until their White colleagues saw a need or "selected" to recognize them.

When I questioned Dr. Jackson, for example, she called her experience "selective invisibility" because the phenomenon she often encountered with white colleagues, which left her invisible until they saw a need or "selected" to recognize her. "It's a kind of a —a selective invisibility, though. *Because when they have problems with minority students, they run to me. —*I don't know what they would do with those minority students if I wasn't here!?!"

Dr. Ruby Zapata was the only faculty of color, although not the only woman in her department. She indicated that she was more visible than invisible. She described how the White colleagues in her department seem to bring minority students to her door. She explains,

It's very interesting, really. Well —sad is probably a better term, you —well, for example, any brown, or semi-brown student, it can be Iranian, Filipino, any student that has a tone of brown to their complexion. And I will get a call, and they will —and I will get the student dumped on me. *If the student has an accent or is brown, then the student is immediately brought to my door!!* And the colleague, dean, or whoever calls me, is very friendly on the phone, saying that they "thought of me", and they're "sending the student right over!" —I've gotten Iranian students with very thick accents come to me —and it wound up that they wanted to talk about *immigration issues!!* This is not my area!! I've had a Filipino student sent to me who had questions about *how to get his DRIVER'S license —not even anything academic,* but —he *couldn't* be understood —and *that's why he was sent to me—because he had an accent!!!* So, —so, *that happens to me all the time!* [sigh].

Anzaldúa (1990) discusses the "racial blank spot" that many White people maintain with regard to people of color. She calls it "selective reality" and describes it this way, "[It is] the narrow spectrum of reality that human beings select or choose to perceive and/or what their culture 'selects' for them to 'see'. Perception is an interpretive process conditioned by education. That which is outside of the range of consensus perception is 'blanked out'" (p. xxi). Anzaldúa's point is similar to what Dr. Zapata raises as problematic for the women of color with regard to how White colleagues conveniently "blank out" their existence, until they are needed. Then, when there is a "minority" concern, the women colleagues of color, who were invisible only moments before, are suddenly visible.

The following women discussed "designated visibility" more in terms of the inability to blend in. Dr. Margaret Baker, in her late forties, in the College of Arts and Letters, is in a department with several other faculty of color. She explains how she encounters a sense of designated visibility.

Well, in my own department there are other faculty of color —but when I go outside of the department —I do get a sense of support, but I also have some sense that I'm a novelty, that I, I —my position is fairly rare . . . uh, so, when I say I'm a novelty in, I don't mean that wholly negatively, but I realize that when I'm present, by no means am I *in*visible, but rather I'm under a glass —ah, a glass cage in the sense that I'm highly visible when I am present.

Here Dr. Baker discusses not only the aspect of high visibility, but also how it creates a sense of being on display. Dr. Zapata extends this by posing this heightened sense of visibility into a frame of not being able to blend. Dr. Zapata's framed her remarks in this manner: "I'm *invisible* when it comes to *intellect.* But when it comes to *physical* things, *I'm right out there. I'm like a beacon!* You know, not too many people on this campus look like me —so, I —*I'm really visible in a lot of ways.*" Dr. Zapata's response reflects her recognition of the coexistence of the two phenomena, invisibility and "designated visibility."

The comments of Dr. Jackson's reinforce those of Dr. Zapata, regarding the aspect of being exceptionally visible and the problematic of not being able to blend. Dr. Jackson notes:

I feel very visible —you know, I'm from a fairly large city in the east. It's very integrated, so there are lots of people of color —then I came to this region —being in an all White place, where not only does no one look like you, but you, —you stand out. Yes, I'd say that there's been quite an impact on my life. —*Incredibly visible* —that's part of the thing I always feel here. No matter what I do —*it's always show time!* Whether I'm on campus or off. I mean, if I go to the store in grubbies [non-professional clothing] *everybody notices how I am dressed.* If a White person goes in grubbies, they're just one of many people that might be dressed that way. No one notices. That's not an option for me. I can't blend. And if I *do* decide to dress casually, there's always the chance that I will be treated differently. —Sometimes I am watched or followed around the store as if I might steal something. *[It just never ends! It —never —ends. sigh]* You know, that's not something White people, certainly not my noted colleagues, ever have to deal with or think about!! For me, it's a daily reality —a daily reality!

Here Dr. Jackson is describing her response to the physical reality of being in a predominantly White environment and how it spills over from her life on campus into her life off campus. While she was matter of fact in her reply, she displayed fatigue in her face as she described her experience. Dr. Baker also describes her experience with how the visibility doesn't end with the professional life, nor is there an ability to blend. She states,

And White folks don't understand how you are *Forever on stage! Forever! Just by virtue of the fact that you're Black.* And some of them are, you know, they're in shock at what can come out of your mouth that makes sense, but ASK them 'why did all of you turn around and look at me [when she spoke to her son's teacher]?', you know, they would say, 'well, we didn't mean anything!' You know, 'we were just . . . and you were sitting over there. . . .' And they *don't realize that their reaction is different from the way they reacted when other [White] folks were in the room were talking.* So, —*if you tell them, then you're "overly sensitive!" Something's wrong with you! So, you're always a problem.*

Dr. Baker's example of her encounter off campus illuminates further how "designated visibility" acts as a double edged sword, by not only making one very visible, but also having the disadvantage of being considered reactionary if one responds to the shock of others.

In her reaction to the question, Dr. Brown brings the discussion back to the campus side of their lives. Still raising the issue of the inability to blend, she begins:

Well, I am extremely conscious of how visible I am. You know, I just —I'm sure that if this were a conversation we were having with say, White women faculty, they would say, "well, we feel very visible too!!" *But it's more insidious. I think, you know? Because, first of all, you're constantly reminded that you're spotlighted. You're foregrounded.* I think *when a blond, blue-eyed woman decides that she's tired of doing whatever it does that registers her protest and sets her aside from the pack, she can close her mouth, and fling her hair.* Or whatever —the tight jeans, and just you know, —*sort of fade, blend. I, on the other hand, am always spotlighted, always visible. So it keeps me sort of borderline crazy.*

Through her comments, Dr. Brown registers her frustration with how "designated visibility" operates in the academy. She raises the point that while White female colleagues may feel very visible as well, they still have White-skinned privileged. They can blend, women faculty of color have no choice. By virtue of their skin color, women faculty of color are always "out there."

While Dr. Brown's response is an example of the how that visibility operates differently for White women faculty from being a woman faculty of color, Dr. Smith shares an example of literally how the physical visibility operates in her life. Dr. Helen Smith, in her late thirties, in the School of Social Sciences, is the first and only faculty of color among the male and female colleagues in her department. She notes,

Well, I do think that it does have an effect! —I think that there is —that *my chair is anxious to make me as visible as possible and to have me to interact with as many students as possible.* And it, it's a mixed bag. *I think a lot of that has to do with my race.* That he wants . . . and I mean, part of his motivation is good. He wants as many of the students as possible in this department to have contact with the *only Black professor* in the department. On the other hand, you know, *there's also the element of "Make me as visible as possible" because that enhances the department's reputation* and all those kinds of things. *And that can be very destructive to people of color and to women.*

The participants discuss the more physical side of being visible, both off and on campus, with Dr. Smith providing an example of how it can operate at the departmental level.

Another aspect of "designated visibility" focuses on being designated as the spokesperson or token member of your ethnic group. In her comments, Dr. Jones captures how the spokespersonship functions. She described how this occurred in relation to her participation in campus-wide committee meetings. She states,

. . . there's a kind of *appropriation of my being there* in a way by some people —it's a certain kind of *invisibility within visibility,* if you understand what I'm saying. *Seeing the individual as a representative of the group* and *not seeing the individual.* So that *the individual is invisible* — because I am seen by some only as a representative of a larger group!! . . . I find among faculty members —that there's a certain kind of baggage that they have, where they tend to think of blacks as a group —and, you know, deny individuality. —You know, *you could be in a meeting where an issue of race comes up and everybody looks at you!* —So I think that's —*that goes on all the time!!! ALL THE TIME!*

Dr. Jones stressed the frequency with which this aspect occurred in her life in the academy. Not only did her white colleagues treat her in meetings as if she had no personal identity, but they further placed upon her the responsibility to be the spokesperson for her race.

Dr. Zapata's comments and experience concur with what Dr. Jones has been saying. Dr. Zapata also encountered this sort of spokespersonship responsibility. She explained,

I am on several campus committees and —and I can go to a meeting and if they're talking —*if they're talking about anything other than minority issues, I'm invisible EVEN WHEN I'M VERBAL.* They *don't want to hear* what I think then. *But, if it turns to minority issues, the talking stops, and the eyes drift down to wherever I am, and I am supposed to expound on "what it is to be a minority"* or *"what Hispanics think"* —[sighs and shakes her head] Here in the Midwest, they're *always saying "Hispanic"* —I don't know any "Hisspanics"! We are Chicanas, Latinas, or Cubans, or Puerto Ricans —but Hispanics? [sigh] But I'm digressing. My point is they *always* want *you to speak for your race!* You know —if I turned it around, and asked them "gee, Dr. So and So, as a white man, tell me, what is it like to be white?" or "Say, Dr. Whatever, as a white woman tell me what all you whites think" —They'd think it was absurd. They don't get it, you know? They *really* don't get it!! I've even gotten in meetings, "Well, Dr. Zapata, what do 'you people' think about that?" —*YOU PEOPLE????* I can only speak for myself, just as they can only speak for themselves. But that *never stops them* from putting it on me!!! And above all, I better not show offense! I mean —*I am supposed to have a temperament and not a personality!* An *even* temperament, and respond a certain way. *Which means that they take me out of a human vein,* out of being happy, sad, and angry —*I just have to be one dimensional* — pleasant, and respectful —and *don't let my voice get loud!* Cause then the stereo's [stereotypes] come, they come into play here! "Loud," "brash," Chicana!

While the two participants above discussed the demand that they be spokespeople, other participants described how tokenism functioned in their lives.

The next two respondents link how tokenism operates in conjunction with demands for service. As Dr. Woods remarks,

... *when they* [white faculty], *WHATEVER they're having on campus, and it seems, and they "need a black,"* you know—[chuckles]—*a black face* —and you know, *they're pulling you in,* and then the students, of course are pulling you in for, you know, your expertise or whatever. So the service here is truly humongous!!

Dr. Lewis also talked about the link of tokens and service. She said, "They demand more service here [predominantly White campus]. Being a minority, even more so. *Cause they are always putting you on a committee to be a token somewhere."* Both of these respondents raise the point about the demands made upon them and the tokenism that feeds it. All in all, these aspects of designated visibility took enormous amounts of the participants' time and energy.

The Sharp Edge: Coexisting Contradictions

On the surface, when confronted with the unexpected phenomena of visibility, in conjunction with invisibility, it would appear that a contradiction exists. After all, physically one either visible or one is not. Yet, social constructions are not always in harmony with physical reality.

Typically, invisibility and visibility are not discussed as coexisting together. It may be difficult to comprehend how one could be both visible and invisible as the same person. Yet, Lorde (1984) posits that for Black women it is not necessarily an either/or dichotomy. "Within this country where racial difference creates a constant, if unspoken, distortion of vision, Black women have on one hand been highly visible, and so, on the other hand, have been rendered invisible through the depersonalization of racism" (p. 42). Lorde addresses the seemingly impossible contradiction of experiencing both phenomena, by pointing out that invisibility and visibility coexist together in the lives of many Black women. By extension, this coexisting contradiction also exists in the lives of many non-Black women of color as well.

At Everwhite University, for these participants, invisibility and visibility emerge as social constructions created by their colleagues. The women faculty of color were INvisible when their colleagues had no pressing need to acknowledge their presence. Their small numbers in the academy can exacerbate this, as small numbers can indicate insignificance—of only peripheral importance. In this way, the women of color at Everwhite could be disregarded, or forgotten. They were not really INvisible, but this invisibility was "imposed" by their peers. In essence, many of their White colleagues *did not expect* to see them. These expectations were imposed upon these women by those in the majority, by those in dominance.

Ironically, at the same time, their small numbers may also exacerbate their visibility. This visibility may be appropriated to tokenize these women. Their physical difference allows them to be readily recognizable as "different," while their personal identity and individuality are lost. As Caplan (1994) pointed out,

> ... in some ways women from non-dominant groups are ignored, but in some ways they are the subjects of intense attention 'not as individuals, but as representatives of their particular ethnic group—as when a minority woman is called upon to give the "black woman's view" of an issue or problem rather than her own view (p. 214).

This contradictory existence of two socially constructed phenomena was frustrating and problematic for the women who encountered it.

With regard to imposed invisibility, the participants described various circumstances involving issues of their colleagues. Many had given examples describing situations where their colleagues had "dumped" students of color at their door, irrespective of considering the needs/problems of the students or whether the participants had the time or the skills to remedy the students' particular circumstances. They raised as problematic becoming "just another Black face" especially when they thought they had built a solid rapport with the colleagues who reacted in this manner.

Designated visibility was problematic for the participants, as well. With designated visibility the problems evolved around two aspects, that of heightened visibility, and tokenism. The women shared incidences where they felt like "a novelty" or that they were "under a glass cage." Several of the women discussed how this heightened visibility affected not only their professional lives, but their private lives as well. Here the emphasis shifted to not merely the visibility, but the inability to "blend," of it "always being show time" or how they are "forever on stage." They spoke of being "foregrounded" and "spotlighted" in ways that their white women colleagues are not. In one instance, a participant shared how she was made as "visible as possible" because she was the department's only Black professor.

The second aspect of hyper-visibility emerges as spokespersonship and tokenism, and as the respondents reveal, an intertwined demand for service. The participants discussed how they encountered "invisibility within visibility" where they were not seen for who they were, but rather as spokespeople for their respective races. Every single respondent raised the demand made upon them for service, whenever a token was needed. These women spoke of burn-out from the added demand for their presence, while juggling all of the other demands that the academy requires of professors and the sense of exploitation this had upon them.

Having to Dance on the Sharp Edge: Consequences of Coexisting Contradictions

What emerged as central for these women were the consequences of the coexisting phenomena upon their lives. The two socially constructed phenomena, imposed invisibility and designated visibility combine to make what Caplan (1994) calls a "crazy-making paradox" (p. 214). Together these phenomena affected collegial aspects of the professional lives of the women faculty of color at Everwhite.

Certainly, the most obvious consequence is stress. Stress can be a heavy weight that may bear upon their lives, as they may encounter alienation and distrust at being treated as second class citizens within their own ranks. This extra weight may be compounded when a woman of color is the "only one" in her department. She may be viewed as a representative of all people of color, or for her ethnic group, rather than as a individual in her department. In turn, her intellect, and the skills and research interests she brings may neither be recognized nor valued. As the "only one" she may also strain under the burden of responsibility that being "first" often carries. That is, the racial tensions and reactions of colleagues may mean unanticipated amounts of time and energy are needed to cope with their ignorance and how that ignorance plays out in behaviors and comments. The contradictory expectations may be frustrating at best, and at worst may be a catalyst for burn-out or attrition. She may encounter exhaustion from having to constantly wage "battles" and cope with the stress of having to select which battles to let go, while often losing those she does select.

Thus, a consequence of socially constructed coexisting contradictions in the professional lives of women faculty of color at a research institution such as Everwhite, may be a sense that they must constantly dance on the sharp edge of the sword (which could be considered a distraction, and high price to pay), while also contending with all the "normal" stresses associated with academe (e.g., competition, publishing, teaching, already full advising loads, research and grants) that their White counterparts also encounter. This consequence also diverts precious time away from the preparation for tenure and/or promotion. Dancing on the sharp edge of a sword that does not exist for fellow colleagues may certainly have an impact upon whether such women deem the cost worth the price of staying in the academy.

However, the power of consequences lay not merely in the costs to women of color who are working to maintain their footing in academe, but in also providing an opportunity to gaze into the mirror and see what it reflects back regarding the status quo (Rains, 1996 a). As Pollard (1997) articulates in her discussion of research:

> I am attempting . . . to reflect on how research on women and men of color
> and white women, just like research on other topics, is, too often, used to
> maintain the status quo when it could be used for liberatory ends and em-
> powerment. I have spent much of my school and professional life, like oth-
> ers, as one of a small number of people of color in a predominately white
> setting. This could be likened to being placed under the glass of other peo-
> ples' expectations which are often based on their perspectives about *your*
> race/gender identity. From time to time, and with increasing frequency, I
> find it necessary to break that glass (p. 8).

Here, the consequences for the respondents also offers an opportunity to examine how the outcomes reflect back upon their colleagues
and the university.

For White colleagues there may be benefits in sanctioning a construction of imposed invisibility. There is, for example, a benefit embedded in
the convenience of such a construction. That is, it may be convenient to
"impose invisibility" upon women faculty of color when the issues discussed in meetings are focused on topics other than race and ethnicity.
In this way, some white colleagues may profit by ignoring the voices of
these women, while conveniently co-opting their ideas and contributions in such meetings.

Another potential benefit that white colleagues may gain emerges
from the cost women faculty of color pay when they resist such constructions. That is, when women faculty of color have the courage to resist the expectation to be silent, some white faculty may take a "blame
the victim" position. In effect, this position absolves such White colleagues from scrutinizing their own complicity in constructing and
sanctioning the role of imposed invisibility for women faculty of color,
while the women may risk being ". . . labeled as belligerent challengers
of the authority and wisdom of traditional faculty members" (Caplan,
1994, p. 69).

Consequences of the social construction of designated visibility may
also hold benefits for White colleagues. Beyond the obvious visibility
that women faculty of color have on a predominantly White campus, the
expectations and behaviors of some of their White colleagues may form
a construction of heightened visibility for these women. This phenomenon may occur while the women are in their offices, or it may occur in
departmental committee meetings.

For example this construction may occur in their own departments
when a student of color arrives at the office of a White faculty member.
This White professor may then deposit this student at the office
doorstep of the woman faculty of color. The responsibility for student
advisement, then, becomes an association by color. That is, the responsibility falls along the color line. The result is that women faculty of color

often have an overload of student advisees. This overload provides dual benefits. The department benefits by students of color being served or "taken care of" by these women faculty of color. While White faculty may profit from a reduced advisee load, having more time to continue their scholarly activities.

The consequence for women faculty of color from this dual benefit for the institution and for the White colleagues comes in the form of work distribution. Women faculty of color may be expected to shoulder both their share of White students, as well as *all or most* of the students of color. In turn, this unequal distribution of advisees may negatively affect their evaluation for tenure and promotion. The institutional reward system does not generally reward individuals for their service even when these services benefit the institution (e.g., Boyer, 1990; Padilla, 1994).

The flip-side of this consequence for women of color is an "unearned advantage" (McIntosh, 1992) or potential benefit to White faculty. Depositing students of color on the doorstep of these women, in effect becomes a convenience. *It relieves White faculty of having to deal with issues of race or diversity.* Thus, White faculty's responsibility is reduced without the loss of their position or privilege in the structural inequalities that undergird racial issues (e.g., McIntosh, 1992; Reyes & Halcón, 1991; Scheurich, 1993). Through such a benefit as this, the location of such White faculty in the traditional hierarchical structure of the academy remains secure and the status quo is maintained.

The social construction of designated visibility also occurs in departmental committee meetings. For example, in such a meeting, if the topic of discussion turns to racial matters of *any* kind, women professors of color are often expected to be the spokesperson for all people of color. Here again, matters of convenience and construction of the roles women faculty of color are expected to play, arise from the expectations of their white colleagues. The women are "needed" and spotlighted, with the expectation that they will perform this constructed role.

Internal to the expectation of "spokespersonship" are several veiled assumptions. One such veiled assumption takes the form of presuming that a single person, regardless of race or ethnicity could possibly speak for, or could even possibly know what all or most people within any group thinks, let alone across several groups. Another assumption embedded within this expectation denies the broad diversity that exists within, as well as across different groups of people of color. Typecasting is the final assumption buried within this expectation of spokespersonship. The presumption functions to put the responsibility upon the woman of color to be the "expert" on all things racial. It is a form of stereotyping similar to assuming that if a man is Black, he "must be good at basketball." These veiled assumptions that are buried within the ex-

pectation of spokespersonship, coalesce to create another costly consequence for these women faculty of color. This consequence operates to
deny their individuality and their personal identity, while denying their
expertise and scholarly interests which may or may not concern issues
of race.

There is an added benefit that White faculty gain when they expect
women faculty of color to be the voice and representative of people of
color. This constructed visibility once again relieves such White faculty
from responsibility of learning or knowing about racial issues and matters. Again, the responsibility for learning may be projected outward.
That is, the locus of responsibility for learning or knowing these issues
may be externalized to women faculty of color. The internal responsibility of such White faculty towards issues of diversity and race, in this way,
may be denied. Not only are women faculty of color held responsible for
knowing about these issues and matters, but the positioning of White
faculty is protected and the status quo upheld.

In many instances the women faculty of color expressed fatigue and
stress when designated visibility materialized by way of being tokenized
for the "bit of color" they brought to departmental or campus-wide
committees, panels, presentations and the like. As one of the women expressed it, "Because everybody *wants one*! Everybody wants a person of
color to be on something or other." The consequences for the women of
color here, similar to spokespersonship, are again tied to benefits for
their White colleagues and the institution itself. The demand for their
presence, often came without regard to their need for protected time for
writing. Many of the women were on as many as seven to fifteen extra
committees or panels and such, beyond what their White colleague
committee/service loads in their respective departments were. When
the women attempted to "just say no" as it were, they were often hit with
the expectation from White colleagues of "Well, that's what *we hired you
for!*" Yet, their extended service was rarely recognized and seldom rewarded in the tenure and promotion process.

Ironically, the construct of designated visibility, here, generates a benefit for such White colleagues, while also creating a benefit for the institution, as well. Tokenism offers many White colleagues a way out of extra
committee duty or panel time, providing many with more opportunity
for scholarly pursuits, such as writing and publishing. At the same time,
the expectation of tokenism that the construction of designated visibility provides, also screens the maintenance of the status quo from view.
Through the designated visibility of women of color and the expectation
of tokenism, the institution is able to provide the illusion of diversity and
integration, when in fact it may be more symbolic than real. The very
nature of tokens indicates small numbers, and in this case, small num-

bers of women of color rarely have the power to "effect change" (Parker, 1986) and shift the paradigms necessary to make integration a reality. The institution, then, profits from the token appearance of diversity, while the institutional structures and status quo remain unchanged.

Is Dancing Faster All There Is?

Life in the academy is challenging, hectic and stressful for most faculty, regardless of gender or ethnicity. When socially constructed, contradictory expectations and demands generate benefits for some White faculty, while the consequences generate costs for some women faculty of color, it adds a layer of strain, intensity, pressure for these women that absorbs valuable time and energy that could be committed to more scholarly pursuits. It would seem that at Everwhite University, equity of access did not always materialize in to equity of treatment in the area of collegial relations. Sandler and Hall (1986) note the chilly climate that many White women in the academy endure. I posit that for many women of color the climate is not chilly, it's a cold sword upon which they must dance, often barefoot, ever faster and faster to survive.

While I think that more people of color are needed in academe, in graduate schools, and in faculty and administrative positions, that would be an overly simplistic response to a complex situation. Such a response would assume that to "color-ize" would necessarily eliminate the sword. That however, would place all the burden of "integrating" the academy upon the backs of people of color. It might merely mean that the sword would become more crowded. In other words, with such a response the status quo would remain intact, the "unearned advantages" (McIntosh, 1992) of White privilege would continue unaltered. As Madrid (1992) points out in his discussion of academic access. He recalls,

> Some of us entered institutional life through the front door, others through the back door; and still others through side doors. Many, if not most of us, came in through windows and continue to come in through windows. Of those who entered through the front door, some never made it past the lobby; others were ushered into corners and niches. Those who entered through back and side doors inevitably have remained in back and side rooms. And those who entered through windows found enclosures built around them. For despite the lip service given to the goal of the integration of minorities into institutional life, what has occurred instead is ghettoization, marginalization, isolation (p. 10).

Equity of access, therefore, should not be confused with equity of treatment. It is quite possible that increasing the number of women of color, or people of color, into the academy will not alone change the status quo that many encounter within the sacred walls.

It would seem that a different solution is in order. Women of color cannot do it alone. What is needed, is nothing short of "restructuring the master's house" (Ford Slack, Rains, Collay, & Dunlap, 1994). Those with the least power within the academy have the fewest tools and means with which to change the structure of academe. If the ivory tower is to become less ivory and more inclusive in ways that do not force more upon the sword, then changes must also come from those who hold power, position, and privilege within. As public schools have had demographic shifts, in particular within the last thirty years, they have begun to rethink such areas as curricula, teaching strategies, support systems, teaching populations and the like. Yet, the academy, grounded in the elite, White, male power structure of medieval monasteries (Rains, 1995) has made few changes as the demographics have begun to shift. While I do not have all the answers, it would seem that a rethinking of the structure of the academy, a rethinking of how equity of access does not necessarily translate into equity of treatment, a rethinking of the need to share responsibilities more equitably, a rethinking of who profits through unearned benefits and who pays the cost and how that translates to maintain the status quo, and other such issues might be a good place to start. Dancing on the sharp edge of the sword remains a high price for many women faculty of color to pay for wanting to participate in the realm of intellectual inquiry and scholarly pursuits. Surely, dancing faster can not be all there is.

Notes

1. My identity is layered and shifts depending on the circumstance. Broadly speaking, I consider myself a woman of color when much of the discussion surrounds issues of Whiteness/privilege. Yet, when the issues are more related to concerns within/about color, I can reveal a different layer where I identify as non-Black "biracial"—Japanese & American Indian. In even more specific circumstances, such as Native rights issues, for example, I identify with the Indian "side" of my identity. For the purposes of this chapter, I may at times shift back and forth.

2. The identification "students of color" is meant to recognize historically oppressed groups [via racism/classism] in the United States (e.g., American Indian, Latinos, African Americans; Asian American).

3. Here I purposefully use "First American" in preference to "Native American." It must be noted that I do *not* speak for all Native peoples instead allowing the power of my deliberate choice to weigh in as it will. One lesson that became abundantly clear during my graduate education, was the great power that exists in ability to name. The ability to "name" can with one fell swoop, empower or

disempower, can either recognize or dysconsciously ignore. So here, I engage in the empowerment of voice to take personal responsibility for naming in a way that, similar to the First Nations of Canada, makes clear the history of location and precedence. This might seem an insignificant point, hardly worth this lengthy explanation. Yet, it was an indirect experience with the Ku Klux Klan that changed my mind. In a documentary of the KKK from a local network in Indiana, several members identified themselves as "Native Americans." When questioned about this designation, these KKK members proudly stated that they were "born here in the U.S. of A." thereby making them the true "Native Americans." While the thought of sharing such an identity with KKK members is abhorrent, there is yet a second reason. The label "Native American" emerged from the ivory tower, and has been perpetuated by scholars and the "politically correct." Meanwhile, many of the Native Nations for whom this label is supposed to "honor" continue to use their Native Nation affiliation primarily, and secondarily, use either "Indian" or "American Indian." Irrespective of Columbus' navigational error in judgment, it is time to clarify precedent with regards to these lands and who is Indigenous and who is not.

4. While generally age, rank, and department/field are revealed in descriptions of the study sample, women faculty of color are so few at research universities (some being the only woman of color at their rank, at their institution or sometimes in the entire nation, in their respective field) it becomes more necessary to protect their identity, even through such otherwise common descriptors. In the case of this study, agreement to participate by almost all of the women was strongly correlated to my word that I would protect their identity.

5. It is important to note that certain Black male scholars (e.g., DuBois, 1903; Douglass, 1855; Woodson, 1933) were critiquing and deconstructing White generated theories about people of color over half a century ago or longer, although the White theories were not always accompanied by studies at that time.

6. All of the names of the participants are pseudonyms.

7. Italic is used to illustrate the emphasis used by the women in their speech patterns. A long dash is used to indicate a natural pause in their conversation.

References

Allen, P. G. (1988). Who is your mother? Red roots of White feminism. In R. Simonson & S. Walker (Eds.), *Multicultural literacy: opening the American mind* (pp. 13–28). St. Paul: Graywolf Press. (Original work published 1986).

Anzaldúa, G. (1983). La prieta. In C. Moraga & G. Anzaldúa (Eds.), *This bridge called my back: Writings by radical women of color* (pp. 198–209) (2nd ed.). New York: Kitchen Table Women of Color Press.

Anzaldúa, G.(1990). Haciendo caras, una entrada: An introduction. In G. Anzaldúa (Ed.), *Making face, making soul, haciendo caras: Creative and critical perspectives by women of color* (pp. xv–xxviii). San Francisco: An Aunt Lute Foundation Book.

Bannerji, H., Carty, L., Dehli, K., Heald, S. & McKenna, K. (1992). *Unsettling relations: The university as a site of feminist struggles*. Boston: South End Press.

Bernstein, A. & Cock, J. (1994, June 15). A troubling picture of gender equity. *The Chronicle of Higher Education*, B1–B3.

Boyer, E. L. (1990). *Scholarship reconsidered: Priorities of the professoriate.* Princeton: The Carnegie Foundation.

Butler, J. E. (1989). Transforming the curriculum: Teaching about women of color. In J. A. Banks & C. A. McGee Banks (Eds.), *Multicultural education: Issues and perspectives* (pp. 145–164). Boston: Allyn & Bacon.

Caplan, P. J. (1994). *Lifting a ton of feathers: A woman's guide to surviving in the academic world.* Toronto: University of Toronto Press.

Carty, L. (1992). Black women in academia: A statement from the periphery. In H. Bannerji, L. Carty, K. Dehli, S. Heald, & K. McKenna (Eds.), *Unsettling relations: The university as a site of feminist struggles* (pp. 13–44). Boston: South End Press.

Chan, S. & Wang, L. C. (1991). Racism and the model minority: Asian-Americans in higher education. In P. G. Altbach & K. Lomotey (Eds.), *The racial crisis in American higher education* (pp. 43–68). Albany: State University of New York Press.

Davis, A. Y. (1983). *Women, race and class.* New York: Vintage Books. (Original work published 1981).

Dill, B. T. (1987). The dialectics of Black womanhood. In S. Harding (Ed.), *Feminism and methodology* (pp. 97–108). Bloomington: Indiana University Press. (Original work published 1979).

Douglass, F. (1969). *My bondage and my freedom.* New York: Dover Publications, Inc. (Original work published 1855).

DuBois, E. C. & Ruiz, V. L. (1990). Introduction. In E. C. DuBois & V. L. Ruiz (Eds.), *Unequal sisters: A multicultural reader in U.S. women's history* (pp. xi–xvi). New York: Routledge.

DuBois, W.E.B. (1994). *The souls of Black folk.* New York: Gramercy Books. (Original work published 1903).

Ely, M. (1990). *Doing qualitative research: Circles within circles.* New York: Falmer Press.

Farmer, R. (1993). Place but not importance: The race for inclusion in academe. In J. James & R. Farmer (Eds.), *Spirit, space & survival: African American women in (White) academe* (pp. 196–217). New York: Routledge.

Ford Slack, P. J., Rains, F., Collay, M., & Dunlap, D. (1994, April). *Can we rebuild the AERA house using the same old tools? The academic vampire chronicles— chronicle III: A reader's theatre on life in academia.* An "experimental" presentation at American Educational Research Association, New Orleans, LA.

Green, R. (1990). The Pocahontas perplex: The image of Indian women in American culture. In E. C. DuBois & V. L. Ruiz (Eds.), *Unequal sisters: A multicultural reader in U.S. women's history* (pp. 15–21). New York: Routledge. (Original work published 1975)

Green, R. (1992). *Women in American Indian Society.* New York: Chelsea House.

Guba, E. G. & Lincoln, Y. S. (1985). *Naturalistic inquiry.* Beverly Hills: Sage Publications.

Harrison, F. V. (1993). Writing against the grain: Cultural politics of difference in the work of Alice Walker. *Critique of Anthropology, 13*(4), 401–427.

Hill Collins, P. (1986). The emerging theory and pedagogy of black women's studies. *Feminist Issues*, 6, 3–17.

Hill Collins, P. (1990). The social construction of black feminist thought. In M. R. Malson, E. Mudimbe-Boyi, J. F. O'Barr, & M. Wyer (Eds.), *Black women in America: Social science perspectives* (pp. 297–326). Chicago: University of Chicago Press (original work published 1989).

Hill Collins, P. (1991). *Black feminist thought: Knowledge, consciousness, and the politics of empowerment.* New York: Routledge.

hooks, b. (1981). *Ain't I a woman: Black women and feminism.* Boston: South End Press.

Hull, G. T. & Smith, B. (1982). Introduction: The politics of Black women's studies. In G. T. Hull, P. B. Scott, & B. Smith (Eds.), *All the women are White, all the Blacks are men, but some of us are brave: Black women's studies* (pp. xvii–xxxi). New York: The Feminist Press.

King, D. K. (1990). Multiple jeopardy, multiple consciousness: The context of a Black feminist ideology. In M. R. Malson, E. Mudimbe-Boyi, J. F. O'Barr, & M. Wyer (Eds.), *Black women in America: Social science perspectives* (pp. 265–296). Chicago: The University of Chicago Press. (Original work published 1988).

King, J. E. (1991, Spring). Dysconscious racism: Ideology, identity, and the miseducation of teachers. *The Journal of Negro Education*, 60(2), 133–146.

LeCompte, M. D.& Preissle, J. (1993). *Ethnography and qualitative design in educational research: Second edition.* San Diego: Academic Press, Inc.

Lewis, D. K. (1990). A response to inequality: Black women, racism, and sexism. In M. R. Malson, E. Mudimbe-Boyi, J. F. O'Barr, & M. Wyer (Eds.), *Black women in America: Social science perspectives* (pp. 41–64). Chicago: The University of Chicago Press. (Original work published 1977).

Lorde, A. (1984). Age, race, class, and sex: Women redefining difference. In A. Lorde (Ed.), *Sister outsider: Essays and speeches* (pp. 114–123). Freedom, CA: The Crossing Press Feminist Series. (Original work published 1980).

Madrid, A. (1992). Missing people and others: Joining together to expand the circle. In M. Andersen & P. H. Collins (Eds.). *Race, class, and gender: An anthology* (pp. 6–11). Belmont, CA: Wadsworth Publishing Company.

McIntosh, P. (1992). White privilege and male privilege: A personal account of coming to see correspondences through work in Women's Studies. In M. L. Andersen & P. Hill Collins (Eds.), *Race, class, and gender: An anthology* (pp. 70–81). Belmont, CA: Wadsworth Publishing Company.

Merriam, S. B. (1988). *Case study research in education: A qualitative approach.* San Francisco: Jossey-Bass Publishers.

Padilla, A. M. (1994). Ethnic minority scholars, research, and mentoring: Current and future issues. *Educational Researcher* 23(4), 24–27.

Parker, K. (1986). Ideas, affirmative action and the ideal university. *Nova Law Journal*, 10, 761–778.

Patai, D. (1991, October 30). Minority status and the stigma of 'surplus visibility'. *Chronicle of Higher Education*, A 52.

Pérez, L. E. (1993). Opposition and the education of Chicana/os. In C. McCarthy & W. Crichlow (Eds.), *Race, identity, and representation in education* (pp. 268–279). New York: Routledge.

Pollard, D. S. (1990). Black women, interpersonal support, and institutional change. In J. Antler & S. K. Biklen (Eds.), *Changing Education: Women as radicals and conservators,* (pp. 257–276). Albany: State University of New York Press.

Pollard, D. S. (1997, March). Breaking glass in multiple places. The 1997 Willystine Goodsell Address. Presented at the American Educational Research Association, Chicago, IL. *Research on women and education newsletter, August 1997,* 8–11.

Public Broadcasting Service (1997, January 9–12). *Shattering the silences.* [documentary video on faculty of color in research universities].

Rains, F. V. (1995). *Views from within: Women faculty of color in a research university.* Unpublished doctoral dissertation, Indiana University, Bloomington.

Rains, F. V. (1996 a, Spring). Holding up a mirror to White privilege: Deconstructing the maintenance of the status quo. *Taboo: The Journal of Culture and Education, 1,* 75–92.

Rains, F. V. (1996b, April). The struggle to maintain who I am. In J. Cooper & M. Benham (Co-Chairs), *Ha'awina No'ono'o [The Sharing of Thoughts]: The Professional Stories of Diverse Women in Academia.* Interactive symposium conducted at the meeting of the American Educational Research Association, New York.

Rains, F. V. (1997, February). *Squaws, princesses, and the power of "myths:" Indigenous women held hostage by entangled ignorances.* Paper presentation at Talking Across the Disciplines: A Feminist Symposium, University of Colorado at Boulder.

Reyes, M. de la L. & Halcón, J. J. (1990). Racism in academia: The old wolf revisited. In N. M. Hidalgo, C. L. McDowell, & E. V. Siddle (Eds.), *Facing racism in education* (pp. 69–83). Harvard Educational Review. Reprint Series #21.

Reyes, M. de la L. & Halcón, J. J. (1991). Practices of the academy: Barriers to access for Chicano academics. In P. G. Altbach & K. Lomotey (Eds.), *The racial crisis in American higher education* (pp. 167–186). Albany: State University of New York Press.

Reyes, M. de la L. (1994, b, April). *Interrupting racism and sexism: White women, women of color and the preparation of teachers.* Paper symposium presented at the annual meeting of the American Educational Research Association, New Orleans, LA.

Sandler, B. & Hall, R. M. (1986). *The campus climate revisited: Chilly for women faculty, administrators, and graduate students.* Washington: Association of American Colleges.

Scheurich, J. J. (1993, November). Toward a white discourse on white racism. *Educational Researcher,* 5–10.

Touchton, J. G. & Davis, L. (1991). *Fact book on women in higher education.* New York: American Council on Education and Macmillan Publishing Company.

Trask, H. K. (1993). Racism against native Hawaiians at the University of Hawai'i: A personal and political view. In H. K. Trask [Ed.], *From a native daughter: Colonialism and sovereignty in Hawai'i* (pp. 201–224). Monroe, ME: Common Courage Press.

Trinh-Minh Ha, T. (1989). *Woman, native, other: Writing postcoloniality and feminism.* Bloomington, IN: Indiana University Press.

Washington, V. & Harvey, W. (1989). *Affirmative rhetoric, negative action: African-American and Hispanic faculty at predominantly White institutions.* ASHE-ERIC Higher Education Research Report no. 2. Washington: School of Education and Human Development, George Washington University.

Williams, P. J. (1991a). *The alchemy of race and rights: Diary of a law professor.* Cambridge: Harvard University Press.

Williams, P. J. (1991, September/October). Blockbusting the canon. *Ms.*, *2*(2), 59–63.

Wilson, R. (1989). Women of color in academic administration: Trends, progress and barriers. *Sex Roles, 21*(1/2) 85–97.

Woodson, C. G. (1933). *The mis-education of the Negro.* [reprinted] Philadelphia: Hakim's Publications.

Yamada, M. (1983). Invisibility is an unnatural disaster: Reflections of an Asian American woman. In C. Moraga & G. Anzaldúa (Eds.), *This bridge called my back: Writings by radical women of color* (pp. 35–40) (2nd ed.). New York: Kitchen Table Women of Color Press.

Yellin, J. F. (1982). Afro-American women, 1800–1910: Excerpts from a working bibliography. In G.T . Hull, P. B. Scott, & B. Smith (Eds.), *All the women are White, all the Blacks are men, but some of us are brave: Black women's studies* (pp. 221–244). New York: The Feminist Press.

Zinn, M. B., Cannon, L. W., Higginbotham, E., & Dill, B. T. (1990). The costs of exclusionary practices in women's studies. In G. Anzaldúa (Ed.), *Making face, making soul, haciendo caras: Creative and critical perspectives by women of color* (pp. 29–41). San Francisco: An Aunt Lute Foundation Book.

10 Negotiating Daily Life in the Academy and at Home

Jean I. Erdman

Introduction

As I was reading Sue Middleton's work, I found myself living out her thoughts about taking on too much administrative responsibility, about the daily demands of mothering, and about the "sometimes terrified vulnerability that comes from public confessions." It is the end of a semester, and as faculty are leaving for winter break, I continue to complete academic/bureaucratic tasks, while thinking of home and wondering whether I should have sent my eleven-year-old to school today rather than allowing him to stay home with a sore throat.

Kristine Kellor reminds us that all discourse is dangerous, and that issues of self, identity, representation and relations of power in the academy are intertwined. We name ourselves through life writings in order to survive. Anger, resistance and discomfort, and excesses of meaning are part of the crisis of witnessing. These words quiet my fears about going public with my poems.

Administrative work in the academy and parenthood have gotten easier, with experience in the roles of department chair and master's program coordinator, with numerous progressive changes on my campus, and with the entry of my younger child into elementary school. Most of the poems to follow were drafted a few years ago.

I share these poems for the comfort and solace that an audience of readers provides. The poems are not intended as a lack of gratitude for the privilege of working in higher education. This week I read in the local paper of another local factory being sold—none of the workers will retain their seniority, job security or benefits. I recognize also the privilege

175

of middle class motherhood. The poetic, including that which is critical, can comfort and inspire us toward something better for ourselves and others.

People Should Be in Their Offices

"People should be in their offices
What would it be like here
If everybody had a two day week?"

> *"But, but, but . . .*
> *everybody has not written 3 books and 14 articles."*
> *If they do*
> *Then they have a two day teaching schedule."*

"But what would it be like
if everybody had a two day week?"

"I remember when Sarah Willard was here
She used to not want 8:00 classes
And her boys were big enough to hit a bear with a stick.
What would it be like if all of us with kids
Refused to teach at 8:00?"

> *"I don't know how it was at your house?*
> *But at my house*
> *My husband is up and out the door*
> *He does not worry about the kids*
> *I'm in charge of the kids."*

"What if everybody
Refused to teach at 8:00?
People should be in their offices
What would it be like here
if everybody had a two day week?"

> *"But, but, but . . .*
> *everybody has not written 3 books and 14 articles."*
> *If they do*
> *Then they have a two day teaching schedule."*

"But what would it be like
if everybody had a two day week?

I remember when Sarah Willard was here
She used to not want 8:00 classes
And her boys were big enough to hit a bear with a stick.
What would it be like if all of us with kids
Refused to teach at 8:00?"

> *"I don't know how it was at your house?*
> *But at my house*
> *My husband is up and out the door*
> *He does not worry about the kids*
> *I'm in charge of the kids."*

"What if everybody
Refused to teach at 8:00?"

> *But everybody doesn't . . .*
> *The inability and refusal to particularize*
> *The advocacy of an authoritarian stance*

"You tell people when they will teach.
You can't always listen to faculty.
You tell them when to meet."

> *"But the department is meeting*
> *When I want*
> *Faculty are being very cooperative."*

"Oh.
You are going to be criticized
Down the road
Other people would like a two day teaching schedule."

> *Wearily I listen*
> *Afterward I anguish*
> *About the sexism of only women scholars*
> *Cited as problems.*

> *I respond*
> *"But if we have to be here every day*
> *Then no more coming in to the office*
> *Turning on the lights*
> *and disappearing for three hours.*
> *And no more male faculty being permitted*

For years, to hold another full time job
With nobody commenting."

My friend from Turkey
Gets the racism
How is the search committee going?
I suppose you think we need colored women
To straighten us out?
I got a call from a black consultant
telling us what we could do for migrant workers
I remember Sarah Wilson
Going out west of here
Getting the migrants all riled up.
Give them a job and a place to stay
That's enough.
Hopefully times are different now.

"You tell people when they will teach.
You can't always listen to faculty.
You tell them when to meet."

"But the department is meeting
When I want
Faculty are being very cooperative."

"Oh.
You are going to be criticized
Down the road
Other people would like a two day teaching schedule."

Wearily I listen
Afterward I anguish
About the sexism of only women scholars
Cited as problems.

I respond
But if we have to be here every day
Then no more coming in to the office
Turning on the lights
and disappearing for three hours.
And no more male faculty being permitted
For years, to hold another full time job
With nobody commenting.

My friend from Cypress
Gets the racism.
"How is the search committee going?
I suppose you think we need colored women
To straighten us out?
I got a call from a black consultant
telling us what we could do for migrant workers
I remember Sarah Willard
Going out west of here
Getting the migrants all riled up.
Give them a job and a place to stay
That's enough."

  Hopefully times are different now.
  We commiserate, my friends
  And postulate our replies
  To verbal racism, sexism
  And I am struck by how
  the telling of these memories
  and assertions of these biases
  As universal
  Is not that different.
  Than the name calling discourse of the rightest commentators
  On CNN, mouthing that PBS
  Is a feminist, gay rights liberal, prowelfare forum.

We commiserate, my friends
And postulate our replies
To verbal racism, sexism
And I am struck by how
the telling of these memories
and assertions of these biases
As universal
Is not that different.
Than the name calling discourse of the rightest commentators
On CNN, mouthing that PBS
Is a feminist, gay rights liberal, prowelfare forum.

Evidence and data to the contrary
Are not the point.
Evidence is beyond the horizons of a worldview
That interprets differing views as
equivalent to a balkanized society

They remain unable to converse.
I have known for sometime of struggle
Of its ongoing and recurring necessity
And certainly the struggle wearies me
As my anxiety surfaces me awake at 4 a.m.
Three to four times a week.

But there is at least
The "yeah buts," the counter evidence
There was before too, I'm sure
From folks who have left here
And others silenced and not so silenced.

Gone through retirement is the person
Who joshed—"You can't have off,
even if it is a Jewish holiday."
And I replied laughingly,
"Emil, No, no, no—
You can't do that."
To the gratitude of my Jewish colleague.
Was it good that I laughed away the anti-Semitism.
Maybe we should hit the discrimination harder
To hell with face-saving
Yet, that's not right
I need cooperation from these guys
And humiliation never feels good.
I have shied away from directness much of my life
Raised to be quiet
Middle child syndrome too
Shy personality, working class modesty
In my background.

I'm getting better
At directness
But I have so far, so far to go
And I'm not sure I'll get anywhere
In higher ed, minimal in its progressive stretch
But perhaps I can make some differences within
Create some wiggle room and win small victories.

I do worry that I'll be frazzled into
Days of interruptedness
Perhaps as long as I am appalled by

"What if everybody . . . " as a line of reasoning
By "You tell people. . . ."
By lack of imagination and control as purpose
And as long as I read and write perhaps . . .

The bottom line is that
is having the seat of your pants
in the seat of your chair
cannot be
the main criteria
for doing
your job.

And others silenced and not so silenced.
Gone through retirement is the person
Who joshed—"You can't have off,
even if it is a Jewish holiday."
And I replied laughingly,
Emil, No, no, no—
You can't do that."
To the gratitude of my Jewish colleague.
Was it good that I laughed away the anti-Semitism.
Maybe we should hit the discrimination harder
To hell with face-saving.

Thoughts on Worrying

I suppose it's hard to give up the worry
A part of who I am
My retrieval process for remembering
The responsibilities of this year's days of life
Easy to forget
That so much is mundane
That people count
That caring for others
That time for myself is a gift
An elliptical slippage
Back into the why am I I? am I I?
am I I? Of my childhood thoughts.

Emerging to consciousness
I think I may be glimpsing

What and who will be me after death
What will count and confront me
At that white light time
Of transcending the body
Into an elusive, nondiscursive
Love of oneness
And I hope
of less worrying.

Patches of Gold Are My Friends

In the midst of a crisis
in the academy
I have discovered
What friends can mean.

I phone Sharon at 9:30 p.m.
Filled with anxiety and stress
Seeking I'm not sure what
Advice, solace, comradery
From this woman from New York
Misplaced here in small town middle America
Seen by some as crazy, at least angry and over the edge . . .

We meet for lunch.
I visit her at home
And I discover
An activist of courage, fighting successfully
Against sexual harassment of female students by professors
And faculty advisor of the campus gay activist student group.

The pale cabbage roses wallpaper
Envelop a home rich with photos of past generations
She is strong, interrupting our conversation
For a phone call with a therapist for her adult step-daughter
Taking care of others
Living on the edge herself.

I find myself in good company.
Sitting on the tan couch
with a gold striped afghan

Staring at the plant stand
of a half dozen purple African violets
Just like my mother's mother grew.

Then there is Betty
My retired partner from teaching teachers to write
project at the university
I walk to her ranch home three blocks away
Her "worst" language for colleagues who miss the point
Is the term "dolt."

Betty taught me to focus my teaching
And to remain calm
She listens amid queries
As I pour out the mishaps
of work conflict.

Back to Sharon
Who informs me
That women who take on the system
are "demonized"
I'm not offended
Physically I'm not big enough
to fill up this term
Which gives me lots of space
Suddenly I feel better.

Julie
My telephone solace
I call after the kids are asleep
She reassures me that everyone
Is not talking about me
That life goes on
That retirements of colleagues will help
As I know will the passage of time.

And so
I have brought women friends
Back into my being
Soul mates
Lost during the first seven
years of motherhood
For lack of time.

These friends are
Hidden patches of gold
Conversations with them
help me
Chip away
at the ineptitude
that fosters
blind-eyed
patriarchy.

A Day in the Life

A day in the life
Something more mundane
than the backdrop political drama
Of Solzhenitsyn's Iven Denisovitch.
Unlike this prisoner, I
Have chosen this department chair work
Yet its intensification
Leaves me sometimes
With the frustration of the hours
of my precollege summer job.
I spent days cutting 700 wire gadgets an hour
They were parts for tv tuners
A gadget, which no longer exists.
Remember changing the channel
By turning the knob
Manually and not from the couch?

The point is, the work just keeps coming
The tasks pile up
And I either work on the tasks
or they bury me
Psychologically
The papers that obscure my desk
Are physical evidence
Of work to do.

I imagine waves washing in
A big one across the Atlantic sunny ocean sand

My long life of much work and few breaks
Brightened by the ocean vacations
Norfolk Beach and Sarasota
I walked the beach , hopping in the waves
Having a blast digging shells
With my five year old—fun!
We surreptitiously bring home a clothes basketful of shells
Bags of them tucked into each piece of luggage
My husband wondering why the suitcases were heavier.

They say negative ions in the salt air are good
for the spirit – something physiological
Must be but it can't hurt
That the paper work can't reach me
At the ocean.
We don't have an answering machine
And don't want one.
Do people really want to return calls?
Not me—a piece of my life for peace
For family—bad enough that my work
Psychologically preoccupies my thoughts
Even when I'm with the kids
Worse to have to bring outsiders
Home.

The undertow of work flow
Wreeks havoc with my emotions
A phone call, 3 documents to study
Fifteen minutes with a secretary
Two more phone calls to undo those three wasted hours
Because somebody else failed
To write down a policy.
An oral culture
Doesn't work.
It leaves no record
And drives me to distraction
To ten minute ranting sessions
With a work sister
Or with my mentor
Also a work sister.

We are all caught in bureaucratic rules
Somewhat of our own making.

I do wonder, as we live out
The effects of additive and addictive reform
And of its flight from purpose
What are we about?

We hope for more democratic action
Located in communities and classrooms
We critique external standards and accountability
As facades for busy work distract us from
Humane administering and teaching relations.

I pursue problem-solving
Six curriculum modifications
For students
Two students get registration help
A memo to move 12 students to an open course section
Reading scholarship information
To prepare to select winners
Reading candidate folders for jobs.

More, more, more!
Seeking advice on resolving
Directions given to a novice professor
Put it in writing or just yell
Dilemmas.
I take them to bed with me at night.
Tomorrow is another chance
I bet.

The Allure of Little Stuff

I could write about psychological
wearout, overall fatigue
About the after effects of
too much being busy
Of shuffling papers, taking phone calls
crossing tasks off my list
I could write about a three-page
to do list
About cleaning my office out of
desperation
A last excuse not to tackle the
hard stuff

The mountain of undone big tasks.

Now I understand why the little
urgencies
Get done
And the important stuff sits
A response to wearout
and the demand and high of
closure
and gratification
For solving a little problem.

The big stuff sits.

Time to rethink.
The job.

Part Time Staff in the Academy

The university women and men, mostly women
who are "ad hoc" staff
The phrase perniciously itself
Conveying temporariness,
an after thought, catch as catch can
In whose jobs title does not follow function
Whose base salaries are 25 to 40% less than faculty . . .
Whose labor is further intensified
By 15 rather than 12 credit hour teaching loads
who cannot vote and
whose efforts are disparaged by comments
We have "too many ad hoc"
Thoughtless remarks, intended to gain resources
Heard by "ad hoc" staff as disparaging
Of their mammoth and sincere efforts
To serve students well-

We delude ourselves.
thinking that faculty
Immersed in all the politics of bureaucracies
Entrenched and poorly led always teach better.
The issue is exploitation more than quality.
This little stuff that absorbs my thoughts is not small.

Solitude

Lack of solitude
Something academic women without young children
Find time to write about
As academic women with young children awaken
at 4:00 A.M., awake 'til 5
to garner space
time for the soul
time to think.
To grasp multiple identities
to resist total positionings
As mother, wife,
bureaucrat.

Bureaucracy smothers
attempts and stabs at
intellectual time
And crunches family and personal time.

Contradictions abound
obscuring the solitude.

Such as "how come
I am now working part-time
And have more
University committee work
Than ever before?"

The work will be there tomorrow
And the next day
Right now I need to savor—
Solitude.

Solitude garnered in the night
But not alone
As my son asks for one more book read aloud before
(hopefully and finally)
falling asleep
While
The baby is sleeping.

4:00 A.M. may be

My only chance
For solitude.

Late Night Phone Call

A running chronology
of painful work events
that only my mother
can be imposed upon
to listen to
on the phone
for nearly two hours.

I hope that
my kids
will not need
my listening ear
for two hours
when they are in their forties.

But if they do
I hope that I
will have
the good
sense
to listen.

11

Feeling Blue, Seeing Red, and Turning Fifty: Moving in from the Margins

Sue Middleton

Thursday, November 14, 1996

I take yet another sip of ginger and lemon (non-caffeinated herbal) tea. Americans pronounce it 'erbal, don't they. I have to think and write American again—a slightly foreign tongue—after months of writing 'naturally' for New Zealand audiences. I look again at this book's prospectus, and at the editors' letter to me way back in May: "We are familiar with your book *Educating feminists: Life-histories and pedagogy*.... perhaps you could select a portion of the book which you could expand and refocus." But that was written in 1991 and published in 1993. Since then many dimensions of my life have been radically transformed—by shifts at the level of national politics; by institutional restructuring; by the computer technology revolution; by the life-cycle and bodily changes of 'later mid-life;' and—enmeshed in all of these—I have moved in new directions in my research, teaching, administration and wider political strategies . . . This paper deconstructs my writing since 1992 by making visible the circumstances in which it has come to form—historical, political, geographical, technological, cultural, discursive, institutional, generational, familial, emotional . . .

I shall use this invitation as an opportunity to experiment with style. Daily diary entries—temporal fragmentations—cut across the apparent linearity that normally characterizes academic discourse. The disciplined sequencing of argument is further interrupted by anarchic intrusions of emotions, memories, fantasies, and dreams. And I bring to the center of my reasoning my 'foreignness' with the aim of unsettling much that is taken for granted by those from the North.

Revisiting Old Texts and Creating New Ones

A salient theme in my work—as teacher, as researcher/writer, and as academic administrator and political strategist—has been to seek a harmony between medium and message (McLuhan, 1964); form and content; overt and covert (or hidden) curricula; to "practice what I preach." In earlier work, I explored the biographical and contextual processes and settings in which were generated the theoretical underpinnings of my (post-World War Two-born) generation of feminists and critical educational theorists/activists (Middleton, 1992a; 1993a, 1993b; 1995). In *Educating Feminists*, I summarized these:

> Many of us—today's feminist and socialist educators—are children of parents from the working or lower middle classes, of ethnic/cultural minority backgrounds, and from rural areas or small towns . . . such students—especially those who were the first in their families to attend institutions of higher education—often felt marginalised within them. My generation's radical sociological and/or feminist perspectives on education had been at least partly theorizations of our experiences of marginality or alienation within it although—as individuals who were to become academically successful—we had sufficient 'cultural capital' . . . to enable this marginalisation to become the basis of an intellectual critique rather than of educational withdrawal or failure. The simultaneous experiences of marginality and the economic circumstances of full employment and teacher shortages created in many Western educationists who had been students in the 1960s and early 1970s a sense of both the desirability and the possibility of progressive or radical educational and social change (Middleton, 1993b, pp. 4–5).

In contrast, of the early 1990s I wrote: "Today, as a university teacher in the 1990s, I watch my students and my daughter moving into adulthood in times of economic recession and despair" (Middleton, 1993b, p. 1):

> Our responses to the New Right have been more than mere intellectualizations. They are underpinned by deep feelings of outrage and loss. The kinds of social-democratic collectivism or socialism that are being attacked and dismantled had characterized the educational and social policies that had made possible for many of us, our own educations and careers. We now see for our children's generation the erosion of such possibilities (Middleton, 1993b, p. 5).

Reading that four years later, I am struck by the strong emotions simmering beneath the surface, and the binary opposition between the 'good life' of the 1960s–70s and the 'bad things happening' in the early 1990s. In the 1960s–early 1970s, although the aspiring educators of my age-group "felt marginalized" and had experienced alienation, we sublimated these into intellectual critiques. It was a positive time of "full employment" which fostered our "sense of both the desirability and the possibility of progressive or radical educational and social change." In contrast, I characterized our experiences of early 1990s politics by "deep feelings of outrage and loss"; the cocoon of social democracy which had nurtured us was being "attacked and dismantled" and we saw an "erosion of possibilities" for our children. *Educating Feminists* was centered around a question posed by Maxine Greene (1986, p. 440): "what might a critical pedagogy mean for those of us who teach the young at this peculiar and menacing time?"

For some, this question has been addressed by means of critiques of educational, and wider social, restructuring and giving students access to these. Yet, as Erica McWilliam (1995, p. 68) points out, "Critical teacher educators are increasingly perceived as conveying little more than a litany of complaints about the very sort of contemporary practice student teachers have to imitate." Like her, I would describe my "overwhelming concern" as "helping my students to understand the power relations in which teachers work without being defeated by them" (McWilliam, 1995, p. 134) . . . Sudden silence as the Ronnie Jordan CD on the CDROM player on my computer ends . . . I select an old Miles Davis—something without words to interrupt my thoughts . . .

In order to subvert the hegemony of undiluted rationalism—to allow emotion to erupt through its cracks and contradictions—feminist writers have attempted simultaneously to construct and to deconstruct our own perspectives by making visible our everyday lives. This chapter affords me an opportunity to continue my experiments with textual collages and counterpoint (Middleton, 1992a, 1993a, 1993b; 1995). Once more, I am creating at times outrageous splicings. I am grateful for what Madeleine Grumet (1988) has referred to as "the promise of word processing" (p. 146)—a technology that encourages intertextuality. It has made practicable my collations and juxtapositions of diverse media . . . orchestrations of multiple voices (Middleton, 1993a, p. 177–178).

As Madeleine Grumet (1988, p. 46) has argued, the word processor "invites us to use multiple texts, splicing them, interweaving them with each other, with our commentaries, with our questions." While writing *Educating Feminists* in 1991, I was resisting "having a modem or a fax" in my home office and feared that these would bring "technological intrusions into my privacy, my space" (Middleton, 1993a, p. 7). Instead, my beloved new 'Power Mac' has taught me the joys of what Dale Spender (1995) has referred to as "nattering on the net," and has opened up new possibilities in transgressive, collaborative, writing. With its help we can explore how e-mail can be used to create dialogues and pastiches (Middleton, 1996a; Middleton & Summers-Bremner, 1997) . . . double click on Interslip, brr brr the dial tone, squeal as it connects; open Eudora, 'check mail' . . .

> Date: Fri, 14 Nov 1996 16:06:06 GMT+1300
> From: Alison Jones [a.jones@auckland.ac.nz]
> Subject: email and you
> To: educ_mid@waikato.ac.nz
> Organization: University of Auckland
> Priority: normal

> Sue—This morning I have been able to check out a response to a student's work from an examiner in Singapore, talk to a colleague in Dunedin who asked me to look over a paper she is preparing for publication, arrange a meeting with someone in Brisbane, rave madly with someone else in London about the impossibilities of being an academic woman at forty-something taking on too much administrative responsibility, and talk to a student about her latest draft. (They were the pleasurable interactions, there were others of the more boring sort.) All on the beloved email! What about you and me? We couldn't have the immediate academic relationship and friendship we have if it were not for the possibilities of words rushing through cyberspace right to where you sit for most of the day. That's a neat snapshot of how I feel about email at this moment. Best, A

Tired, I spend the next hour or so clearing the less interesting messages.

Friday, November 15, 1996

A stormy Friday. Too wet to go out for my early morning walk . . . Coffee in hand, I shall tackle theory now, when I feel fresh . . .

A Materialist Girl

(with apologies to Madonna . . .) Like a number of other feminist curriculum theorists, historians, and sociologists of women's education (Arnot & Weiler, 1993; Weiner, 1994; Weiler, 1988; Yates, 1993), I have come to identify my theoretical and methodological orientation as 'feminist materialist'—a blending of Marxist historical materialism, socialist feminism, the structuralisms and phenomenologies which coalesced in the 1970s as the 'new' sociology of education, and Foucaultian versions of post-structuralism. To be consistent with this position, this paper must demonstrate the methodology it espouses. "[M]aterialist feminist theory embraces the authority of its narratives in the knowledge that its mode of reading, like any new practice, is *in* history and so provisional, always circulating in a field of contesting discourses that challenge and redefine its horizons" (Hennessey, 1993, p. 138).

This paper too is 'in history'—has been 'interpolated,' or 'hailed' into existence (Althusser, 1971) at a specific moment. It is brought into being within the international capitalist relations which produce academic texts (including critical feminist ones such as this); by the academic power relations which both constrain and make possible the form and content of what may be written for such texts; by the circumstances within the United States which enabled the editors of this text to initiate it and to invite me to contribute; and by the local and particular conditions within New Zealand that provide me with the opportunity to write it and with the 'content' of what I am writing.

In 1993, New Zealanders voted for a revolutionary change in our political constitution—from the 'first past the post' Westminster system of party government to a German-style (MMP) Mixed Member Proportional system. The first MMP election was held on October 12, 1996 and, as I write, the splintered, multiple and overlapping fragments of what once was a neat two party (right/left) binary, jostle for position and coalitions. The modernist 'left-right' binary doesn't fit our fluid coalitions of the late 1990s . . .

At the institutional level, the parts of the University of Waikato in which I work have been restructured. The teachers' college and the university have amalgamated to form the School of Education and the former dominance of 'theory over practice' in the B Ed degree is being overturned. As, in Basil Bernstein's terms (1971) interdisciplinarity ('integrated knowledge codes') is made difficult by the imposition of neoliberal/rationalist agendas of accountability. University administration has been devolved in ways which force departments and faculties to compete against one another for students (the reimposition of what Bernstein called the 'collection knowledge code'). The once trans-faculty women's studies program has become more tightly bounded and encapsulated within the School of Social Sciences in which it is forced to compete for students against the 'other' departments with feminist courses which once gave birth to and sustained the program (Middleton, 1987).

And, at a personal level, I have been promoted to an academic management position, started and completed a major research project, and am in the process of reviewing and redirecting my teaching priorities. The daily demands of mothering are behind me—my daughter, Kate (who, at age fourteen, had small walk-on parts in *Educating Feminists*), is about to turn twenty and is now overseas in New York. I have had a hysterectomy. I turn fifty on July 31, 1997 . . . I am momentarily distracted by the unseasonable early summer gale outside my study window. I am glad I can stay inside. Teaching for the academic year has ended, my grades are at the Registry, and I am on study leave for the summer—until February 1, there is time at home to write and reflect . . .

I pause to read what I have just written. I note my use of 'here' and 'there'—that I am positioning my American readers as outside my New Zealand horizon, resisting the temptation to reach out across the vast Pacific Ocean to address 'them' as 'you', and thereby to embrace 'them' in the 'we', as I did in my 'American book', *Educating Feminists* (Middleton, 1993b). That book was designed to court, to seduce, an American audience. Now that many Americans are used to reading my work, I want 'them' ('you') to experience the way 'we' (New Zealanders and others of the 'South') are positioned in/by what count as key texts, to write for once spontaneously 'from the center' instead of self-consciously 'from the margins' . . .

From on the Margins of in the Middle

I am one of those women who "are tired of researching and politicizing their marginality. Women of all colors, it seems to me, want to take charge of the rules and of those discourses that define center and margin, insider and outsider, ruler and ruled . . . . instead of the more common, largely ineffective feminine strategies of consensual negotiations, subtle persuasions, and silent postcards from the edge" (Luke, 1994, p. 227). We have found that to experience, research and theorize marginalities is to face the contradictions of being positioned simultaneously 'inside and outside'— and, as David Harvey (1990, p. 345) has expressed it, "the exploration of contradictions always lies at the heart of original thought." Much as I have tried in this paper to get away from the theme of marginalities, it continues to structure my thoughts, and to generate strong emotions—anger, resentment, grief, stubbornness. . . . I like Carmen Luke's image of 'postcards from the edge', but mine will be anything but silent . . .

I glance back at the abstract which I wrote for the editors of this volume on June 15, 1996—so long ago—and read from what I wrote then:

> Since 1992, when my university and the local teachers' college amalgamated, the School of Education has had a predominantly female faculty and a feminist woman dean. Over 90% of the students are women and they have access to feminist courses in Education and on the campus more generally. Within this new environment, I have been promoted into a senior academic rank and a middle-management administrative role. As a senior

feminist academic, who teaches feminist courses, does feminist research, and writes feminist books in a predominantly female environment, am I still in any way 'on the margins' of academia?

I have been an academic since 1980. I now hold the rank of Associate Professor (Reader). Our nomenclature follows the British—not the American—model. In 1994, 8.2% of the Associate Professors were women and 7.6% of the Professors (Wilson, 1995). In keeping with international trends (Acker, 1995; Bagilhole, 1993), as one proceeds 'down' the hierarchy of seniority, the proportion of women increases. Predictably, the most female-intensive Schools (our word for Faculties) are Education and Humanities/Social Sciences. My own School of Education has 105 staff holding positions of .5 and above—58 women and 47 men. There are 3 professors (2 male plus the female dean); 3 Associate Profs (myself plus 2 men); 45 Senior Lecturers (18 women and 27 men); and 50 Lecturers (34 women and 16 men).

I am now in 'middle-management.' My present position has two components. For 0.2 of my time, I am Assistant Dean (Graduate Studies). In this capacity I represent the School on four University committees, and am also on nine School committees. I am responsible for the development of the School's graduate programs and structure; for advising graduate students with respect to their programs, for writing information, and recruitment. To apply for this position was a conscious choice—I wanted a cross-departmental policy position rather than to be a departmental chair, which would have involved me in competition with other departments for scarce resources. Now I don't believe in a 'woman's way of leading', but . . . . The other .8 of me is a member of the Education Studies Department—and it is that .8 which does teaching and research . . .

MEMO
Sunday, October 20, 1996
TO: Director, Personnel and Management Services
FROM: Sue Middleton
Dear Sir:
This is in response to your memo of October 17 announcing "a deduction of half a day's salary from salary payment due 14 November." You have asked me (and presumably all AUS [union] members), "If you did not strike, and met your normal employment responsibilities, there will be no salary deduction provided that you give notice in writing through the office of your dean etc. . . . "
As a member of AUS I abided by the collective decision of my union and spent the morning of Wednesday October 9 in industrial action, so I am not seeking to be treated any differently from my fellow union members. However, there are assumptions in your memo which I wish to challenge . . . .

The assumption I am questioning is the concept of "half a day's salary." I note from my pay slip that my salary is seen as remuneration for 75 hours a fortnight, which translates to 37.5 hours per week. The assumption in your phrase "If you did not strike, and met your normal employment responsibilities" is that those of us who went on strike did less than the 75 hours that we are required to do.

You will see from the attached time sheet that in fact I worked 114 hours that fortnight: 58 hours in the week of October 7 and 56 in the week of October 14. If I am employed to work a 75 hour fortnight, and if my pay is calculated by the hour or half-day, then it would seem reasonable for me to regard the university as owing me 39 hours of overtime. One could, then, well argue that, in your words, I have "not met my normal employment responsibilities"— but, rather, have exceeded them by 52% . . .

. . . I feel angry again re-reading that . . . I decide not to include the 'timesheets' in this paper . . . My neck stiffens. I've been sitting here rather rigidly for too long. Breathe in, stick tailbone back into the chair, breathe out . . . out . . . out . . . look at the ceiling . . . open mouth . . . out . . . Feldenkrais postural techniques to prevent the recurrence of neck pain and tendonitis in my 'mouse arm' (OOS they call it—Occupational Overuse Syndrome—they don't call it RSI any more) . . . I wonder if/ when I'll be able to play my digital keyboard again. I can no longer write and play piano—too much stress on my back; too much sitting—it's computer or piano, but not both. Sequential monogamy . . . But I will play again when the book is complete . . . 6:30—time for *Restoration*, a movie at our new Art House cinema. We walk there in the summer twilight.

Saturday, November 16, 1996

An early morning start. Piles of journals on the cork-tiled floor of my home office—in preparation for this paper, I've reviewed some recent writing by and about academic women. Much of it focuses on marginalities—on women's under representation in positions of power in academic hierarchies (Bagilhole, 1993; West & Lyon, 1995); on the exclusion, trivialisation or distortion of women's experiences and perspectives in male-centered disciplines (Aisenberg & Harrington, 1988); and on feminist struggles to create, and clear spaces for, women-centered sets of knowledges and pedagogies (Maher & Tetreault, 1994). There are analyses of how women's (particularly feminists') marginalisation in universities may be affected by 'New Right' governments' policies (Acker, 1994, 1995). A rapidly-growing body of post-structuralist work has deconstructed the homogenizing term 'woman' to explore how— within feminist academic knowledges and pedagogies—the unequal opportunities and visibilities between women of different social classes, races/cultures, sexualities, body shapes, and beliefs are reproduced (Luke & Gore, 1992). Like critical pedagogy and other discourses of empowerment and emancipation, feminist theories and pedagogies are increasingly being studied as technologies of surveillance and normalization which privilege some students and ideas and marginalise others (Luke & Gore, 1992; McWilliam, 1995).

When I received the invitation to write this paper, my first instinct was to add to these discussions about marginality by writing about the peculiar marginalising experiences created by my circumstances as a Pakeha (white) New Zealander reading and writing in the international forums and networks of 'education feminism' (Stone, 1994). I glance at the abstract which I wrote for the editors of this volume on six months ago—and read what I wrote then:

> To become available and to be given status and credibility locally, my research and writing must pass through the filters of an academic discipline (education studies) which is configured by the economic, political and cultural relations of international capitalism. In particular, American conferences, journals, and book publishers structure the possibilities for what is written and talked about in New Zealand university classrooms. As a New Zealander, whose research and teaching are organic to the local context, I have to 'translate' when I write for an international audience, and I have to 'translate' from the jargons of American academe into the everyday language of those for whom I write (my students).

At the time I wrote this, I was remembering my first visit to the United States—as a Fulbright scholar in 1991. It was a time when the reality of capitalism in academic publishing hit me hard. I met American doctoral students who were aiming for academic careers. They were working with powerful (usually male but sometimes female) supervisors, some of whom had contracts with the big international publishing companies to edit series of education books, but all of whom had the necessary contacts to facilitate the eventual publication of the student's work. These students knew that if they wrote competent theses, the next step could be a book.

. . . . New Zealand doctoral students work very much alone. Although one university now has an Ed D degree, in the other six (including my own), there is no doctoral course work and a Ph D is by thesis only. It can be a lonely experience—one has only one or two supervisors and most of us in Education Departments did our doctoral theses part-time while also employed as full-time lecturers. Our theses are almost never published. Mine was turned down by New Zealand publishers as 'too academic' and by the British as unmarketable because of its New Zealand content. During the 1980s, many of us found that while American and British work was often assumed to be of universal interest, ours was often regarded as parochial, local, and of no international concern.

There are only 3.5 million people in New Zealand—a country the geographical size of Britain or Japan. To publish academic books here, one must write for the undergraduate textbook market. Yet, to extend one's ideas, one needs to write also at the higher academic levels—for postgraduate students and ones academic staff peers. While it is not difficult to have New Zealand papers accepted for international journals or chapters in edited books, it can be extremely difficult to break into the academic book market if one's topic and orientation is explicitly grounded locally. Our work falls between the cracks. As academic job markets tightened around the world, academics from the northern hemisphere began flocking to the southern nations for jobs. Because they researched and wrote about and for the huge northern markets, their doctoral theses were far more likely than ours to have been published. This gave a young American or Briton an 'international book' which put them far ahead of most New Zealanders of the same age in the job market and served to reproduce the colonialist power relations in academic disciplines such as education and women's studies . . .

One of the ironies about the dominance of 'New Right' political influences in the West, and New Zealand's 'pioneering' status in trialing New Right ideas, is that suddenly books about New Zealand's restructuring became objects of international interest. Anthologies of essays about New Zealand education were published overseas (Lauder & Wylie, 1990), and New Zealanders' perspectives are more often included in international readers. The seeming 'closing down' of opportunities for academics under the 'New Right' in fact propelled New Zealanders onto the international stage . . . I gave up thinking about the 'New Right' in 1992, but now it is time to confront them again . . . tomorrow . . .

Sunday, November 17, 1996

A sparkling day. Why spoil it with the Right? I'll write fast and get them out of the way, then venture out into the summer sun . . .

Why the Men of the Right Make Me Feel Blue and the Men of the Left Make Me See Red

Throughout the 1980s and through into the early 1990s, my main academic strategy can be summarized as "Creating spaces and finding voices" (Miller, 1990). I started New Zealand's first university course on 'women and education' (Middleton, 1992a, 1993b) and this required me to produce my own curriculum. Other women started similar courses and this created a market for local undergraduate textbooks, compilations of indigenous work (Middleton, 1988; Middleton & Jones, 1992). Because my courses straddled both the education (B Ed, BA, and B Soc Sci) and the women's studies programs, I also found myself inserting 'education' as a topic, and feminist educational theory as a field of study, into women's studies courses and texts (Du Plessis et al., 1992). As I came into contact with like-minded women in other countries, I began to be invited to contribute 'New Zealand' chapters to international feminist readers and journals (Arnot & Weiner, 1987; Weiner & Arnot, 1987).

As feminist theses, research projects, courses, and texts became evident in university Education Departments, male colleagues began to invite feminists to contribute chapters to the edited readers which were textbooks in undergraduate core courses in Education. Feminists got 'wheeled in' to education classes to 'do feminism' or 'women and girls' in single sessions or blocks of lectures. However, as many others have written, this level of recognition of our work seldom went further to produce 'gender inclusiveness' or androgynous theories in the (sociological, historical, philosophical, psychological, etc.) education 'disciplinary mainstream' or core. The situation in Education Studies in the 1980s and early to mid 1990s is easily recognizable in this account by feminist geographer, Gillian Rose, who sees the relationship between feminists and 'others' in her field

> not as a series of conversations between equals, but more as a series of brush-offs. Feminism has been consistently marginalised by mainstream geography . . . Papers may contain a one off reference or two to feminist authors, and a feminist chapter or two, written by some combination of the valiant few feminist geographers, is obligatory now in most edited collections, but there is hardly ever a sustained engagement with feminist work (Rose, 1993, p. 3).

As Carmen Luke puts it, "To cite 'key' feminist authors in the burial site of the bibliography is not the same as knowing or using their work" (Luke, 1992, p. 40).

During the late 1980s to early 1990s, many feminists in education from across the 'western' world devoted huge amounts of energy to critiquing the policies driven by 'New Right' political agendas. With two others I edited a book which collated examples of 'left-wing' critiques of New Zealand's reforms (Middleton, Codd & Jones, 1990). Of the thirteen chapters, five were by women—and four of these were written from feminist perspectives. Reviews of the book, however, usually ignored the feminist chapters altogether—male Marxists used the review space to fight each other and thus erase feminist critiques. . . . As I write, I feel the red heat of anger. I shall not reference these reviews—I do not want to give these men the 'honor' of being in my bibliography. Let them be rendered invisible . . .

The men of the right and the men of the left have several things in common. Both 'New Right' educational critics and Marxist researchers see 'the economy,' or the relation between schooling and the workplace, as the central issue. Ironically, Marxist critiques—that public schools have served to reproduce class inequalities—have been quoted by the Right in support of their arguments for increased privatization of schooling (NZ Treasury, 1987) . . .

. . . This is the first time for four years that I have engaged in critiquing the Right. For four years I have exercised my right to do other things, to choose my own questions and research agenda. Now, once more, I take up arms. In my 'absence' New Zealand's National Government developed a National Curriculum Framework for all schools and the curriculum statements for individual subjects are being written, trialled, and critiqued (Ministry of Education, 1993). Critiques of the Framework and of the guidelines for social studies, English, science and technology, have been developed from the Right and the Left . . . Our use of 'new right' implies a continuity with regimes in Britain and the United States. They have common strands, but are not the same. I must explain, translate . . . I find myself lapsing into disembodied exposition as I construct this brief account—for foreign (non-New Zealand) readers—of the political context that has been so formative of the constraints and possibilities for my creative work.

The term 'New Right' in New Zealand usually signifies economic libertarianism—what Peters and Marshall (1996) recently described as 'busnocratic rationality.' New Zealand's economic libertarians have often tended to be liberal on 'moral' issues like homosexuality and abortion. Some also support government intervention on 'equity issues,' such as equal opportunities, or human rights. The social conservatism of Reganism or Thatcherism has not been a central feature of New Zealand's restructuring, which began under the 1984–1990 Labour Government (Middleton, Codd & Jones, 1990). Conservatives on moral or social issues were in both major parties, were very much in a minority, but tended to congregate in National more than in Labour. Feminists were found in both parties, although those in National were fewer and of the liberal feminist persuasion, while Labour attracted more radical and socialist feminists (Middleton, 1992c).

As the first MMP election approached (October 12, 1996), the traditional binary between a more socialist (but basically liberal) Labour Party and a more conservative (but increasingly liberal) National Party collapsed. ACT (Association of Consumers and Taxpayers) was formed by extreme economic libertarians from Labour and joined by Maori radicals who saw the free market as a way for Maori to take control of their own economic destiny—ACT commanded only 5% of the vote. The socially conservative Christian Coalition (in part a splinter group of National) failed to win any seats in Parliament. National (minus most of its social conservatives) and Labour (minus most of its libertarian economists) can both be seen as centrist urban liberal parties, although Labour still advocates some slightly more protective legislation for workers. The far left have split to 'New Labour' (a splinter group started by former Labour MP, Jim Anderton, in the late 1980s), but this group is subsumed under the umbrella of The Alliance (which won 15% of the vote)—a loose confederation of former Social Crediters, Greens, and Mana Motuhake (a Maori Party). Holding the balance of power is New Zealand First, a party initiated in the early 1990s under the charismatic leadership of Winston Peters—a Maori, a lawyer, and a former National MP. It is an extraordinary alliance of Maori nationalists and white middle-class superannuitants. Although National won the highest number of votes, it does not have a majority without the support of New Zealand First. But Labour (under feminist Helen Clark) could govern if both New Zealand First and the Alliance entered a coalition with it. Until coalition partners are decided—talks are proceeding at the time of writing—we have a (National) caretaker Government. Whichever way Winston Peters jumps, we will have a government of the Center and radical change (some say decisions of any kind) will be extremely difficult. 'Northern' binaries of left/right; conservative/radical etc. are increasingly irrelevant—collapsing, splintering, as new groups form, coalesce, split, and flow in new directions.

The curriculum debate is introducing a strong tone of social conservatism into the political/educational scene—and this is being directly imported from Britain. There is an orchestrated campaign from an organization of New Zealand's richest men, the Business Round Table. This group supports a conservative 'Think Tank', the Education Forum, which sponsors 'overseas experts' (usually of British origin and known social conservative persuasion) to 'review' New Zealand education. As I write, a Briton, who lives in Australia, has been commissioned to review teacher education. Snook (1996) has argued that those commissioned reports which the Round Table do not like (those favorable to New Zealand's public schools) have been suppressed (Snook, 1996). The Business Round Table has made submissions on the various curriculum documents—and these have been summarized recently by Michael Irwin (1996), The Round Table's Policy Analyst.

Irwin has won favor from some of New Zealand's leftist critics because he is critical of the Framework's emphasis on economic, as distinct from educational, aims: "Irwin's work signals a new sophistication in the work of the Forum/Roundtable" (Snook, 1996, p. 49). Like the Left (e.g. Codd,

1996; Peters & Marshall, 1996; Snook, 1996), Irwin attacks recent innovations in curriculum and assessment for their 'skills-based' vocational tendencies and their under-emphasis on the development of rationality—knowledge and understanding of the traditional academic disciplines. As Snook points out, however, Irwin sees academic knowledge as objective, and dismisses the ideas of those who address its perspectivity (feminists, Maori, and constructivist teachers) as contaminants. He attacks the requirements of the Ministry for teachers to address the "noneducational concepts" (p. 7) of gender inclusiveness, biculturalism and multiculturalism in their handling of the curriculum. These he describes as mere obeisance "to current, politically correct, emphases" (Snook, 1996, p. 6) which aim to teach "children what to think and not how to think, and the use of schooling to serve external purposes such as social reconstruction" (p. 14). Yet, the leftist men who praise Irwin for his attacks on the 'commodification' of the curriculum, have paid little attention to his attacks on equity and seldom—if ever—acknowledge that feminists have produced sustained critiques which could be incorporated into their responses to both Irwin and the new curricula.

To be fair, some male Left critics have at least *mentioned* that 'equity' is an issue of concern in recent curriculum policy shifts. Under National (1990–1996), the results of feminist initiatives over the last 20 years were steadily chipped away (Leahy, 1996). Special units within the Ministry of Education were disestablished; and the requirements of school charters to address 'equity issues' were made optional (Middleton & Jones, 1992). In recognition of this, Peters and Marshall comment that "The Minister of Education de-emphasised all issues pertaining to equity and empowerment and has made a commitment to repeal the statutory requirement that schools include equity clauses in their charters" (Peters & Marshall, 1996, p. 36). They do not, however, mention or reference (let alone engage with) any of the now large body of local critique and research by feminists and Maori about the discursive underpinnings and historical antecedents of contemporary notions of equity, or current political struggles concerning it (Alton-Lee & Densem, 1992; Jones, 1991; Middleton, Codd & Jones, 1990; Middleton & Jones, 1992; Middleton, 1992b, 1992c, 1992d; 1993; O'Neill, 1992; Leahy, 1996).

As in Britain (Weiner, 1993), New Zealand's social conservatives are continually chipping away at 'equity issues' in the National Curriculum. 'Leftist' philosopher, Ivan Snook acknowledges this when he comments on the Business Round Table's submission on the English curriculum (written by Carl Stead) :

> Stead's view that the new English curriculum moves into 'social policy' is naive. Two decades of curriculum sociology and sociological analyses of education have demonstrated that every curriculum does that. In the other

documents, the term 'social engineering' is reserved for those who want to promote a more *just* society or a fairer society. It is never acknowledged that the most blatant form of social engineering is that which has been imposed on new Zealanders for the past ten years (Snook, 1996, p. 54).

What Snook fails to acknowledge is that this point has already been made many times by New Zealand feminists in scores of submissions, conference papers, published articles, and books. As usual, we do not *even* make it into the "burial site of his bibliography" (Luke, 1992).

Although (albeit so mildly) questioning of Irwin's dismissal of 'equity questions', the instinct of some of New Zealand's 'Left' has been to join with Irwin in his attacks on vocationalism. Peters and Marshall, for example, commend Irwin for his celebration of the Enlightenment 'man of reason' as a counterfoil to the 'consumer' model of commodified education: "the form of individualism offered by the autonomous chooser is not the free person offered by Enlightenment thought and liberal education . . . Liberals and the liberal left in New Zealand have had no real response to these changes, either intellectually or in practice, except to provide critique and/or to repeat the principles and policies of the past (Peters & Marshall, 1996, p. 44). They seem oblivious of the twenty years of international and local feminist scholarship and critique of Enlightenment models of rational autonomy. Yet look at the blatant ignorance and misogyny of some of the Round Table's submissions to the Ministry on some of its curriculum statements. (I am using Irwin's (1996) summary of all of the submissions; although he expresses support for all of these, some are quotations from documents which he may not have personally authored):

We are not told explicitly the criteria by which we should recognize 'highest quality' in the curriculum, but presumably they include being "gender-inclusive, non-racist, and non-discriminatory . . ." and having a substantial element of biculturalism and multiculturalism. Much of this is mistaken at best and, at worst, encourages the wrong sort of education—one that seeks to inculcate certain views rather than give students the knowledge and concepts with which to arrive at their own opinions. The required emphasis may, for example, discourage critical engagement with historical accounts involving Maori and women in New Zealand society. They reflect current politically correct emphases which, in their present form, may well not prove durable (p. 8)

[I]f the aim is to give the same amount of attention to recorded female and male activities in social studies programs, massive omissions and purges of major areas of human experience would be required. Whether or not this state of affairs should now be referred to as 'just', the fact is that the overwhelming bulk of activity recorded in any fields of human endeavour has been carried out by males. . . . any attempt to balance the choice of [literary] texts as between male and female authors [in the English curriculum] would be to misrepresent literary history since women writers were relatively few prior to the twentieth century. That it is fashionable to deplore this fact does nothing to alter it, nor to supply a shortfall of good pre-twentieth century texts by women (p. 10)

Similarly, with respect to questions of the Treaty of Waitangi, biculturalism and multiculturalism, Irwin condemns the Ministry's "reluctance to confront the unattractive features of traditional Polynesian culture; the requirement that teachers value traditional Maori family relationships and forms of land ownership, but not the typical nuclear family of those of British descent and modern forms of property ownership which have been so germane to economic and social progress" (p. 11). My response to the overarching sexism which unites the men of the Left and those of the Right is rage and despair. It is the kind of response that tempts me back to an essentialist radical feminism—to reclaim Dale Spender's (1982) claim that it is the "patriarchal paradigm" which unites 'mainstream' educational theory . . . But now I can go out into the summer sun. George and I walk along the cobbled paths beside the wide Waikato River.

Monday, November 18, 1996

Transitions

I had my hour and half morning walk—got home just as rain set in. It's cold enough for me to have turned the heater on. Might as well write all day, although I still have to finish marking that doctoral thesis . . . Taking a swig of chamomile tea, I pick up my battered copy of *Educating feminists* and think of how writing it was my first peak academic experience . . . In 1992 I gave up responding overtly to both Right-wing and Left-wing agendas. For five years my research and theorizing had been dictated by Government policy—I was continually reading through turgid policy documents and writing critiques—submissions to decision making bodies (Middleton, Codd & Jones, 1992); empirical research on the impact of restructuring in schools (Middleton, 1992c); and theoretical critiques of key concepts (Middleton, 1992b, 1992d). It was time to set my own agenda again.

It is difficult to expand one's thoughts when forced to confine them to a 5,000 word—or, at the most, a 10,000 word, journal article or book chapter. To develop and sustain an idea or style, one needs the wide open spaces afforded by a whole book. By 1990, I was struggling with the idea of reworking the various phases of my work into a coherent text—

the doctoral thesis on feminist teachers, discourse analyses of 'New Right' and earlier education policy texts; research with school Boards of Trustees; snippets of autobiographical/reflexive writing about doing feminist academic work. But how could I persuade an international publisher that, although my life and works were grounded in New Zealand, I could speak in terms which an international audience could relate to? I had a miraculous stroke of luck.

Maxine Greene spoke in Wellington at a Fulbright Foundation anniversary seminar— at which I was a keynote speaker (Greene, 1993). Had Geraldine McDonald—a feminist who has mentored many younger New Zealand women—not invited me to that seminar, *Educating Feminists* may never have been written . . . In 1977—as a 'mature student' with a preschool child—I had been struggling to conceptualize my masters thesis on feminism, phenomenology and education. I had no women lecturers in my Masters program; and knew of no women writing in philosophy of education. Maxine Greene's writing was alone in being by a woman and about the complex interweaving between educational theorizing and everyday life. I adored her work. Now, fifteen years later, I was to meet her. I could not believe it when she warmed to my paper, asked me for my other papers, read them, talked through my book proposal, and advised me on whom to send it to for review in the United States. By mail she mentored and encouraged me through the writing process. And so, *Educating feminists* was written and I loved every moment of writing it . . . It gave me the freedom of wide-open spaces—the chance to bring together the personal, political, and theoretical dimensions of my life/thought and to project my dreams across the wide Pacific Ocean . . .

We women of the post–World War Two baby boom have continually theorized 'our generation' of feminists. As we turn fifty, our academic research and life-writing turns to mid-life (Drewery, 1995) and the more commercial writers amongst us are producing a new wave of self-help books. In one of these, New Zealander, Sandra Coney, describes us as "a singularly adventurous generation of women who fearlessly explored new territories . . . My generation of women are warriors, pioneers, ground breakers and survivors from way back. The journey has been tough, there have been suffering and casualties along the way, but like steel seasoned by fire, we have grown through experience" (Coney, 1996, p. 9). I know that I have to talk about the time when "the journey got tough." No, Sandra Coney, we were not 'fearless'—we were, and still are, sometimes terrified. I fear writing the next section—fear the vulnerability that comes from personal confessions in public spaces—from exposing frailty. I shy away from disclosures about deep personal things. I do not expect my students to do this either—dislike the voyeurism of teaching which requires students to keep journals—do not feel comfortable with the panoptic surveillance of 'the personal' (Foucault, 1977, 1980). This may surprise those who read me as a 'confessional' writer—those who respond to *Educating Feminists* with "I learned so much about YOU from that book" and read it as a personal, rather than as a methodological, political and theoretical, text . . . I did not conceptualize *Educating Feminists* as a 'personal' text, but as a feminist historical materialist one. My aim was to write an open text which simultaneously constructed and deconstructed its own arguments and assertions. In this—as when I offer students the chance to create 'archaeologies' of their own schooling (with photographs, report cards etc)—my aim is to create explicitly 'situated' accounts. It is Foucaultian discourse analysis, but with the added dimension of exploring the power relations between discourses. For, as Rosemary Hennessey (1993, p. 119) has expressed it, "situating the problematic out of which historical narrative is constructed within the discursive field of the present encourages feminist history to account for its own historicity."

Falling Over the Edge

To continue this paper—a discourse analysis of my own intellectual production over the past five years—I have to 'confess' to the bodily and spiritual illness that afflicted me in 1993 and nearly cost me career—even my life. But, in hindsight, it enabled me (as my therapist put it) to put down forever some heavy baggage from my past and to walk forward into new projects—new research, new courses, and new political strategies—no longer in bondage to the old anxieties and insecurities that came from years of feeling 'out of place' . . . It started with a shocked recognition of mortality as my strong and healthy female body failed me for the first time. *Educating Feminists* was written in 1991 and was 'in production' in 1992. That year I was 'written out'—exhausted, and beginning to feel afraid that I had used up all my creativity—as if that were a finite pool . . . When a book is in production, and for months after it is launched, there is a silence. It is as if one's life work has disappeared down a black hole, spinning out, out, and over the edges of the universe . . .

I spent 1992 in constant menstrual pain, which I tried to ignore, thinking that it was probably 'normal' at my stage of life (I was then 45) and that it would stop by itself at menopause. But, after being taken ill at a conference in Australia, I spent the Christmas of 1992 in hospital having an abdominal hysterectomy . . . Some women who visited me thought that to have one's womb removed was a spiritual crisis—but I laughed. To me it was a relief—freedom from the worries and inconvenience of contraception and menstruation . . . No more pain.

I recovered quickly over the summer and went back to work to begin my new position as Assistant Dean in February (the start of our academic year). While I was in hospital the contents of my office were moved from the former university Education Studies Department across the football field, and into what used to be the Teachers' College and which is now the amalgamated School of Education. There were tensions between some of the former university and some of the former college staff. I was happy not to 'live' in the midst of them, but to reside in the administration corridor with responsibilities to create a 'graduate culture' amongst staff and students across all departments. I would need strength, charisma, inspiration, and confidence . . . But my body was tired—from years of unacknowledged pain which had made me sluggish, stop exercising and gain 30 pounds in weight; from the surgery; and from years of overwork.

Some of you may remember my daughter, Kate, who flitted in and out of the pages of *Educating Feminists* . . . At sixteen she dropped out of school and took to the road. For weeks and months I did not know where she was . . . remembering my murdered niece, Karla, six years ago—raped, battered, and buried alive on a polluted beach by the sewer outfall near Wellington . . . I fell into the fear. My forty-sixth birthday/ spiritual deathday. Down, underground in a mine tunnel with no ends— no light—cowering, shaking. Prozac sent me screaming further down . . . The roof of the tunnel collapsed—buried alive . . . I had to heal without drugs—not even wine or coffee . . . Three calming voices—all men—my husband, my doctor, my therapist . . . You will be all right. You're exhausted. It has a name—Major Depression—and it passes . . . But their voices are out there somewhere—I don't believe. I'm a useless mother, a failed woman, a finished writer, deserve to die . . . Against advice, I mechanically perform my daily routines. Walk to work. I have nothing to teach, nothing to say—I listen, am (not) 'there' for students. Tutorials— afraid to speak, like some of my students. I get the students to run classes themselves. Wonderful seminars on taboo topics in my new course, 'education and sexuality' at level 200—for, and about which, in 1996, I am now producing texts (Jones & Middleton, 1996; Middleton, 1996c). I am only a mask, yet my students' evaluations of the courses are high. I have come back to the 'neo-progressive' pedagogies from which academia's loud demands to act (pretend to be) 'the authority' had torn me (Middleton, 1996b) . . . It was those undergraduate students' enjoyment of 'education and sexuality' and the care of three men that gave me the 'outside' support I needed to work my way back to health . . . Breathe in, and out, in and out . . . meditations, affirmations . . . Long walks by the river or the sea . . . losing the thirty pounds . . . Maori people have a word, wairua, which is usually translated as 'life-force' or 'spirituality'

(Pere, 1988). Image of a coiled fern-frond piercing through from cradling darkness to light . . . Slowly, gently, through—and changed forever. Leaving behind the years of 'misplacement'— living on the edges, straddling fault-lines—time to come in from the cold . . .

The curled fern-frond—the life-force—how do 'ordinary' people come to form their theories, ethics and values in the course of their everyday lives? How do teachers develop their educational ideas in the course of their daily activities? Why it is it that some philosophies of education 'take'—get taken up and developed by large numbers or small groups of teachers—at particular times and places? How can I help my students to find what will work for them from the competing and incommensurable array of concepts and theoretical fragments 'in the air' around them in the course of their training and later careers? My crisis brought me back to life-history—but centered my own by meeting and embracing the shadows of the 'demons' who lurk in the seething pit of panic. There was nothing there after all . . . Out of that came the research and pedagogical project—an oral history of educational ideas in New Zealand—which has absorbed me for the past three years. It was this project that helped me 'come in from the margins.' But before telling you about the project, I would like to speak briefly about the institutional politics in which it has been created.

Coming in from the Margins

Writing about the Australian situation, Erica McWilliam (1995, p. 4) notes that "In six years I have seen the demise of the foundational disciplines as educational 'theory'. Psychology, sociology, and philosophy have been doled out in increasingly small measure because more pedagogical territory was demanded for curriculum 'basics' and fieldwork." International commentators are arguing that, increasingly, the rationalist educational policies and commodified curriculum packages of western countries are being transmitted to student teachers as 'fact', rather than as the (critique-able) theoretical assumptions of a dominant political grouping at a particular time and place. Canadian researchers Jean Clandinin and Michael Connelly (1995, p. 9) describe this phenomenon: "For the most part a rhetoric of conclusions is packaged and transmitted via the conduit to the teacher's pre-formed knowledge landscape."

This is happening in New Zealand as well. Our (Waikato's and other universties') four-year B Eds are now in competition with three year B Ed degrees as the new NZQA (NZ Qualifications Authority) exerts control over 'qualifications' and grants 'other' tertiary institutions (teachers' colleges, polytechnics, and private providers) the right to award degrees (Codd, 1996). In order to compete with shorter (cheaper) degrees, the institutions with four-year programs will probably soon be forced to shorten them by a year. As NZQA tightens its hold over teacher education, it gains control over its curriculum. The freedom promised private and state providers to compete for students is reduced to the freedom to deliver standardized (prepackaged) 'unit standards' which are designed and approved by NZQA. The new degrees offered by non-university tertiary institutions are under NZQA control. Where Waikato—a university with a teacher education program—stands is at present confusing. What does seem likely, however, is that—in a shortened program in which there are so many externally determined requirements—there will be fewer spaces in which students and staff can spend concentrated amounts of time thinking through issues which are contextual or philosophical and which may not be of immediate 'use' in the school-based practicum.

My own department is Education Studies, the former university department which moved into the former teachers' college upon amalgamation. Its staff do not supervise practica and have the mandate to teach the theoretical/disciplinary courses rather than the subject-based curriculum courses or professional practice courses. It is extremely vulnerable because not only are theoretical courses being squeezed within the B Ed, but the Education Studies majors in Social Science (B Soc Sci) and Humanities (BA) degrees are also at risk as those schools question the practice of 'their' students taking courses in 'another' School (Education) and thereby diverting EFTS funding across the campus to us. Despite this, my 'education and sexuality' and 'women and education' undergraduate courses have a more secure base in the BA and B Soc Sci programs than they do in the B Ed. They remain as 'electives' in women's studies because my department allows 'our' (Education) B Soc Sci majors in education to include one of their (Women's Studies Department) courses as part of their Education Studies major if they also take my two courses and core Education courses to complete an Education Studies major with a 'gender emphasis.' In return, Women's Studies allowed my courses to remain within their women's studies major—even though EFTS follow my students across the campus into 'our' School. The administrative structures in which Schools (Faculties) must compete for students has almost destroyed cross-faculty interdisciplinary possibilities (Bernstein, 1971; Middleton, 1987) . . .

Even within departments this structure encourages competition between colleagues and political tensions over the structure of Majors. For example, in Education Studies the shrinking space for theory courses in the B Ed program is contested between those who cling to compulsory 'core disciplines' and those of us whose courses are relegated to the (optional) fringes of the B Ed degree. 'Women and education' and 'education and sexuality' are structurally situated as less important than 'mainstream' sociology, history, or philosophy of education.

As a teacher-educator I have abandoned the 'flat map' approach to the teaching of theory—in which students are positioned as spectators, looking in at the range of 'other people's' theories. Instead, I want to introduce B Ed students to educational theories as teachers experience, choose, and live them in the everyday settings in which they work. Engagement with 'other' people's educational life-histories (as students and/or teachers) can help student teachers to deconstruct the educational and other possibilities of their own lives and to view themselves as active and creative educational theorists, who will not merely mimic what has gone before, but create new amalgams of the theories and concepts which they encounter in the course of their professional lives to create pedagogies and educational strategies which are their own.

The life-history based pedagogy I have developed in 'women and education' and written about previously (Middleton, 1993a; 1993b) is suited to a core teacher education course. Accordingly, I have offered to run such a general 'Educational Perspectives' course at level 100 and to give up 'women and education' to a collective of women to develop in their own way. (I shall keep 'education and sexuality' and my graduate course on 'women and education'). This offer has proved controversial—some argue that it would lower standards and deprive B Ed students of the breadth of perspectives they gain from contact with BA and B Soc Sci students in the present shared compulsory course on history, sociology and philosophy of education. But I see it as a way of harnessing theory to practice in a way that welds them inseparably together and as providing a course which the enemies of theory might be unwilling to drop when/if the program is shortened.

Students will choose someone older than they are to interview about their own schooling or their professional lives as teachers; they will do historical literature reviews (to provide context of the time and place); they will study the ideas behind the education policies which gave form to the institutions in which their interviewee studied or taught; they will explore questions of social structure which gave shape to the person's educational experience (race relations, social class, gender, sexuality); and they will weave it all together into a final report (study good writing techniques). It will be a true discourse analysis because it will place the interviewee's perspectives and experiences within the historical etc. context which gave it form. I prefer this to the teaching of 'bare theory'—I like my theories clothed. As Michele Barrett (1991, p. 128) put it:

[T]here is a world of difference between the detailed historical researches that Foucault himself undertook when seeking to recast our understanding of particular discourses (medical, penal, sexual etc.) and the extremely superficial labelling that often goes on in which, for example, sociology becomes 'sociological discourse' without any substantive elaboration of what the discursive ordering and regularities might be (Barrett, 1991, p. 128).

As I write this, I do not know if the department will accept my idea. But if they do, there will be a text which we can use as a stimulus. A new book—*Teachers talk teaching* (Middleton & May, 1997) to which I have devoted nearly all my research and writing time for the past three years . . .

I am nervous about this paper—its disclosures. But I have done what the editors asked me to do—to contextualise my academic work. Writing it has purged me of the past four years . . . I feel lighter . . .

In the Pink

"Will Americans and Canadians understand if I include "in the pink" in my title with 'feeling blue and seeing red?" I asked my Canadian friend, Jody. "I don't think so", she said and explained that (as it does here also), 'pink' is used there to mean 'pinko' or 'left-wing.' But here it also has another meaning: to be 'in the pink' means 'to feel full of health and life and energy'—to be at one's peak. Which is how I feel as I approach the age of fifty.

Tuesday, November 19, 1996

Time to finish packing my suitcase. I look forward to the luxury of a good novel on the long train ride to Wellington. I love gliding through places instead of flying over them—revel in the braiding of narratives along the way; how the whodunnit I'm reading entwines with my fantasies and is interrupted by the 'road movie' through the window—erupting volcanoes, cows in green fields, wild mountains, verandahed shops in country towns . . . I am going to spend a week with Helen May—the friend and colleague who has worked with me on this huge project over three years. This week we will tidy up the final draft and send it to Palmerston North to Dunmore Press . . .

Throughout 1994 and 1995 Helen and I did interviews with 150 teachers and former teachers, ranging in age from 21 to 97, about their educational ideas and where they came from. Our overall aim has been to map the tides and currents of educational thought as 'lived' and created by teachers in the course of their everyday lives. Teachers are viewed not 'from the top' as passive recipients of the ideas of policy-makers but as creative strategists whose theories-in-practice are products of their own agency within the constraints and possibilities afforded them by their biographical, historical and material, cultural and geographical situations and the theoretical, conceptual or discursive resources to which their circumstances afford them access (Middleton, 1996b, 1996c). While Helen interviewed 75 early childhood and infant educators, I interviewed 75 teachers of secondary, intermediate, and older primary school children. We had over 3,000 pages of transcript and used the NUD-IST software package to code and organize it (Middleton, 1996a) . . . the microwave beeps, signaling that my cold cup of coffee (one of five I allow myself each day) has reheated . . .

I shall do my ironing in front of the daytime soaps on TV—a luxury of study leave to adapt one's diurnal rhythms . . . I carry my coffee into the lounge. The six-foot cardboard cutout of Kate looks at me from the corner—brown eyes beneath a white skateboarders' hat; black singlet; white Levis; arms behind her head; no makeup on her brown face; tattooed 'bracelet' clearly visible around her upper arm . . . I am grateful to the local *Denim and Blues* store for giving me the cutout when they no longer needed it for their shop window display. She did the photo shoot for fun—does casual jobs when she wants money, educates herself through travel . . . In my photo album I have a photo of the 'real Kate' just before she flew off to Wales, and one of me with 'virtual Kate', the cutout in the store . . . Real Kate phones sometimes from New York which—as I do—she loves . . . I turn on the TV and begin to iron my black jeans. So excited about finishing the Dunmore book. And thinking about the new one I shall start writing for New York's Teachers' College Press in the warmth and flowery brilliance of a January mid-summer . . . It will be 1997, the year George and I—and some of our friends—turn fifty. As a group we plan to hire a hall and have a huge mid-winter party—I shall dust off the keyboard, get the band back together, play old rock 'n roll. . . .

November 21, 1996

I had to leave this for a day—to distance myself from it before proofreading. I double click on the Interslip icon . . . click on 'connect' . . . type in my username and password. In seconds this paper flies from my converted laundry-room study in a New Zealand summer morning, through cyberspace and onto the editors' computers somewhere in an American winter night . . .

Post-script

Six months have gone by—it is now May 21, 1997. I am doing the editors' required corrections to the draft of this paper I sent them back then—

feeling somewhat distant from what I wrote. Since then the bodily sensations of menopause have occupied me more as—sharing new-found knowledge with same-aged colleagues—I read of, and experiment with, ancient herbal, and other natural, remedies and find that they work . . . It has been a momentous week—the end of an era for me. The first copies of the oral history book (Middleton & May, 1997) arrived on Monday. On Tuesday I received and responded to the copy-editor's queries on the text of my book for Teachers' College Press, *Disciplining sexuality—Foucault, life-histories, and education.* I have a publication date— February, 1998. I feel 'written out'—happy to rest from writing for a while, to focus on my work as Assistant Dean (Graduate Studies)—to create systems and structures that nurture the writings of others. And I've cut my coffee intake down to four cups . . .

References

Acker, S. (1994). *Gendered education*. Buckingham and Philadelphia: Open University Press.

Acker, S. (1995). Unkind cuts: Reflections on the U.K. university experience. *Ontario Journal of Higher Education 1995*, 55–74.

Aisenberg, N. & Harrington, M. (1988). *Women of academe: Outsiders in the sacred grove*. Amherst: University of Massachusetts Press.

Althusser, L. (1971). Ideology and Ideological State Apparatuses. In L. Althusser (Ed.), *Lenin and philosophy*. London: Monthly Review Press.

Alton-Lee, A. & Densem, P. (1992). Towards a gender-inclusive school curriculum. In S. Middleton & A. Jones. (Eds.). (1992b). *Women and Education in Aotearoa 2*. Wellington: Bridget Williams Books.

Arnot, M. & Weiler, K. (Eds.). (1993). *Feminism and social justice in education: International perspectives*. New York and London: The Falmer Press.

Arnot, M. & Weiner, G. (Eds.). (1987). *Gender and the politics of schooling*. London: Hutchinson.

Bagilhole, B. (1993). How to keep a good woman down: An investigation of the role of institutional factors in the process of discrimination against women academics. *British Journal of Sociology of Education, 14* (3), 261–274.

Barrett, M. (1991). *The politics of truth: From Marx to Foucault*. Cambridge: Polity Press.

Bernstein, B. (1971). On the classification and framing of educational knowledge. In M.F.D. Young (Ed.), *Knowledge and control*. London: Collier McMillan.

Clandinin, J. & Connelly, F.M. (1995). *Teachers' professional knowledge landscapes*. New York: Teachers College Press.

Codd, J. (1996). Higher education and the Qualifications Framework: A question of standards. *Delta, 48* (1), 57–66.

Coney, S. (1996). *Feeling fabulous at 40, 50 and beyond: A handbook for mid-life women*. Auckland: Tandem Press.

Drewery, W. (1995). *Directions at mid-life: Women theorize their lives*. Hamilton: Unpublished D. Phil thesis, University of Waikato.

du Plessis, R; Bunkle, P; Irwin, K; Laurie, A. & Middleton, S. (Eds.) (1992), *Feminist voices: Women's studies texts for Aotearoa/ New Zealand*. Auckland: Oxford University Press.

Foucault, M. (1977). *Discipline and punish: The birth of the prison*. Harmondsworth: Penguin.

Foucault, M. (1980). *A history of sexuality, Vol 1*. New York: Vintage.

Greene, M. (1986). In search of a critical pedagogy. *Harvard Educational Review, 56*, 427–441.

Greene, M. (1993). Foreword to S. Middleton, *Educating feminists—Life-histories and pedagogy*. New York: Teachers' College Press.

Grumet, M. (1988). *Bitter milk: Women and teaching*. Amherst: University of Massachusetts Press.

Harvey, D. (1990). *The condition of postmodernity*. Cambridge Massachusetts & Oxford, UK: Basil Blackwell.

Hennessy, R. (1993). *Materialist feminism and the politics of discourse*. New York & London: Routledge.

Irwin, M. (1996). *Curricular confusion: The case for revisiting the New Zealand Curriculum Framework*. Paper presented at the Seminar on Implementing the Curriculum, Principals' Center, University of Auckland.

Jones, A. (1991). *At school I've got a chance*. Palmerston North: Dunmore.

Jones, A. & Middleton, S. (Eds). (1996). *Educating sexuality. Special Issue of New Zealand Women's Studies Journal, 12* (1).

Lauder, H. & Wylie, C. (Eds.). (1990). *Towards successful schools*. New York & London: Falmer.

Leahy, H. (1996). *Focusing on a faultline: Gender and education policy development in Aotearoa New Zealand, 1975–1995*. Wellington: unpublished M Ed thesis, Victoria University.

Luke, C. (1992). Feminist politics in radical pedagogy. In C. Luke & J. Gore (Eds), *Feminisms and critical pedagogy*. New York & London: Routledge.

Luke, C. (1994). Women in the academy: The politics of speech and silence. *British Journal of Sociology of Education, 15* (2), 211–30.

Luke, C.& Gore, J. (Eds). (1992). *Feminisms and critical pedagogy*. New York & London: Routledge.

McLuhan, M. (1964). *Understanding media*. London: Routledge and Kegan Paul.

McWilliam, E. (1995). *In broken images: Feminist tales for a different teacher education*. New York: Teachers College Press.

Maher, F. A. & Tetreault, M. (1994). *The feminist classroom*. New York: Basic Books.

Middleton, S. (1987) Feminist academics in a university setting: A case study in the politics of educational knowledge. *Discourse 8* (1), 25–7.

Middleton, S C. (Ed.). (1988). *Women and education in Aotearoa*. Wellington: Allen & Unwin/Port Nicholson Press.

Middleton, S. (1992a). Developing a radical pedagogy : Autobiography of a New Zealand sociologist of women's education. In: Goodson, I. (Ed), *Studying teachers' lives.* London: Routledge (in Association with Teachers College Press, New York).

Middleton, S. (1992b). Equity, equality, and biculturalism in the restructuring of New Zealand schools: A life-history approach. *Harvard Educational Review, 62* (3), 301–322.

Middleton, S. (1992c). Gender equity and school charters. In S. Middleton, J. Codd, & A. Jones, (Eds.), (1990) *New Zealand education policy today: Critical perspectives.* Wellington: Allen & Unwin/Port Nicholson Press.

Middleton, S. (1992d). Schooling and the reproduction of gender relations. In J. Lynch, S. Modgil & S. Modgil (Eds.), *Cultural diversity and the schools: equity or excellence?* Lewes: Falmer.

Middleton, S. (1993a), A post-modern pedagogy for the sociology of women's education. In M. Arnot & K. Weiler, (Eds.), (1993), *Feminism and social justice in education: International perspectives.* New York & London: The Falmer Press.

Middleton, S. (1993b) *Educating Feminists—Life-histories and pedagogy.* New York: Teachers' College Press.

Middleton, S. (1995) Doing feminist educational theory—A postmodernist perspective. *Gender and Education, 7*(1), 87–100.

Middleton, S. (1996a). Doing qualitative educational research in the 1990s: Issues and practicalities. *Waikato Journal of Education, 2,* 1–23.

Middleton, S. (1996b). Towards an oral history of educational ideas in New Zealand as a resource for teacher education. *Teaching and Teacher Education, 12* (5), 543–560.

Middleton, S. (1996c). Uniform Bodies? Disciplining sexuality in school 1968–1995. *N.Z. Women's Studies Journal, 12* (2), 9–36.

Middleton, S. (1998). *Disciplining sexuality: Foucault, life-histories and education.* New York: Teachers College Press.

Middleton, S; Codd, J. & Jones, A. (Eds). (1990). *New Zealand education policy today: Critical perspectives.* Wellington: Allen & Unwin/Port Nicholson Press.

Middleton, S. & Jones, A. (Eds). (1992b). *Women and education in Aotearoa 2.* Wellington: Bridget Williams Books.

Middleton, S. & May, H. (1997). *Teachers talk teaching 1915–1995: Early childhood, schools, teachers' colleges.* Palmerston North: Dunmore Press.

Middleton, S.& Summers-Bremner, E. (1997). Feminist pedagogy: A conversation. In R. du Plessis & L. Alice (Eds), *Crafting connections/defining difference.* Auckland: Oxford University Press.

Miller, J. (1990). Creating spaces and finding voices: Teachers collaborating for empowerment. Albany: SUNY Press.

Ministry of Education. (1993). *The New Zealand curriculum framework.* Wellington: Learning Media.

N.Z. Treasury. (1987). *Government management: Vol 2, Education.* Wellington: N.Z. Treasury.

O'Neill, A.M. (1992). Educational policy initiative for girls and women: Are we included in the decent society? In *NZ Annual review of education.* Wellington: Department of Education, Victoria University, 35–69.

Pere, R. (1988). Te wheke: Whaia te maramatanga me te aroha. In S. C. Middleton (Ed), *Women and education in Aotearoa*. Wellington: Allen & Unwin/Port Nicholson Press.

Peters, M. & Marshall, J. (1996). The politics of curriculum: Busnocratic rationality and enterprise culture. *Delta, 48* (1), 33–46.

Rose, G. (1993). *Feminism and geography: The limits of geographical knowledge*. Minneapolis: University of Minnesota Press.

Snook, I (1996). The Education Forum and the Curriculum Framework. *Delta, 48* (1), 47–56.

Spender, D. (1982). Education: The patriarchal paradigm and the response to feminism. In D. Spender (Ed.), *Men's studies modified*. New York: Teachers' College Press.

Spender, D. (1995). *Nattering on the net: Women, power and cyberspace*. Melbourne: Spinifex.

Stone, L. (Ed.). (1994). *Education feminism*. New York & London: Routledge.

Weiler, K. (1988). *Women teaching for change: Gender, class and power*. New York: Bergin & Garvey.

Weiner, G. (1993). Shell-shock or sisterhood: English school history and feminist practice. In M. Arnot & K. Weiler (Eds), *Feminism and social justice in education: International perspectives*. London & Washington DC: The Falmer Press.

Weiner, G. (1994). *Feminisms in education: An introduction*. Buckingham & Philadelphia: Open University Press.

Weiner, G. & Arnot, M. (Eds.). (1987). *Gender under scrutiny: New inquiries*. London: Hutchinson.

West, J. & Lyon, K. (1995). The trouble with equal opportunities: the case of women academics. *Gender and education, 7* (1), 51–68.

Wilson, M. (1995). Academic women in the 1990s. in N. Alcorn (Ed.), *Education and the equality of the sexes—Twenty years on*. Hamilton: School of Education, University of Waikato, 61–71.

Yates, L. (1993). Feminism and Australian state policy: Some questions for the 1990s. In M. Arnot & K. Weiler, Kathleen (Eds.), (1993), *Feminism and social justice in education: International perspectives*. New York & London: The Falmer Press.

Against the Grain: Reflections on the Construction of Everyday Knowledge and Uncommon Truths

Linda K. Christian-Smith & Kristine S. Kellor

Everyday knowledge and uncommon truths: women of the academy evolved from a chance meeting between co-editors Linda Christian-Smith and Kris Kellor who had not met nor heard of one another's work prior to presenting their papers at Session 24 of the 20th Annual Research on Women and Education Conference in St. Paul, Minnesota on October 28th, 1994. The conference, publicized under the theme "Understanding Self, Understanding Others: Observing Others Through Our Individual Lenses," focused on a discernment process: Who am I as a teacher researcher? Where did my question come from? What do I bring to the question? How do I interpret what I see? How does that interpretation affect my future actions?

Kris's Story

That Linda and I addressed these questions by self reflexively deconstructing critical life events which we believed influenced our feminist, activist perspectives was not surprising. Yet, we and women in the audience were visibly startled by strong similarities in the powerful autobiographic narratives Linda and I had constructed as a way to situate our intellectual labor in the academy. Linda presented first. As her story unfolded, I felt shivers running through my body. The hair on my forearms stood up. I knew I was giving witness to a transformative testimony. I was thrown off center as I listened autobiographically for the feminine resistance (Felman, 1993) in the life stories Linda shared as a way of addressing the discernment process. The particularities of the childhood and young feminist peacemaking experiences she described were remarkably similar to the life stories I related in my paper; yet, her interpretations of the life events which had strongly influenced her academic work and research were far different from the stories I had constructed regarding my graduate school experiences at the University of Wisconsin-Madison.

Later, a graduate school friend commented to me on the "sparking"—the visceral union—she observed forming between Linda and myself as we listened to each other's stories. Yes, there was a strong and, for me, unexpected bond forming between Linda and myself. I also sensed connections between the audience and Linda and myself as we presented. It seemed obvious that something unusual was happening as we listened to each others stories. I had previously experienced phenomenon similar to this in my work with autobiographic life stories as curriculum which invites and permits working across socially formed difference; yet, I hadn't expected my or another's conference presentation to be so moving.

Linda and I spoke briefly after the session. Moved by the afternoon's experience, we agreed to meet the next morning. Over coffee we hoped to learn more about one another's work. The next day, as we exchanged stories, I was struck by strong similarities in the trajectories of Linda's and my nineteen sixties and seventies feminist activism. I was especially interested in those experiences which centered on our anti-war activities in 1968 and 1969. Each of us seemed to believe that the actions we took to protest the Vietnam War were integrally tied to our feminist perspectives. It was our sense that our current perceptions of our work as feminist educators and researchers were strongly influenced by our political activism in the 1960s and '70's. In the course of our conversation about political activism in the academy, I mentioned my interest in learning whether and how involvement in women's liberation and anti-war movements in the late nineteen sixties and early seventies influenced current feminist research, teaching, and pedagogy in the academy. I suggested that I would like to investigate this issue, hopefully editing an anthology of autobiographic narratives written by feminist educators who associated their current feminist practices, at least in part, with their 1960s and '70's antiwar, resistance activities. Linda replied that she would be happy to help me with such a project—offering to function in whatever capacity I desired. I was surprised, pleased, and flattered by her offer to work with me. I was unpublished; outside of my twenty minute conference presentation, she knew nothing of my work. We did however know that we undoubtedly shared critical theoretical assumptions since we each had completed doctoral coursework in Curriculum and Instruction at the University of Wisconsin-Madison. Although Linda and I didn't make any definite plans for proceeding with the anthology, it was clear to me that we had committed to the project. Parting, we agreed to keep in touch with one another, possibly getting together at the April AERA Conference in San Francisco in the Spring. In April, 1995, we met briefly in San Francisco over sandwiches and soup to discuss and outline "next steps" for working on the project. The anthology was now in the soup pot—bubbling, stewing; neither Linda nor I had time to devote to the project until summer.

During the three years Linda and I have negotiated and actively worked on the anthology, each of us has encountered a plethora of major life events within and outside our work in the academy. We know that several chapter contributors, while working on their chapters, also grappled with crises and other significant changes in their lives. I know that these critical life incidents irreversibly influenced my work on the anthology. I find it productive to retrospectively examine them as a way of noticing how they may have influenced the structure and texture of my intellectual labor in the academy. Reflection on the experiences reminds me that I entered the academy with a storied body. My understanding of this fact was so strong I decided early in my graduate studies to make personal experience the primary object of my graduate studies. *Everyday knowledge and uncommon truths* is an extension of my master's and doctoral studies—but, with a critical difference. In my work on the anthology, I have found myself speaking openly, and without apologies. My work on the book has been marked by a remarkable self confidence which I believe is not egotistical. I haven't questioned my right to speak authoritatively about my knowledge of narrative inquiry and experiential learning. This is not to say that I view my perspective on these issues as ideologically correct. Rather, I am aware that my understandings of them are idiosyncratic—my personal interpretations of and reflections on an evolving area of inquiry. I have quite simply hoped that the anthology might serve as a forum for women wishing to give witness to the power of story in working across socially formed differences.

Working on the anthology, I have lost a great deal of my self consciousness in speaking openly in the academy. I've also become quieter inside and more patient. Like my dissertation, this book has had a long gestation. It has become woven into the everyday textures and pulse of my life. In the ways it takes up a certain amount of space in my file cabinets, in my allocation of time, and in my responses to the perennial question "Are you working," the anthology has to a degree become incorporated into my sense of self. But, to date I have not mistaken my self for my work on *Everyday knowledge and uncommon truths*. I continue to be surprised by the remarkable lack of ego investment I have in seeing this anthology through to publication—my work on the text seems necessary and right— work arising from my heart rather than my intellect. Like many of the chapter contributors, I have observed that working on the anthology has been healing—a corrective to academic silencing, as well as a way to give witness to and honor one's experiences of self and other.

After our brief meeting at AERA in San Francisco, Linda and I didn't meet face to face again until late summer. In early August, I traveled by bus to her home near Milwaukee, Wisconsin. She picked me up at the Park and Ride Lot and gave me a scenic tour of the hills and vales surrounding her home. We ate a lovely lunch she had prepared; after lunch, Linda and I visited her flower and vegetable gardens and played with her cats before settling in for several hours of concentrated work. I knew Linda and I had a great deal of work to accomplish that day and I was on some levels eager to get started. In spite of this, I found her decision to take time to welcome me into her private space—feeding me home prepared food at her kitchen table, introducing me to her cats, showing me her home, yard, and neighborhood—set a tone and framing for our work together which I found refreshing and alarmingly unfamiliar in most of my collaborative work with academics. The ways in which Linda welcomed me into her living/working space suggested to me that she valued and trusted me as a woman as well as an academic colleague with whom she was about to collaborate. Mutually shared generosity and trust have marked all aspects of our work together on the anthology.

I was surprised by the similarities in our domestic life; I had expected her to be a hard core intellectual with little concern for the beauty of the world outside of books. A guest in her home, I noticed that she, like me, beautified her home with furnishings she had sewn; her garden like mine provided a peaceful respite from the work of the mind; her devotion to her cats was obviously as strong—maybe stronger than mine. Chatting with Linda while becoming a bit familiar with her home bearings, I had the strong sense that we had connected on some deep— maybe transpersonal—levels. Spending time with Linda in the place she calls home, I knew too that there were many commonalities in our lives. Neither of us had been born into worlds where the intellect ruled; yet, even as young schoolgirls longing for independence we each pursued lives of the mind as one way to gain entrance to worlds which would otherwise have been closed to us.

We shared other commonalties as well. As we settled in to begin our discussion of the anthology we hoped to construct, I chuckled as I noted that she, like me, stashed her projects into cast off computer paper boxes, labeling them with black magic marker. I enjoyed seeing the box labeled "Kris and Linda book." I liked the commitment it signified! Linda invited me to speak first; this surprised me. She was a published, tenured professor and I an unpublished, doctoral student. I believe I had been prepared to defer to her suggestions. I liked the sudden shift in perspectives her asking me to speak first created. I read Linda the list of issues I hoped we could address before I headed back to Madison later that afternoon; Linda added a few items. We methodically worked our way down the list. Two and a half hours later we had accomplished much. In addition to dealing with the general logistics of working with each other, we had shared our thoughts and insights regarding the theoretical framing, content, depth, breadth, pitch, and scope of the anthology we envisioned.

Having discussed the overall "feel" of the anthology we were envisioning, we spent an hour or so identifying women whose work we might wish to include in the anthology. We divided up the tasks associated with locating articles, book chapters, conference papers, and so forth representative of work currently being done by prospective contributors. We agreed to read select texts written by each person we wished to consider for inclusion in the anthology. The afternoon turned to early evening; we had to hurry through rush hour traffic to meet my bus at the Park and Ride lot. We scheduled a second face to face meeting at Linda's home; during this meeting, we planned to discuss the readings, narrow the list of prospective contributors, and begin to construct the book prospectus. We agreed that it was imperative that we compose a prospectus which would invite theoretically complex, yet self-reflexive and readily accessible texts.

Preparing the prospectus turned out to be easier than I had thought it would be. To a large extent this was due to Linda's facility in conceptualizing and articulating compact, pithy theoretical position statements. Also, potential contributors were an absent presence which heavily informed our work on the prospectus; we prepared the prospectus with a particular group of contributors in mind. In our letters of solicitation, we invited each woman to re-visit from the perspective of the discernment process issues she had addressed in her earlier work. Linda and I worked hard to construct a prospectus in which the women we invited to contribute a chapter would readily recognize the relevance of their work for the anthology. Although Linda and I held firm convictions regarding the elements we wished to build into the prospectus, we also wished to avoid putting closure on the form and content of contributed chapters. We were interested in seeing how the issues we outlined in the prospectus played out in the intellectual labor of women's work in and outside the academy. We suspected that the discernment process incorporated into the book prospectus would insure a narrative approach to the anthology.

Everyday Knowledge and Uncommon Truths: Women of the Academy

We had a strong response to the prospectus; of 15 women invited to submit work to the anthology only three declined; each informed us that she did so not out of disinterest but, rather, due to time constraints imposed by already too heavy commitments in her academic and private lives. As chapter abstracts arrived, Linda and I were struck by the strong similarities in the themes and issues the women proposed they would address in their chapters; yet, we noted the particularities of the experiences the women brought to their intellectual labor varied significantly as did the contexts in which they performed their work. After reading the abstracts, Linda and I changed the working title of the anthology to "Everyday Knowledge and Uncommon Truths: Women of the Academy"; a title we believed more accurately captured the tone and textures of the evolving text. Early in our work together, Linda assured me that a well-crafted prospectus would greatly minimize the work we needed to do once we had chapter drafts in hand; she was correct. The specificity of the tightly constructed book proposal also seemed to result in remarkably sound fits between our needs and hopes for the anthology and the authors' interests and concerns.

Working on chapter edits, I began to feel a bit uncomfortable about the privileged positions from which Linda and I read and edited the chapter drafts. While I had up until this point felt little personal ownership of the anthology, it became more apparent that there was no way I could escape the knowledge that my editorial comments had constitutive power. The beliefs, perspectives, and limitations I brought to my readings could potentially greatly influence the scope, tone, composition, and so forth of the collaborative text. Linda, I sensed, shared these insights; I believe we were struggling with gatekeeping implications of editing. Reading the chapter drafts, I began to viscerally appreciate what before I understood so well intellectually. *All discourse is dangerous. There are no innocent readings.* Editing contributors's chapter drafts, I felt great responsibility to them, to Linda, to myself and to potential readers of the anthology. It was clear that our editorial comments had the potential to construct knowledge in ways different than the contributors may have intended or wished. We were engaging in serious, risky business. Hoping to assist in creating a text which did not close down meaning—which left room in which readers could insert themselves and their lived experiences (Mairs, 1994), which might be read oppositionally (Chambers, 1991) and autobiographically for feminine resistance (Felman, 1993), my concerns regarding responsible editing went beyond the personal. While I did not wish to inadvertently offend and/or alienate the women who graciously agreed to contribute their work to the anthology, my over-arching concerns centered on constructing a non-ideological, soulful text which would experientially address women's work in higher education.

From my perspective, it was in the chapter editing that Linda and I did some of our most productive work together. When we didn't agree on which edits to propose to contributors, Linda and I discussed our concerns—sometimes over the phone, occasionally by mail, often through e-mail. Through these conversations, I gained deeper understandings not only of the work I hoped this anthology would perform, but also of biases, blind-spots, and strengths I brought to my work on the anthology. Deeply committed to the agenic possibilities of narrative self representation, in my editing, I found myself wanting authors to maintain a narrative voice throughout their chapters. I realized I feared they were abandoning their experiences of self when relinquishing an autobiographic voice in their text. Yet, I wondered if in suggesting this to them, I might take their experiences from them.

Understanding Self, Understanding Others: Observing Others Through Our Individual Lenses

Recently, over a two day period, I read all of the revised chapter drafts in the order Linda suggested we might wish to place them in the anthology. I was struck by the rightness of her decision. Without intending to, I found myself simultaneously reading the texts on several levels—through one another. I began to discern subtexts occurring across the chapters; I wondered if Linda had been aware of these when she suggested the ordering of the chapters. As I constructed this section of what we originally believed would be the introductory chapter, Linda worked on the final section in which she discussed themes contributors take up in their chapters. I was eager to see if the themes and subtexts Linda identified would be similar to those I perceived; I suspected they might be, but I knew I would not be surprised if they differed. I recognize that I read women's life writings autobiographically for the feminine resistance in the text (Felman, 1993).

I have experienced other forms of resistance as I have worked on the "Kris's Story" section of this chapter. Recently, Linda and I suggested—in e-mails which crossed in transit—that each of us contextualize our work on the anthology. This necessarily meant I must self-reflexively recall and analyze a difficult three year period of my life. I was surprised to find I did not want to revisit experiences associated with this period. I realized that I had moved on from these experiences and had no desire to re-examine them for this chapter. Yet, I knew I must; along with Linda, I believed that the contexts in which we have worked on the anthology are of significant import to the text we were producing. Fortunately, I found this re-membering was not as difficult as I thought it might be— in fact it has been productive in many ways. I have new appreciation for the depth of my current sense of being present to my experiences of self. Also, working on this section, I felt the absence of the sense of soul-murder I experienced as a graduate student. Upon earning my doctor-ate, I was relieved but still felt soul murdered. It had been my sense then that through the very act of participating in an oral defense of my re-search I was in ways complicit with my own violation of self. This feeling was so strong, it prevented me from attending graduation ceremonies. I believed there was little to celebrate. I knew there was still much work to be done in academe; I was uncertain whether I was up to continuing my work in this context. A year later, I find myself an employee of my alma mater. In my work as curriculum design specialist in the Office of Hu-man Resource Development, I have been charged with coordinating the design and implementation of academic leadership workshops for de-partment chairs, project and center directors. Many of the workshops focus on ways to improve the educational climate at the University of Wisconsin-Madison. In this work, I am discovering, in the flesh, what I already knew intellectually: academic silencing goes beyond individu-als—it is an institutional phenomenon intricately tied to relationships between power/discourse/knowledge. Faculty too feel discursively si-lenced and/or unheard. Somewhat oddly, understanding this has signif-icantly lessened the terrible sense of loss of self I experienced while in graduate school. Now, I no longer fear speaking openly in my work in academe and I seldom mistake myself for my ideas.

Given this, I have been taken off guard by my strong reluctance to ex-plicitly state and/or outline the theoretical framework informing this an-thology. On my writing table, lie more than a dozen pages of notes in which I describe and discuss my understandings of theories I believe frame this inquiry. Yet, I find myself incapable of putting them into this text. I begin to understand that there are several reasons for this. First, this is a collaborative inquiry and I cannot speak for others whose work is represented in this text. I think it quite possible that I might mis-identify theories individual authors believe inform their work. Chapter authors have taken great care to incorporate rich theoretical analysis into their autobiographic responses to the questions posed in the discernment process. Second, although co-editor Linda Christian-Smith and I locate our work in similar discourses and practices, our understandings of narrative inquiry, literary theory, discourse analysis, and so forth are quite divergent at times. It is my sense that in the book prospectus Linda and I described the general theoretical framework informing this anthology. Third, for some time now, I have found myself firmly resisting requests to identify, label, or name specific theories informing my or others' work. I find this discursive practice repugnant especially in the ways such labeling excludes the experiences of many and/or closes off meaning. Finally, my approaches to academic research, practice, and writing call for embodied, experiential engagements with theory which I believe are best described through biographic and autobiographic narratives.

I am highly aware that in working on this anthology, my interests have centered almost exclusively on examining and learning more about the transformative potentials of narrative inquiry in higher education. Even more specifically, I have found myself focusing on performative, narrative texts which Denzin (1995) suggests double back on themselves. For several years my research and teaching have centered on experience as an object of study and on narrative self representations of socially formed differences such as race, class, gender, sexual preference, ethnicity, physical and mental ability, and so forth. I brought these theoretical perspectives to my work on the anthology. At some point about five years ago, I recognized that in my research it is impossible for me to separate theory, method, content, and process. It is my sense that in narrative inquiry they are intricately intertwined. This belief informed my readings of *Everyday knowledge and uncommon truths*.

Reading the original and especially the revised chapter drafts, I was struck by the excessiveness of the texts. These were shivery texts—reading them alone and together I felt the hair stand up on my forearms, my torso twitching a bit with the ripple of recognition that these were sacred stories. These were performative texts which caught me up—engaging me autobiographically. Denzin (1995) believes readers change as a result of becoming participants in such texts. This has certainly been true of my readings of the chapters comprising the anthology. For that, I thank Linda Christian-Smith and the women who have contributed their stories to this anthology.

Linda's Story

The idea for this book was suggested by Kris during conversations we had at the Research on Women and Education Conference in St. Paul,

Minnesota, in October, 1994. Kris's recollections of the circumstances of our meeting and the uncanny similarities between our papers perfectly conveys the recollection I also have. As we talked later over coffee at a nearby restaurant, I felt I had found a new friend and colleague. My memory of the several hours of conversation is clouded by time, but I do recall feeling that our lives so intertwined. The sixties, the anti-war and early feminist movements were pivotal events for both of us. As Kris shared the ramifications of her former spouse's decision to fully resist the draft, I recalled my family's state of readiness to drive my brother to Canada should he draw a low draft number. I can also recall the relief we all experienced when we learned that he had drawn a high number. However, my present feelings are tempered by the fact that other young men from working class households like my husband's neither possessed the financial means nor the familial support to resist the draft. Ken was drafted into the Marines in 1969 and was stationed in Da Nang, RVN for the duration of his duty. He and I had not yet met during those times. What Kris and her young husband shared in the prison letters, Ken and I have lived out in the aftermath of a war that has scarred several generations. On the positive side, it made Ken a social activist and provided me with a partner in my struggles against social injustices of many kinds and an important balancing force in my life. Another cup of coffee poured and other similarities between us emerged. Kris and I pursued doctoral studies at the same university and department during middle age. We both have many familial responsibilities, very supportive partners and find comfort in the company of our aged cats. Yet, there are differences between us that I thought would make friendship and collaboration very interesting. Kris possessed knowledge and insights that I did not have and has taught me so much. I have come to greatly appreciate her attention to detail and efficient organization. She reminds me of myself early in my career. Kris and her husband made a conscious choice years ago to simplify their lives and surroundings. This is serving as a guide to me as I endeavor to do the same.

What intrigued me about this conference was the focus on the discernment process in which women reflect on the connections between their backgrounds, teaching and research. I had just started to use life history and autobiography in my research and writing. Kris had been using and deconstructing autobiographical narratives in her dissertation for some time. As she linked her discussion of her doctoral work and dissertation to the discernment process, I was convinced that I wanted to be part of a larger project dealing with these issues. I was also encouraged by the conference presenters who spoke candidly about their experiences in higher education. Laughter occurred and heads nodded as I replied in a session that if many doctoral students really knew what academe was like for faculty, they would run screaming from our doctoral schools and these places would go out of business. Working on this book has strengthened my voice and my determination never to be silenced again.

Dancing in the Mine Field

While Kris has discussed our approaches to the book and the work involved in preparing the prospectus, securing contributors and the myriad of other activities surrounding the preparation of this edited book, I want to turn to what has emerged as the most compelling and disturbing aspect of the book for me. As I read the early drafts of the chapters, I was gripped by fear, disgust and anger over the continuing chilly climate of higher education for women and the toll that this takes on one's spirits, body and personal life. Contributor after contributor described the overt and subtle means through which patriarchy is maintained in the academy and its devastating effect on women faculty, their careers and families. However, I felt some relief in reading Jennifer Gore's story of a smooth transition into higher education and a satisfying overall experience. I thought, "There is some hope." Yet, the other papers continued to haunt me. I was literally fearful for Kris and other women who are embarking on a career in higher education about the damage that this work can do to women's minds and bodies. I was disgusted by the many instances of harassment and disrespect towards women of color that Frances Rains and Lori Ideta and Joanne Cooper recounted. Anger surged over me as the words of Ava McCall, Magda Lewis and Carmen Luke tapped into my own experiences in higher education. Kris's metaphor of "soul murder" loomed large.

During the three years that Kris and I have been working on this volume, so many of the events of which the contributors write came to the fore in my life. During my twelve years in higher education, I have become increasingly disenchanted with higher education and alienated from the factory model of schooling dominating so many postsecondary institutions. There are speed-ups, more and more work to do, salaries at an all time low, little recognition for quality work and a political climate as slippery as a river bank after a downpour. For faculty at primarily teaching institutions who are involved in ambitious research and publishing agendas, the very long days and weeks take a tremendous toll. Years of my family and personal time have been sacrificed for tenure and an endowed professorship. As a survivor of three rare physical disorders, the stress in my workplace has further weakened my already fragile body and spirits. Several years ago I took the position that an important part of my career would be research and publication despite the fact that proper faculty work was defined as being in the office Monday–Friday from 9–5 in a noisy work atmosphere not conducive to unraveling in writing the complex findings from my research projects. My decision to work at home on scholarship on non-teaching days caused complaints to my dean and cautions about tenure expectations despite my already extensive publication record. This harassment increased with the stand I took regarding my negative tenure vote involving a male faculty member in my department during the tenure of my former dean. These and other events have caused me to think more than twice about whether I want to continue in this career. Lori Ideta and Joanne Cooper's discussion of college administration who contribute to and condone a hostile work climate strongly resonated with me. While things have vastly improved through several retirements and the efforts of my present department chair and our present dean, mismatches between what is said and delivered on continue while old practices remain that make systemic change slow and difficult.

References

Chambers, R. (1991). *Room for maneuver: reading /the/ oppositional /in/ narrative.* Chicago: University of Chicago.

Denzin, N., Kincheloe, J., Lather, P., Lincoln, Y., Pinar, W., Polkinghorne, D., & Tierney, W. (1995, April). *Representation and the text: Reframing the narrative voice.* Interactive symposium conducted at the American Educational Research Association Conference, San Francisco, CA.

Felman, S. (1993). *What does a woman want? Reading and sexual difference.* Baltimore, MD: Johns Hopkins University.

Mairs, N. (1994). *Voice lessons: on becoming a (woman) writer.* Boston: Beacon Press.

About the Editors and Contributors

Linda K. Christian-Smith is Oshkosh Foundation Professor of Curriculum and Instruction in the College of Education and Human Services at the University of Wisconsin, Oshkosh. She has published widely on issues of gender, class, race, ethnicity and sexuality in schooling as well as cultural politics, feminist theories and the development of literacies and femininities among women through reading popular children's and adolescent fiction. She is the author of *Becoming a woman through romance* (Routledge), *Texts of desire: Essays on fiction, femininity and schooling* (Falmer Press) and co-author of *Becoming feminine: The politics of popular culture* (Falmer Press) and *The politics of the textbook* (Routledge). She is currently researching popular children's and adolescent horror fiction and its impact on the formation of masculinities.

Joanne E. Cooper is an Associate Professor of educational administration at the University of Hawai'i at Manoa. She teaches courses in qualitative research, organizational theory, curriculum in higher education, adult learning, and critical reflection. Her research interests focus on women and leadership, multicultural issues, and qualitative methods, specifically the use of narrative. She is the co-author of "The constructivist leader" (1995) and of "Let my spirit soar: Narratives of diverse women school leaders" (in press). She is also involved in a Kellogg Grant Project to gather indigenous educators from across the USA, Canada, New Zealand, and Australia to discuss educational issues for native peoples.

Jean I. Erdman is an Associate Professor, a co-founder of the Fox Valley Writing Project, graduate advisor, and chair of the Curriculum and Instruction Department at the University of Wisconsin, Oshkosh. She has been named 1996 Wisconsin Teacher Educator of the Year, is a poet laureate for the Wisconsin State Reading Association Journal, and has written with Linda Christian-Smith about the construction of childhood in relation to children's reading of *Goosebumps*. She is married and has two elementary school aged sons.

Jennifer Gore is Associate Professor in Education at the University of Newcastle, Australia. Author of *The struggle for pedagogies: Critical and feminist discourses as regimes of truth* and co-editor (with Carmen Luke) of *Feminisms and critical pedagogy*, her current research focuses on issues of power and pedagogy. Her teaching, in the broad areas of sociology of education and teacher education, enables her to link her research interests with her practice. She is also Assistant Dean, Director of Academic Matters, in her Faculty. She longs for more time to think, read and write.

Lori M. Ideta is the assistant to the dean of students at the University of Hawai'i at Manoa here she serves as a source of advice and assistance in regard to matters of discrimination, academic grievances, conduct, and sexual harassment. Her research interests center around qualitative methodologies, Asian affairs, women's issues, and higher education.

Janice Jipson is a Professor of education at National Louis University. She received her Ph.D. in Curriculum and Instruction from the University of Wisconsin in 1984. Her recent books include *Repositioning feminism and education: Perspectives on education for social change* (1995) with Petra Munro, Susan Victor, Karen Froude Jones, and Gretchen Freed Rowland, *Daredevil research: Re-creating analytic practice* with Nicholas Paley (1997), *Resistance and representation: Rethinking early childhood education* with Richard Johnson (in preparation), *Questions of you* with Nicholas Paley (accepted for publication), and *Intersections: Feminisms/early childhoods* with Mary Hauser (in press). Her professional interests include curriculum theory, early childhood education, literature-based curriculum and research issues related to intersubjectivity and representation.

Kristine S. Kellor completed a Ph.D. in Curriculum and Instruction (1996) and a Master's in Continuing and Vocational Education at the University of Wisconsin, Madison. Her research focuses on textual self representations of women's experience in academe; autobiographic narratives as curriculum in postsecondary education; and on the work of the unconscious in experiential knowledge, embodied theorizing, and representations of Self and Other. Strongly committed to working across social and cultural differences, Kristine divides her time between employment as a curriculum design specialist in the Office of Human Resource Development at UW-Madison, course facilitator of "Life-Writing as Spiritual Practice" at Edgewood College in Madison, WI, and independent research and writing.

Magda Lewis is Queen's National Scholar and Associate Professor in the Faculty of Education and the Institute of Women's Studies at Queen's University at Kingston, Canada where she teaches Sociology, Cultural Studies and Feminist Theory. She has numerous journal publications and book chapters in her field of study. Her book *Without a word: Teaching beyond women's silence* (Routledge), signifies a focal point for her interest in the examination of the situation of women in the academy. Her current teaching, political work, public addresses, ongoing scholarship and personal life is dedicated to the unraveling of the workings of power as the beginning place from which might be imagined a world embracing of social justice and generosity of spirit.

Carmen Luke is Associate Professor in the Graduate School of Education at the University of Queensland in Australia. Her current research projects include women in higher education in south-east Asia, the cultural politics of interracial families, and gender and knowledge politics in emergent cyber-technologies. Her most recent book is *Feminisms and the pedagogies of everyday life* (1996), State University of New York Press.

Ava L. McCall is an Associate Professor in the Curriculum and Instruction Department at the University of Wisconsin, Oshkosh, USA where she teaches social studies methods and issues in education and supervises clinical students and student teachers. Ava's scholarly interests include caring in teaching, feminist pedagogy, students' responses to feminist, multicultural ideas, and incorporating women's voices in the curriculum through textile arts. After spending several years researching teacher education students' responses to feminist, multicultural ideas in her courses, in the fall of 1997, Ava engaged in a collaborative action research project with a fourth-grade teacher to study children's responses to the feminist, multicultural curriculum they team taught in the fourth-grade classroom. Articles based on the research of education students' responses to multicultural, social reconstructionist ideas have been published in the *Journal of teacher education, Equity & excellence in education,* and *Action in teacher education* (co-authored with Ann Andringa) and articles focused on incorporating women's voices through textile arts in teaching history and culture have been published in *Social studies and the young learner* and *Theory and research in social education.*

Sue Middleton is Assistant Dean (Graduate Studies) in the School of Education at the University of Waikato, Hamilton, New Zealand, where her teaching includes courses on "women and education" and "education and sexuality." Sue has published widely in Britain, Australia, New Zealand, and the U.S. Her American publications include two books: *Educating feminists: Life histories and pedagogy* and *Disciplining sexuality: Foucault, life-histories and education.* Sue has recently completed an oral history of educational ideas in New Zealand. She loves jazz, traveling, and walking. Sue is married with a twenty year old daughter.

Petra Munro is an Associate Professor of Education and Women's and Gender Studies at Louisiana State University. She is teaching courses in curriculum theory, qualitative research and secondary social studies. Her research focuses on narrative analysis of curriculum history, women's life histories and the discourses of qualitative research. She is the co-author of *Repositioning feminism and education: Perspectives on educating for social change* and *Subject to fiction: Women teacher life history narratives and the cultural politics of resistance.*

Frances V. Rains (Choctaw/Cherokee & Japanese) is an Assistant Professor at The Pennsylvania State University, with a split appointment in Curriculum & Instruction and Educational Policy Studies/American Indian Leadership Program. She teaches courses on social studies; race, class & gender; women theorists of color, and American Indian education, federal policy and contemporary issues. Her research emphasis is in social justice and equity issues linked to race, class and gender in American education, with special interests related to women of color and American Indian issues. She has contributed an article to *Taboo: the journal of culture & education* and has a chapter forthcoming in *White reign: Learning & deploying whiteness in America.*

Index

Acker, S., 197–198, 215
Aisenberg, N., 64, 79, 81, 129–130, 144, 198, 215
Alcoff, L., 121–122, 126
Allen, P. G., 151, 169
Althusser, L., 195, 215
Alton-Lee, A., 204, 215
Anzaldúa, G., 33, 42, 151, 157, 169
Arnot, M., 194, 201, 215, 218
Astin, H. S., 129, 144

Bacon, C. S., 100, 103, 108
Bagilhole, B., 197–198, 215
Bailey, C., 29, 31, 43–44n
Banks, J. A., 95, 107
Bannerji, H., 79, 81, 151, 169
Barrett, M., 212–123, 215
Bauer, D., 11, 14
Belenky, M. F., 87–88, 90, 92, 107, 110–111, 115, 119, 121, 126, 132
Bensimon, E. M., 8, 15
Benstock, S., 46, 57
Bentley, R. J., 89, 107
Berger, J., 75, 81
Berman, S., 95, 107
Bernstein, A., 150, 170
Bernstein, B., 195, 211, 215
Blackburn, R. T., 89, 107
Bloom, L. R., 46, 57, 142–144
Bollas, C., 26–28, 42–43
Bordo, S., 144
Boyer, E. L., 165–170
Britzman, D., 71, 81
Brookes, A-B., 79, 81
Bunkle, P., 201–216
Burton, S., 132, 145

Butler, J. E., 151, 170
Butler, J., 30, 33, 43, 124, 126, 141

Canaan, J. E., 22–23
Cannon, L. W., 152, 173
Caplan, P. J., 149, 153, 156, 162–164, 170
Card, C., 86, 105, 107
Carpenter, M., 12, 15, 79, 81
Carter, D. J., 129, 144
Carter, K., 132, 144
Carty, L., 79, 81, 151, 153, 169–170
Chambers, R., 225, 230
Chan, S., 151, 170
Chilly Climate Collective, 79, 81
Christian-Smith, L. K., xiii, 42, 45, 52–53, 57, 219, 227
Chun, K. T., 129–130, 145
Clandinin, D. J., xii, xiv, 130–131, 145, 210, 215
Clark, V., 4, 15
Clinchy, B. M., 87–88, 90, 92, 107, 110–111, 119, 121, 126, 132, 144
Cock, J., 150, 170
Codd, J., 201–204, 206, 210, 215
Collay, M., 168, 170
Collins, P. H., 132–133, 145
Coney, S., 207, 215
Connelly, F. M., xii, xiv, 130–131, 145, 210, 215
Cooper, J. E., xiv, 145, 229–230
Corrigan, P., 70, 79, 81

Davies, B., xii, xiv
Davis, A., xi, xiv, 151–152, 170
Davis, L., 149, 172
Dehli, K., 79, 81, 151, 169

Dellabough, R., 96, 107
Denfield, R., 6, 11, 15
Densem, P., 204, 215
Denzin, N. K., 227, 230
Dill, B. T., 151–152, 170, 173
Douglass, F., 169–170
Drewery, W., 207, 216
du Plessis, R., 201, 216
Duane, J., 101, 105, 108
DuBois, E. C., 151, 169–170
DuBois, W. E. B., 170
Dunlap, D., 168, 170
Dunn, K., 101, 107

Edelman, L., 60, 81
Edgerton, S., 126
Elbaz, F., 131, 145
Elbow, P., 98, 107
Ellsworth, E., 17, 23, 38–39, 111, 117, 126
Ely, M., 150, 170
Emechita, B., 112, 125–126
Erdman, J., xi, xiii–xiv
Erdrich, L., 112, 126
Escueta, E., 129, 145

Fairclough, N., 46, 57
Farmer, R., 149, 153, 170
Fay, E., xi, xv
Felman, S., xii, xiv, 25, 37, 39, 43, 220, 225
Fillion, K., 6. 15
Fine, M., 144–145
Firestone, S., 112, 126
Fiske, J., 38, 43
Ford Slack, P. J., 168, 170
Foucault, M., 18, 23, 33, 36, 43, 208, 216
Frank, A., 66, 82
Frankenberg, R., 133, 145
Fraser, N., 74, 81
Freed-Rowland, G., 119, 127
Friedan, B., 118, 126
Froude Jones, K., 119, 127
Fuss, D., 33, 43

Garber, L., 79, 81
Garner, H., 4, 6, 12, 15

Gavey, N., 46, 57
Gee, J., 46, 57
Ghandi, M., 33, 43
Gilmore, L., 38, 43
Glaspell, S., 76, 81
Goldberger, N. R., 87–88, 90, 92, 107, 110–111, 119, 121, 126, 132, 144
Gore, J., xi–xii, xv, 1–2, 15, 18, 23, 110, 126, 199, 216
Grant, C. A., 84, 94–95, 97, 108
Green, R., 151–152, 170
Greene, M., 118, 121–122, 126, 193, 207, 216
Griffin, G., 125, 127
Grossman, P., 131, 145
Grumet, M., 111–112, 115, 119, 121, 127, 193, 216
Guba, E. G., 150, 170

Halcón, J. J., 148, 165, 172
Hall, R. M., 167, 172
Hall, S., 1, 15
Harraway, D., 64, 81
Harrington, M., 64, 79, 81, 129–130, 144, 198, 215
Harrison, F. V., 151, 170
Harvey, D., 196, 216
Harvey, W., 149, 173
Hatch, J. A., 45, 57
Heald, S., 79, 81, 151, 169
Heck, R. H., 145
Heckle, S., 76, 81
Heilbrun, C. G., 132, 145
Hekman, S., 124–125, 127
Helle, A. P., 132, 145
Hennessy, R., 195, 208, 216
Higginbotham, E., 152, 173
Higonnet, M., 4
Hill Collins, P., 151–152, 171
Hirsch, M., 5, 15
Hoagland, S. L., 103, 107
Hoffman, N., 90, 108
hooks, b., xii, xiv, 79, 81, 84, 87–89, 92–101, 103, 105, 108, 132, 145, 151–152, 171
Houston, B., 86, 105, 108

Hsia, J., 142, 145
Huberman, A. M., 145
Hull, G. T., 151, 171

Ideta, L., xiv, 229–230
Irwin, K., 201, 216
Irwin, M., 203–206, 216
Jipson, J., xiv, 110, 119, 127
Jones, A., 201–202, 204, 206, 208, 216
Jung, C. G., 30, 33, 43

Kaplan, A., xii, xiv
Katrak, K., 4
Keller, E. F., 5, 15
Kellor, K. S., xiii-xiv, 29, 43–44n, 175, 219
Kelly, L., 132, 145
Kincheloe, J., 230
King, D. K., 151, 171
King, J. E., 151, 171
Kirby, S., 62, 81

Lather, P., xi, xiv, 46, 56–57, 103, 108,
    111, 127, 230
Laub, D., xii, xiv, 39, 43
Lauder, H., 200, 216
Laurie, A., 201, 216
Leahy, H., 204, 206
LeCompte, M. D., 150, 171
Leland, C., 129, 144
Lessing, D., 112, 118, 125, 127
Lewis, D. K., 151, 171
Lewis, M., xiii-xiv, 51, 61–62, 82, 229
Lincoln, Y. S., 150, 170, 230,
Longhurst, D., 57
Lorde, A., 87, 101, 108, 132–133, 145,
    152, 161, 171
Luke, C., xi, xiii-xv, xvii, 1–2, 7, 9, 15,
    51, 196, 199, 201, 205, 216, 229
Luke, H., 9, 15
Lyon, K., 198, 218

MacDonald, G., 79, 82
Madrid, A., 167, 171
Maher, F. A., 198, 216
Mairs, N., xii, xv, 225, 230
Marshall, J., 204–205, 217

Matthews, J. J., 11, 15
May, H., 213, 215, 217
Maynard, M., xi, xv
McCall, A. L., xiii-xiv, 51, 95, 108, 229
McIntosh, P., 165, 167, 171
McKenna, K., 62, 79, 81, 151, 169
McLuhan, M., 192, 216
McWilliam, E., 193, 199, 210, 216
Merriam, S. B., 150, 171
Middleton, S., xii-xiii, xv, 25, 43, 51,
    117, 127, 175, 192–196, 200–202,
    204, 206, 209, 211–217
Miles, M .B., 145
Miller, J., 200, 217
Mitchell, C., 72–73, 82
Modgil, S., 217
Morgan, G., 141, 145
Morrison, T., 112, 125, 127
Mossman, M. J., 79, 82
Munro, P., xiv, 46, 57, 110, 119, 127,
    141–142, 144

Nakanishi, D. T., 129–131, 133, 138,
    140–142, 145
Nelsen, R., 79, 82
Ng, R., 79, 82
Nicholson, L., 74, 81, 117, 127, 132, 146
Noddings, N., 96–100, 105, 108, 121, 127

O'Brien, E., 129, 145
Okazaki, S., 130, 146
Olsen, T., 112, 122, 127
O'Neill, A. M., 204, 217
Opie, A., 46, 57
Orner, M., 110, 127

Padilla, A. M., 165, 171
Pagano, J., 59, 82, 125, 127
Paglia, C., 6, 15
Parker, K., 166–167, 171
Parson, L. A., 101, 105, 108
Patai, D., 156, 171
Pearce, L., 46, 57
Pere, R., 210, 218
Pérez, L. E., 171
Peters, M., 204–205, 218
Peterson, B., 95, 108

Phelan, P., xii, xv, 38–39, 43
Pinar, W., 230
Polakow, V., 121, 127
Polkinghorne, D., 230
Pollard, D. S., 151–152, 163, 171
Powell, P., 59, 82
Preissle, J., 150, 171
Proulx, E. A., 123–124, 127
Puka, B., 84, 86, 105, 107–108
Purkey, S., 104, 108
Purvis, J., xi, xv

Rains, F. V., xiv, 147–149, 152, 163, 168, 170, 172, 229
Rakow, L. F., 103, 108
Ram Dass, B., 33, 43
Raywid, M. A., 104, 108
Regan, L., 132, 145
Rethinking Schools, 96, 108
Reyes, M. de la L., 148, 151, 165, 172
Rhoades, K., 11, 14
Richer, S., 79, 82
Rose, G., 201, 218
Ruddick, S., 115, 127
Ruiz, V. L., 151

Sadker, D., 88, 108
Sadker, M., 88, 108
Sandler, B., 167, 172
Sands, R. G., 101, 105, 108
Savage, G., 122, 127
Schaafsma, D., 29, 31, 43, 44n
Scheurich, J. J., 165, 172
Scott, J.W., 23
Sedgewick, E., 66, 82
Shrewsbury, C., 111, 119, 127
Simeone, A., 106, 108
Simon, R., 61–62, 82
Sleeter, C. E., 84, 94–95, 97, 108
Smith, B., 104, 108, 151, 171
Smith, D. E., 133, 146
Snook, I., 203–205, 218
Sommers, C., 6, 15
Spender, D., 193, 206, 218
Stacey, J., 46, 57
Steedman, C., xii, xv, 39, 43
Stone, L., 199, 218

Sue, S., 130, 146
Summers-Bremner, E., 194, 217
Suzuki, B. H., 129–130, 146
Swadener, B., 127
Tarule, J. M., 87–88, 90, 92, 107, 110–111, 119, 121, 126, 132, 144
Tetreault, M., 198, 216
Thayer-Bacon, B., 100, 103, 108
Tierney, W., 8, 15, 230
Tokarczyk, M., xi, xv
Touchton, J. G., 149, 172
Trask, H. K., 152, 173
Trinh-Minh Ha, T., 151, 173
Tripp, D., 146
Trubek, J., 43–44n

Victor, S., 119, 127

Walkerdine, V., 120, 127
Wang, L. C., 151, 170
Washington, V., 149, 173
Watts, A., 33, 43
Weber, S., 72–73, 82
Weedon, C., 30, 33, 43
Weiland, S., 132, 146
Weiler, K., 111, 127, 194, 215, 218
Weiner, G., 194, 201, 204, 215, 218
Weir, L., 79, 82
West, J., 198, 218
Williams, P. J., xii, xv, 151, 156, 173
Wilson, M., 197, 218
Wilson, R., 129, 144, 149, 173
Wisniewski, R., 45, 57
Wohlgemut, S., 73, 82
Wolf, N., 6, 15
Woodson, C. G., 169, 173
Woolf, V., 76, 82
Woolgar, S., 46, 57
Wylie, C., 200, 216

Yamada, M., 151, 173
Yates, L., 194, 218
Yellin, J. F., 173
Young, M., 5, 15

Zinn, M. B., 152, 173